GW00374273

CASS LIBRARY OF WEST INDIAN S·

No. 9

ST. LUCIA

CASS LIBRARY OF WEST INDIAN STUDIES

ST. LUCIA

HISTORICAL,
STATISTICAL AND DESCRIPTIVE

BY

HENRY H. BREEN

FRANK CASS & CO. LTD.
1970

Published by
FRANK CASS AND COMPANY LIMITED
67 Great Russell Street, London WC1

First edition   1844
New impression   1970

ISBN 0 7146 1930 2

Printed in Great Britain by Clarke, Doble & Brendon Ltd.
Plymouth and London

ST. LUCIA:

HISTORICAL, STATISTICAL,

AND

DESCRIPTIVE.

BY

HENRY H. BREEN, ESQ.

(THIRTEEN YEARS A RESIDENT IN THE ISLAND.)

LONDON:

LONGMAN, BROWN, GREEN, AND LONGMANS,

PATERNOSTER ROW.

——

1844.

INTRODUCTION.

Of all the insular possessions of Britain there
is none so little known as St. Lucia; and while
each has repeatedly attracted the attention of the
traveller and the historian, this Island has either
not been noticed at all, or has been dismissed
with a cursory glance. Amongst recent writers
on the West Indies, Mr. Mackenzie's sphere of
observation appears to have been confined to
Hayti; Colonel St. Clair's to Demerara and Ber-
bice; Mrs. Carmichael's to St. Vincent and
Trinidad; Colonel Flinter's to Porto-Rico; Dr.
Madden's to Barbados, St. Vincent, Grenada, and
Jamaica; Sir Andrew Halliday's to Barbados,
Guiana, Trinidad, and Tobago; Mr. Turnbull's
to Cuba; and the Rev. Mr. Philippo's to Jamaica. Neither of these writers has the slightest

mention of St. Lucia. Of those who have noticed it, Coleridge has given the impressions of a four hours' loitering under the roof of Government House; F. W. N. Bailey the imaginings of half-an-hour's ride to Morne Fortuné; and Sturge and Harvey the gleanings, mostly taken at second-hand, of a whole day's excursion to the valley of Roseau. Even Montgomery Martin, who should be supposed to have sought access to every available source of information, has contented himself with copying from Coleridge the brief notice which he has given to the world of this interesting Colony.

Not only is there little known respecting St. Lucia, but even that little is generally incorrect. In confirmation of this I may mention that Mr. Bailey places the Pitons, or Sugar Loaves, in Gros-ilet Bay—a distance of twenty-five miles from their actual situation; that Mr. M. Martin represents the superficial extent of the island to be 37,000 acres, instead of 158,000; and that Messrs. Chambers, in their "Information for the People," describe Pigeon Island as being at a distance of six miles from St. Lucia, instead of one-third of a mile.

And yet there are few of the sister islands that have higher claims to attention. As a military station it is of considerable importance, not only from its proximity to the French Settlement of Martinique, but from its central position amongst the islands, and its natural facilities of defence both by land and by sea. Inferior to Trinidad in territorial extent, and to Barbados and Antigua in density of population, it is second to none in the number and capaciousness of its harbours, and the richness and resources of its soil. We may form some idea of the value attached to it by the French from the vast sacrifices, both in troops and treasure, which they never scrupled to make for its capture or in its defence. "Had France not been deceived, it was her intention to have made it the capital of the Antilles, the general market of the Windward Islands, and the Gibraltar of the Gulf of Mexico.*

The want of information respecting St. Lucia

* Report of Governor Noguès to First Consul Bonaparte.

was never so sensibly felt as at the present day, when every question connected with our Western Empire receives a three-fold degree of added interest, from the recent abolition of slavery, the still pending experiment of free labour, and the all-engrossing topic of colonization. In attempting to supply this want I have availed myself of a personal acquaintance with the Island during a residence of thirteen years, in which time the whole of the public records have passed through my hands, including the Registry of Slaves, the Compensation and Manumission Papers, the Parish Registers, the Records of the several Courts of Justice, those of the Mortgage Office, the Government Office, the Legislative Council, and the Public Treasury.

The information thus placed within my reach is presented to the public in the following pages. Although the details are chiefly connected with St. Lucia, yet, from the identity of the West India Islands, in condition and prospects, I venture to trust that the volume may be found to possess much matter of general interest, especially in reference to the French Colonies. The statistical tables I have carefully compiled from the most authentic sources; the insurrection in Martinique I witnessed on the spot, and the account of the earthquake in Guadaloupe, originally derived from the published reports, I had an opportunity of revising during a visit to the scene of desolation six weeks after the occurrence.

London, 1st August, 1844.

CONTENTS.

CHAPTER 1.

CHAPTER II.

CHAPTER III.

CHAPTER IV.

CHAPTER V.

CHAPTER VI.

CHAPTER VII.

CHAPTER VIII.

CHAPTER IX.

CHAPTER X.

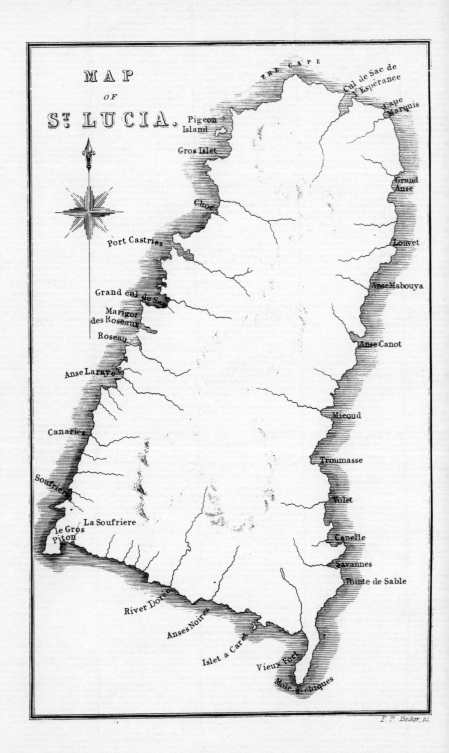

MAP
OF
ST. LUCIA.

THE CAPE

Cul de Sac de
l'Espérance

Cape
Marquis

Pigeon
Island

Gros Islet

Grand
Anse

Choc

Louvet

Port Castries

Anse Mabouya

Grand cul de Sac

Marigot
des Roseaux

Roseau

Anse Canot

Anse Laraye

Micoud

Canaries

Troumasse

Soufriere

Volet

La Soufriere

Canelle

le Gros
Piton

Savannes

Pointe de Sable

River Dorée

Anses Noires

Islet a Caret

Vieux Fort

Mole à chiques

F. P. Becker, sc.

ST. LUCIA,

&c.

CHAPTER I.

St. Lucia is one of a string of islands commonly
called the Lesser Antilles, or Caribbean Islands,
which extend in the shape of a horse-shoe across
the entrance of the Gulf of Mexico, between the

greater Antilles on the north-west, and the main
land on the south-east ; it is 13 deg. 50 min. north
latitude, and 60 deg. 58 min. west longitude.
The most easterly of the whole group except
Barbados, it is situated at a distance of twenty-
four miles to the south-east of Martinique, and
twenty-one to the north-east of St. Vincent ; with
the exception of Gaudaloupe and Trinidad, it is
the most extensive of the lesser Antilles.   It is
forty-two miles in length, and twenty-one at its
greatest breadth, and exhibits a circumference of
one hundred and fifty miles, and a superfices of
158,620 acres.

This island is proverbially known for its wild
and romantic scenery.   Viewed from the sea,
whether to windward or leeward, to the north or
the south, its appearance is equally grand and
picturesque.   From the bold, majestic *Piton* that
shoots its peak aloft to the skies, and seems to
defy the fury of the elements and the wreck of
ages, down to the humble coffee plant that seeks
shade and shelter at the hands of man, the whole
is one chequered scene of sombre forests and
fertile valleys, smiling plains and lowering precipices, shallow rivers and deep ravines—one vast
panorama where nature alternately assumes her
wildest attitudes and most enchanting forms.

The principal mountains* (or rather chain of mountains) extend longitudinally over the centre of the island, dividing it into windward and leeward districts. They are densely clothed with forest trees, and at their greatest points of elevation bear the distinctive names of *Sorciere, Paix-Bouche,* and *Barabara.* From either side of the chain, several mountains of lesser altitude diverge towards the sea, forming in the intermediate space, plains, valleys or ravines, according to their direction and distance from each other.

The *Pitons* are two pyramids of solid rock, of the most remarkable and picturesque character, standing on the south side of the entrance to the beautiful bay of Soufriere. One of them is computed to be 3,300 feet above the level of the sea, and the other about 3,000. They appear to be wholly unconnected with the other mountains, and, with the exception of their western side, which is laved by the sea, their base is fringed with verdure and cane fields in the highest state of cultivation. There are many interesting legends of the attempts made to ascend them ; but owing to their perpendicular formation I feel convinced no one has ever succeeded in reaching the summit.

* In the French Antilles, mountains are commonly called *mornes*, a name which they still retain in St. Lucia.

These mountains bear evident traces of volcanic
origin, and from their proximity to the *Soufre* or
half extinct volcano, are regarded as the remains
of an eruption which is supposed to have occurred
at some remote period. Not far distant from the
Soufriere Pitons is a mountain, called the *Piton
des Canaries*, which is also about 3,000 feet in
height. It occupies somewhat of an inland position, and is encompassed by dense forests and
precipitous ravines.

The height of these different mountains has
never been accurately ascertained ; and various
are the opinions of the natives on the subject.
Those of Soufriere, from their detached and isolated position, appear to surpass the others ; but,
if computed from the level of the sea, there is no
doubt that the *Sorciere* would be found to exhibit
the greatest altitude.

Intersected though St. Lucia be by numerous
precipices and ravines, it possesses, nevertheless,
two beautiful plains. The one is situated at the
northern extremity, in the parish of Gros-ilet,
and the other in the southern extremity, in the
parish of Vieux Fort. Each plain contains
a swamp of some extent, overgrown with various
aquatic plants, and the resort of game in the
shooting season. Due south of the Vieux Fort

plain extends the promontory of Mole-à-chique, whose highest point is 1,076 feet above the level of the sea.

The principal valleys are situated transversally on either side of the central chain of mountains. The most extensive to windward is called the valley of *Mabouya*, and that to leeward the valley of *Roseau*. Besides these, which are equally remarkable for their extent, fertility, and insalubrity, there are others of minor importance, such as the valley of *Grand-cul-de-Sac* to the north of Roseau, and the valley of *Fonds* to the south of Mabouya.

The greatest natural curiosity in St. Lucia is the *Soufriere*, or sulphureous mountain, situated in the parish to which it has given its name. It is about half an hour's ride from the town of Soufriere, and two miles to the east of the Pitons. The crater appears at an elevation of 1,000 feet above the level of the sea, between two small hills, totally denuded of vegetation. It occupies a space of three acres, and is crusted over with sulphur, alum, cinders, and other volcanic matter ; in the midst of which are to be seen several cauldrons in a perpetual state of ebullition.* In

---

* The number of boiling fountains varies according to the intensity of the action of the crater. I counted fourteen of them in 1842.

some the water is remarkably clear; but in the larger ones it is quite black, and boils up to the height of two or three feet, constantly emitting dense clouds of sulphureous steam, accompanied by the most offensive and suffocating stench. From the comparative heaviness of the circumambient air, these clouds generally ascend to the summit of the hills, and then shoot off horizontally in the direction of the wind. After remaining stationary for three minutes on any part of the crust, the subterraneous heat is sensibly felt through the strongest shoe—a circumstance which would seem to indicate that the volcanic focus is not confined to the boiling fountains. Indeed, it is only necessary to remove a small portion of the crust to the depth of eighteen inches or two feet, and the water underneath will find a vent to the cavity and transform it into a cauldron. Occasionally, fresh fountains spontaneously burst forth, and then some of the lesser ones are reduced to bubbling pools of liquid matter, which gradually subside and become quite extinct in appearance.

There is a peculiar feature about the Soufriere, which does not belong to any other volcano. Of course, it can bear no comparison with Etna, Vesuvius, and other celebrated volcanoes, for the intensity and violence of their eruptions, or their terrific grandeur even in a state of quiescence; but it surpasses all others by its uninterrupted manifestation of the volcanic process. Even the Geycers in Iceland, to which it would seem to bear a striking resemblance, only play at intervals, whilst the Soufriere is in a continuous though less violent state of eruption. What it was three hundred years ago it is at this moment, and will probably be three hundred years hence. From the chaotic appearance of the surrounding objects, and particularly of the Pitons, there is no doubt that this spot was once the centre of some awful convulsion of nature; but at what period there is now no means of ascertaining. It must have occurred long before the discovery of the island, as no chronicle of any such event has been handed down to us by the Caribs.

Another peculiarity of this volcano is the perennial supply of water which it commands. It is supposed that this water is received through some subterraneous passage from the *Etangs*, or lakes, situated at a distance of half a mile to the south-east of the volcano; nor does this supposition appear wholly unwarranted, when it is considered that the water in the Etangs is visibly decreasing year after year. Surely neither the

rivulet at the foot of the crater, nor any springs
in its immediate vicinity, could have supplied for
ages the quantity of water which is daily ab-
sorbed by the unremitting action of this extraordinary work of nature.

The hot springs and mineral waters of the
Soufriere were celebrated in former days for their
medicinal properties, and continue to be advantageously used by convalescents even to this day.
The first who appears to have taken any notice of
them was the Baron de Laborie. Soon after his
assumption of the Government in 1784, he caused
the waters to be analysed by the " Médecins du
Roi" in St. Lucia and Martinique ; and in consequence of their favorable report Louis XVI.
granted a sum of money towards the construction
of baths and the requisite buildings, " for the use of
His Majesty's troops in the Windward Islands."
This humane undertaking was confided to the
Baron de Laborie, under whose superintendence
it was completed in the course of the year 1785.
The baths were established upon an extensive
scale between the volcano and the town of Soufriere, at a distance of little more than a mile from
the latter place, and they continued for many years
to be the resort of invalids from the neighbouring
islands.

In December, 1836, some steps were taken by
Sir Dudley Hill to restore the Soufriere baths, but
his exertions were defeated by Mrs. Alexander,
the owner of an adjoining estate, who put forward
a claim to the portion of land formerly occupied
by the works. In an action for trespass against
the Governor, the Royal Court decided that " the
baths and circumjacent land were the property of
Dame Alexander ; and that, consequently, the
works commenced thereupon by the local government should be discontinued, and matters put
back in *statu quo.*"

St. Lucia is watered by innumerable rivers and
rivulets, which ever and anon arrest the traveller's
progress. They have their source in the Pitons
and mornes, whence they meander over hill and
dale, in the most fantastic courses, irrigating and
fertilising the plains below. During the wet
season, and after heavy showers, some of these
streams descend impetuously the steep sides of
the mornes, tearing up the brushwood and trees
by the roots, and precipitating whole masses of
earth and rock upon the roads and fields in the
valleys. Nor is this power of devastation confined
to the mountain streams. On these occasions
the rivers in the low grounds overflow their banks,
and forcing their way through gullies and rocks,

sweep before them every species of vegetable production. The principal rivers are those of Castries, Grand-cul-de-Sac, Roseau, Anse Laraye, Canaries, Soufriere, Anse l'Ivrogne, Choiseul, the River Dorée, Balambouche, Piail, Anses Noires, Vieux Fort, Canelle, Troumassé, Volet, Dennery, Louvet, Marquis, Esperance, Choc, and Vide Bouteille. With little labor and expense some of these rivers might be rendered navigable for small craft, to the incalculable advantage of the contiguous estates.

In the dry season the volume of water contained in the smaller streams being insufficient to force a passage into the sea, their embouchures are dammed up by mounds of sand and gravel, formed by the action of the waves. These basins of stagnant water are called Lagoons. The beach between them and the sea is generally of a compact nature, and affords a safe passage to all who are fond of a ride along the beautiful belts of sand that encircle the coast. Not so when the heavy rains set in : then the embouchures overflow, and the beach, without undergoing any apparent alteration, is converted into a series of quicksands, which often prove fatal to the incautious traveller.

There are several bays in this island which afford excellent anchorage for ships of every size.

The most remarkable to windward are those of Marquis, Grand'Anse, Louvet, Dennery, Praslin, Micoud, Troumassé, Volet, Canelle, and Savannes, and to leeward those of Gros-ilet, Choc, Castries, Grand-cul-de-Sac, Marigot, Roseau, Anse Laraye, Soufriere, and Vieux Fort. The bays to windward are somewhat dangerous and difficult of access, owing to the rugged formation of the shoals, and the prevalence of boisterous winds from the Atlantic. The most singular of them all is the bay of Marigot, with its double basin formed like two rings of a chain, the inner of which is entirely concealed from view on the coast side.

The principal station for the shipping is the Port of Castries, one of the safest and most extensive in the Antilles.* It is adorned with an excellent quay, and possesses a sufficient depth of water to allow the largest vessels to come to anchor close to the wharf. Its entrance is one-third of a mile between the headlands of the Tapion and the Vigie; and it is a mile and a half in receding depth. From the invariable direction of the trade wind, and the consequent difficulty of approaching the bay, no more than one vessel can enter at a time, whilst the largest fleet might

* In compliment to this port the seal of the island bears the legend, " Statio haud male fida carinis."

safely ride at anchor within the basin, and stand out to sea at an hour's notice.

St. Lucia is formed into two great divisions or districts. The eastern side, which is exposed to the trade winds and the Atlantic Ocean, is called the Windward District; and the western side, which looks out upon the Caribbean Sea, is called the Leeward District.* It is subdivided into eleven *quarters* or parishes, viz. : Castries, Anse Laraye, Soufriere, Choiseul, Laborie, Vieux Fort, Micoud, Praslin, Dennery, Dauphin, and Grosilet. At the period of the introduction of the apprenticeship system, there were three stipendiary magistrates allotted to this island, and it was accordingly divided into three districts. The first comprised Castries, Gros-ilet, Dauphin, and Anse Laraye; the second, Soufriere, Choiseul, and Laborie; and the third, Vieux Fort, Micoud, Praslin, and Dennery. At a later date the number of stipendiary magistrates having been increased, the island was divided into five districts. The first included Castries and Anse Laraye; the second, Gros-ilet and Dauphin; the third, Soufriere and Choiseul; the fourth, Vieux Fort

---

* The terms *Cabesterre* and *Basseterre* have long since been disused ; if, indeed, they were ever employed to express any division of St. Lucia, which there is good reason to doubt.

and Laborie; and the fifth, Micoud, Praslin, and Dennery. The last division holds good to this day, as regards the jurisdiction of the stipendiary magistrates; but the old division into parishes is the only one recognised in practice, and adhered to in the agricultural relations of the country and the proceedings of the Courts of Law. Each parish contains a town or a village, situated at the extremity of its principal bay, and the same name applies alike to all three. The villages are remarkable for nothing save their lonely little churches and deserted streets. They are chiefly inhabited by females of retired habits, fishermen and other idlers of the male sex, and the infirm of both sexes and of all ages.

Castries, the principal town in the island, and the seat of Government, is situated at the extremity of the beautiful bay of that name. It was originally called the " Carénage "—a name commonly assigned to careening places in the West Indies. The name of " Castries " was first given to it in 1785, in honor of Marshal de Castries, the French Colonial Minister of the day. Subsequently, when the Republican rage for altering names and abolishing institutions extended to St. Lucia, the name of Castries, of aristocratic origin, was suppressed, and the more homely one of " Carénage " substituted. In the struggle for preponderance which ensued, as often as the island fell into the hands either of the British or the Republicans, the appellations of " Castries " and " Carénage " were respectively adopted by the dominant party. Hence the latter has been disused since the capitulation in 1803.

The plain on which the town stands is in some places below the level of the sea, and consists chiefly of alluvial formations, and what is called " made land." In former days a practice was adopted by the local executive of granting certain portions of the *land under water*, on condition that the lots should be filled up and enclosed. These grants have been the means of wresting from the empire of the ocean a considerable portion of the space now occupied by the western extremity of the town; but those who obtained concessions in the northern division have not exhibited the same zealous exertion, and to their negligence, in great measure, is to be attributed the existence of swamps in that part of the town.

Castries is bounded on the north by an inlet of the bay and the lands of *Sans Souci;* on the east by the *Chaussée* and the lands of *Leslie;* on the south by the river and *Morne Fortuné*, and on the west by the Harbour. It has the form of a quadrangle, and contains 600 houses and a population of 4,000 souls. The streets are wide and well laid out, extending in parallel lines from east to west and from north to south. Most of them are paved, and some are ornamented with foot-paths. The upper part, or *Chaussée* division, is chiefly occupied by the humbler orders, and the houses are all built of wood and covered with shingles. The lower, or *Bord-de-mer* division, is the resort of the wealthier classes. Here the houses are constructed of stone, brick, or wood, according to the taste of the owners, or the pre-vailing anxiety to guard against the consequences of fire, hurricane, or earthquake.

The river on the south side of the town, from enjoying the privilege of traversing the "capital," is converted into a noxious swamp. Not only is the upper portion of it used as a general washing-place by all classes of the community, but the river itself, at the back of the streets, is estab-lished by law as a reservoir for every description of filth. Besides this swamp, there are several others of greater extent to the north-east of the town. These are covered with mangrove bushes, are occasionally inundated by the sea, and for several days after a heavy fall of rain, are found to contain a quantity of stagnant water. Dr. W. J. Evans, a physician of acknowledged ability, who resided several years in St. Lucia, attributes the insalubrity of Castries chiefly to these swamps, and to the miasma which they engender. Of course, as new streets are opened in that direction, the nuisance will gradually disappear. Nothing, however, but the extension of the town to the base of the surrounding hills, from *Sans Souci* to the *Four à Chaux*, will effectually eradicate the evil, and it will require ages of improvement to produce that result.

Castries possesses a *Place d'Armes*, or square, 336 feet from east to west, and 292 from north to south. To that active Governor, Sir Dudley Hill, this square is indebted for much of its importance. He it was who planted its ornamental trees; removed the old Court House (an eye-sore that formerly stood in the centre); and thence transferred the market to its present advantageous and more suitable position at the north-west corner of the wharf.

Two officers, styled "Town Wardens," are appointed to enforce the regulations as to cleanliness, and superintend the reparation of the pavements, the removal of all obstructions from the wharves, and of all buildings in a state of decay. This office

was established by a local enactment on the 24th
of August 1835. The Town Wardens are appointed annually, receive neither salary nor emolument, and are bound to perform the duty under a
penalty of £50 sterling. The office is, nevertheless, very inefficiently executed, as every stranger
that visits Castries cannot fail to observe from the
filthy state of the streets.

An Inspector of Police, having three serjeants
and twenty men under his orders, is invested with
a direct surveillance over all matters affecting the
public tranquillity. This office was created by a
local enactment on the 6th of May 1839 : but the
duties are so loosely defined, and so much confusion has been superadded in the shape of comment
and explanation by subsequent regulations, that the
Inspector is frequently perplexed as to the actual
extent of his powers. And, moreover, he has so
many conflicting authorities to deal with, from the
Governor down to the driver of the chain gang—
each exercising a concurrent or co-ordinate jurisdiction—that he is perpetually encroaching upon
the province of some functionary or other. Thus
we find him at one time metamorphosed into a
police magistrate, taking depositions in criminal
cases ; and at another time transformed into a
public prosecutor, indicting offenders before the

Court of Police. Meanwhile, the Governor exercising the Queen's prerogative, the Royal Court with its supreme jurisdiction, the Attorney-General as "Chef de la Magistrature," the Council wielding the legislative authority, the Stipendiary Magistrates holding special privileges, and the local Justices claiming exclusive rights—are all contriving to usurp the vaguely-defined authority of the Inspector of Police. The contrariety and confusion which must inevitably result from such a system are amongst the least of its abuses.

There is no regulation for the assize of bread—nothing to determine its weight or the quality of the flour. The consequence is that the bread sold in Castries is frequently of the very worst description. There is no inclosure to the Protestant or Catholic Cemetery, and the former has the additional disadvantage of being situated to windward of the town—a circumstance that should have been carefully guarded against in a tropical country. Until very recently there was no shamble or slaughter-house, the butchers being allowed to slaughter in the most frequented parts of the town; and the little improvement that has been effected in this important branch of municipal economy, is entirely owing to Colonel Clarke, the present Lieutenant-Governor. In the event of a fire the

town would be found in the most destitute condition as to the means of averting the ravages of
that terrific and destructive element. Formerly
there were two fire-engines, and a company of the
Militia was specially appointed to preserve them
in working order. But the Militia have been
disbanded, and the engines left to rust and
rot. It is now nearly four years since they were
examined by a competent person, and pronounced
totally unfit for use; and although his report was
laid before the Governor in Council at the time,
no steps have yet been taken to remedy this crying evil.

The public buildings that deserve to be noticed
in connection with Castries, are the Government
House, the Protestant Church, the Asylum, the
Government Offices, the Catholic Church, and the
Gaol.

Government House, commonly called the *Pavilion*, is a spacious wooden structure, tastefully laid
out, and fitted up in a style of elegance worthy
the representative of the Sovereign. It is situated
at the western extremity of Morne Fortuné, on a
plateau or terrace, which commands one of the
most picturesque views in this eminently picturesque island. The prospect, at all times strikingly grand, is seen to the greatest advantage an

hour or two after sun-rise. Below lies the bay
of Castries, gently rocked to rest by the morning
breezes—the wide-spread town with its shingled
houses glittering in the sun—the quay skirted
with vessels of every size—then Vieille Ville and
the Vigie, clothed in undying verdure, as they jut
into the sea—farther on the coast indented
by a succession of lovely little bays—on the
right several eminences topped with gardens and
negro huts—in the distance Pigeon Island—and
straight across the channel, as far as the eye can
reach, the gray cliffs and woody mountains of
Martinique. The prospect is bounded on the
left by a bright expanse of ocean, and on the
right by a curtain of "mornes" fantastically drawn
up before the rising sun, which is seen gradually
to emerge behind their cloudy summits, shedding
alternate tints of light and shadow on the scene
around.

The Protestant Church is situated at the north-
east corner of the town, in the centre of the
extensive swamps which I have already described.
It is seventy-eight feet in length from east to
west, and thirty-two in width; and is calculated
for the reception of two hundred persons. The
first stone of this edifice was laid in 1830, during
the temporary administration of Colonel Far-

quharson, and it was finished in 1832, at an expense of £2,980 sterling. Its steeple was struck by lightning during a severe thunderstorm on the 11th October 1833, and shivered from the summit to the base.

The site of this church appears to have been selected without any regard to health or convenience. If Colonel Farquharson had been commissioned to devise the best means of checking the growth of Protestantism in St. Lucia, he could not have succeeded more effectually, than by erecting the church in the heart of a swamp. Nor is this all : owing to its distance from the houses of the respectable inhabitants, they are compelled to traverse the town under a broiling sun, and the state of fatigue and perspiration in which they reach the church, must predispose them to inhale more of the poison of miasma from the surrounding atmosphere, than of the spirit of God's holy word. Finally, in 1834, as if to put a climax to the infection of this locality, the Protestants, discontinuing their former commendable usage of interring their co-religionists side by side with their Catholic neighbours, commenced the formation of a cemetery for themselves within four yards of the church.

The asylum stands upon a small estate called

Vieille Ville, forming, together with the glacis of Fort Vigie, a peninsula at the north side of the harbour of Castries. This property, consisting of ninety acres of land, was purchased in 1840 on behalf of the colony for the sum of £1,700 sterling. The principal building is used as an asylum for the destitute poor : it is a spacious, substantial structure, consisting of two stories and a garret, and built of brick. It is sixty-four feet long from east to west, and thirty-two feet wide. There are several minor buildings and offices attached, besides a lime-kiln, an alley of cocoa-nut trees, and an extensive tract of pasture ground. This delightful little spot, the favourite resort of maroon parties, commands an interesting view of the town, the harbour and the surrounding hills.

Formerly the different public offices were scattered through the town, each functionary being permitted to keep his office at his private residence. This abuse was reformed by Sir Dudley Hill in 1835, since which period the officers of Government have been established under one roof in Mr. Muter's extensive premises in Mongiraud-street. The principal building is 106 feet long by 39 wide, and consists of two stories and a garret. The ground-floor is appropriated to the

offices of Colonial Treasurer, Attorney-General,
Solicitor-General, Registrar of the Courts, and
Provost Marshal ; and the upper story is occupied by the Court House, the Council Chamber,
and the Secretary's Office.

The Government buildings have been materially
damaged by earthquakes. After that which occurred on the 11th January 1839, the east angle
had to be taken down and reconstructed ; and
there are fissures still conspicuous in many portions of the building, which render it very unsafe
in the event of another earthquake or hurricane.

The Catholic Church, situated on the eastern
side of the *Place d'Armes*, is a substantial stone
structure, 111 feet long and 54 wide, capable
of containing eight hundred persons. It appears that the original projectors had proceeded
to lay the foundation without any fixed plan
as to ulterior execution ; and when the walls
were erected, the span of the building was
found too great for any description of roof that
could be devised. Sorely did this puzzle the
ingenuity of the St. Lucia architects, and many
were the schemes proposed and rejected, until at
length recourse was had to a carpenter from Barbados, under whose directions the present roof
was planned and put up. It is a most complex

affair—knit together in a curious fashion, and supported by eighteen pillars, which serve the double purpose of solidity and ornament.

To the zeal and perseverance of the late Rev. Florent Chevalier the inhabitants of Castries are indebted for the erection of this church, and in compliment to him it is dedicated to Saint Florent, who was Bishop of Strasbourg in the seventh century. It is adorned with a picture of the Saint, and one of Saint Andrew, recently presented by the Scotch members of the community. Both are from the pencil of Mademoiselle David, and are considered creditable specimens of art. It also possesses a marble altar, and a *chaire*, or pulpit, of mahogany, fifteen feet high. The latter, a piece of workmanship of singular beauty, was manufactured by Mr. Nicholas, a native, and self-taught cabinet-maker. The church is richly supplied with vestments and utensils for religious worship : the chancel is paved with marble, and the altars are ornamented with a variety of gilt and plated candlesticks and a profusion of artificial flowers.

The Gaol, usually styled the Royal Gaol, stands on the south side of the Castries river. It is a massive stone building, 78 feet in length, from north to south, and 36 in width, consisting of

two stories and a garret, and having a covered
gallery or verandah in front.   The ground floor
is divided into ten cells, which are used as
cachots, or places of solitary confinement.   The
upper floor contains seven rooms, besides two
apartments for debtors ; and the garret is divided
into three large rooms, generally allotted to
females not confined in the cachots.   This building was commenced in 1824 and finished in
1827, at an expense to the colonial revenue of
£5,417 sterling.   It is well ventilated, is surrounded with a strong wall, and provided with a
residence for the Gaoler, apart from the inmates.
There is a surgeon attached to the establishment,
who visits the prisoners every day.

   This Gaol is one of the best in the West Indies,
and in point of cleanliness, order, and general
management, has been creditably conducted by
Mr. W. Morrison, the present keeper. A right of
superintendence and control was formerly exercised by the Provost Marshal, and a Gaol Committee, composed of the Governor, the Chief
Justice,   the   Attorney-General,   two   Puisne
Judges, two unofficial Members of Council, the
Protestant and Catholic Clergymen of Castries,
and two Justices of the Peace.   This unwieldy
and complex machinery was set aside in 1837 by

an Act of the Imperial Parliament " for the better government of prisons in the West Indies," and the supervision of all matters relating to the Gaol is now vested in one officer, styled an " Inspector of Prisons."

Next in importance to Castries is the improving little town of Soufriere, unrivalled for the beauty and diversity of its tropical scenery. The most fascinating view is from the ridge of a perpendicular hill, 1,200 feet it height, which overhangs the town on the road to Castries. From this elevated position the traveller's bewildered eye descends into the valley, and rapidly glancing over the town, is irresistibly attracted by the *Pitons*, standing in their lonely and imposing grandeur on the opposite side of the bay. Returning to the plain, he follows the little town, as it spreads up the side of the hill, interspersed with gardens of flowers and fruit-trees, and overtopped by the cocoa-nut and the palm in full vigour and luxuriance. Rising still higher he lights on the picturesque and perpendicular ascent, called the " Chemin de la Croix," recently formed on the side of the hill ; and carrying the eye into the clouds, he reaches the ridge of a morne, of equal elevation to that on which he stands, clothed with the verdure of the cane to its very summit. Descending again into the valley he is struck with the most singular vicissitude of scenery : the back ground, to the east of the town, presents an extensive amphitheatre, encircled by steep, cloud-capped hills, and laid out into cane-fields of vivid green. And the whole is studded with the pretty little villas of the different proprietors, and their characteristic accompaniment of negro huts.

The town of Soufriere contains 220 houses, and a population of 1,500 souls. The streets are badly paved, but there is more attention shown to cleanliness than in Castries. Here is a very pretty church, recently somewhat enlarged, but still too small for the wants of the population. Its steeple of cut stone, erected at the expense of the labourers of the district, was thrown down by the earthquake of 11th January 1839, and a neatly painted wooden spire now occupies its place. The prison is a small stone building on the slope of the hill : it is used as a place of confinement for prisoners on their way to the Gaol of Castries, and for the reception of offenders convicted by the local Magistrates.

The principal fortresses are those of Morne Fortuné, commonly called Fort Charlotte, the Tapion, the Vigie, Pigeon Island, and Vieux Fort.

Morne Fortuné is a hill about eight hundred feet in elevation, situated on the south side of the town and harbour of Castries, and commanding a magnificent view of different portions of the island, and an extensive prospect along the coast and out to sea. Its ridge is studded with fastnesses and fortifications, as well as barracks and buildings of every description for the accommodation of the troops, the artillery and engineer departments, and the Ordnance Store-keeper. The barracks are a cluster of brick buildings of one story, situated within Fort Charlotte, and capable of receiving 240 men. The hospital is 140 feet long from east to west and 27 wide, containing four wards for the sick, and surrounded with an open gallery. But the chief ornament of Morne Fortuné is an edifice called the " iron barracks," constructed for the accommodation of the officers. It was commenced in 1829 and finished in 1833. It is 120 feet in length from east to west, 25 in breadth, and two stories in height. The walls are built of ashlar stone, held together by means of iron bars. There is an iron gallery to each story, and an exterior iron staircase from the ground to the roof. The iron barracks are considered hurricane proof; but unfortunately hurricanes are not the only casualties that St. Lucia is exposed to.

Earthquakes, too, are of common occurrence, and this building was somewhat damaged by that which occurred on the 11th January 1839.

Morne Fortuné, whether with reference to its difficult position, the extent and elegance of its buildings, or the strength of its defences, was once regarded as one of the most important military posts in the Antilles ; and the foreigner who visited it was no less struck with its imposing appearance, than with the clean, comfortable, English look of every thing about it—its neat cottages, smiling flower-gardens, ever-green fences, smooth grass-plots, and gravel walks ; but, of late years, its gardens are sadly neglected, and its fortifications are fast falling into decay.

The entrance to Port Castries is guarded on the south by the Tapion and Half-moon batteries, and on the north by the Vigie. These defences command every approach to the bay, and with the aid of their natural ally, the trade-wind, can oppose an insuperable barrier to the ingress of any hostile fleet.

Pigeon Island lies 700 yards westward of the northern extremity of St. Lucia, at a distance of seven miles from the Tapion. It is three-quarters of a mile in length from north to south, and somewhat less than half that extent at its greatest breadth : it contains about forty acres of pasture ground. The barracks are capable of accommodating six officers and one hundred men. Fort Rodney, the principal defence, is situated on the southern eminence, and commands the bay and town of Gros-ilet, on the opposite shore. Pigeon Island has always been considered a most salubrious locality, and it was in contemplation to use it as a convalescent post for invalids from the military stations in the other islands; but in consequence of the ravages committed there by yellow fever in 1842, this scheme appears to have been relinquished. Communication by telegraph is regularly carried on between this fort, the Vigie, and Morne Fortuné ; and no vessel can pass the channel, between St. Lucia and Martinique, or enter the harbour of Fort Royal, without being distinctly descried from Pigeon Island. In the distance stands the Diamond Rock, celebrated in the history of our naval exploits in these seas.

Vieux Fort, which has given its name to the quarter in which it is situated, at the southern extremity of the island, was a fortress of some importance at a remote period. It must have been abandoned long before the colony fell into the hands of the British, as the name would appear to indicate. I visited this fort in 1833, and again in 1841 : it is now overgrown with shrubs and brushwood, and the works are totally dismantled.

Until late years St. Lucia enjoyed the merited distinction of having the head quarters of the white and black troops at Morne Fortuné. Since 1838 it has been deprived of that advantage by the withdrawal of both, and their removal to stations of much less importance. The actual strength of the troops at Morne Fortuné on the 1st January 1844 was seven officers, eleven non-commissioned officers, and two hundred and fifteen rank and file ; and at Pigeon Island one officer, one non-commissioned officer, and thirty-three rank and file. These, together with twenty-six artillery-men, constituted the whole forces in the Colony.

What further aggravates the difficulties of this situation is the total absence of any organised body of native troops, and the utter impracticability of organising them on any emergency. The St. Lucia Militia, a respectable, good-looking corps, and brought to a state of efficiency by the skilful drilling of Major Kearney, and the judicious superintendence of Sir Dudley Hill, was disbanded on the 16th February 1839, under a local enactment, subsequently confirmed by the Sovereign. The motives of policy that are sup-

posed to have operated the suppression of the
Militia were less applicable to this island than to
many others ; and I feel persuaded that the
re-organisation of that corps would be attended
with beneficial results. For that purpose it
would be necessary to obtain a fresh supply of
arms and accoutrements : there are about eight
hundred stand of arms, which are considered
serviceable ; but the old accoutrements have
been destroyed as unfit for use.

The rugged and mountainous formation of the
island, combined with a want of energy on the
part of some proprietors of estates, presents great
difficulties in the construction of roads. The
consequence is that the internal communications
are generally very bad, and in some places
dangerous. There are three principal roads, viz.,
that which extends from Castries to Vieux Fort,
through the leeward districts, a distance of sixty
miles—taking in Morne Fortuné, Roseau, Soufriere, and the Etangs ; 2dly, the road from
Castries also to Vieux Fort, through the windward districts, a distance of forty-five miles, including the *Trace*, the *Barabara*, and the *Bamboos;*
and 3dly, the road from Castries to the town of
Gros-ilet, at the northern extremity of the island
—a distance of nine miles.

The piece of road from Castries to Morne Fortuné, winding up the acclivity of the hill, is kept in excellent condition by the military department, although a portion of it is included within the range of the Town Wardens' authority. The drains in some places are but ill-contrived for carrying off the water, and in the rainy season the road becomes furrowed ; but this damage is easily repaired. Mr. Coleridge* has given an amusing account of the fright he was thrown into whilst ascending this hill in 1825; and one cannot help smiling at the exaggerated terms in which that gentleman's love of the marvellous induced him to represent the danger and difficulty of the ascent. The road, however, both as regards its nature and construction, was in his day what it is at this moment—what it has been since it was first formed—neither perpendicular nor precipitous, neither dangerous nor difficult. Even the most timid and delicate females daily ride up and down, without the slightest apprehension of danger.

After crossing Morne Fortuné, the traveller descends into the valleys of Grand-cul-de-Sac and Roseau, and to the discredit of all concerned, both proprietors and Road Commissioners, the

* " Six Months in the West Indies."

roads in these valleys are the worst in the island. The descent is over the slope of several hillocks, intersected by numerous chasms and ravines, which are spanned by a bridge (as it is abusively called) formed of loose hurdles, and covered over with clay. The road itself is made of clay, and after a shower of rain becomes a perfect quagmire, while the bridges disappear altogether into the bottom of the ravine.

In the month of September 1841 Governor Graydon, accompanied by Captain Ormsby, his private secretary, M. G. Laffitte, Esq., Special Justice, and myself, completed a tour of the island by a short visit to the valley of Roseau. After an early breakfast with Mr. Muter at the Cottage, we started for the Anse Galet estate, in the direction of Soufriere, with the intention of returning to partake of that gentleman's hospitality at dinner. In the course of the day we were visited by a shower of rain, which no one imagined could have had any other effect than that of imparting some degree of coolness to the atmosphere. Great, however, was our surprise on reaching Roseau valley at six o'clock, to find that the bridge we had crossed in the morning, at a place called *Ravine Rouge*, had been swept away, and that a mountain torrent was rolling between us and our dinner

within a few yards of Mr. Muter's house. One of
the party, regardless of his situation after a fatiguing ride, proposed to breast the torrent ; while
another, with a more commendable attention to
health, suggested a retreat upon Anse Galet. At
length, after canvassing both plans in a council of
war, the retreat was resolved upon and effected
by ten o'clock at night. Next morning, just as
we returned to Roseau, the architects of the valley
were giving a finishing dash of mud to a new bridge
of hurdles over the Ravine Rouge.

The road between Roseau and Soufriere is the
best bridle road in the island. It was constructed
in 1786 by a corps of French Artillery, under the
directions of General de Laborie. A considerable
portion of it is scarped from the solid rock : it is
partially shaded with forest trees, and here and
there its sides are flanked by detached fragments
of rock, which, like so many trophies, stand recording to the end of time the honoured name
and enterprising spirit of Laborie. The actual
distance from Castries to Soufriere is no more
than fifteen miles in a direct line ; but the length of
road to be travelled over may be computed at thirty-
five miles, owing to its interminable windings and
a continuous altenation of ravine and promontory,
forming a sort of horizontal zig-zag along the
coast.

After ascending the hills which overhang the
town of Soufriere the road to Vieux Fort assumes
an eastward direction, extending across a comparatively level country. The most remarkable
feature of this road is the scenery of the *etangs*,
or lakes, which although inferior to that of other
districts in grandeur and variety, is nevertheless
of a highly interesting character. Here the traveller who has visited in succession the plains,
and the Pitons, the valleys, and the volcano, may
contrast with their striking sublimity the soothing
loveliness of the humble landscape; its gardens
and grass-plots, clothed in the richest verdure; its
luxuriant coffee bushes, spreading their branches
and berries in endless profusion under the protecting foliage of the plantain; and its stately " peu-
pliers" and palms overtopping the chequered
scene.

The road from Castries to the windward part of
the island is called the *Trace*, or mountain track.
Starting in an eastern direction you gradually
ascend to the summit of a hill, connecting Morne
Fortuné with the central chain of mountains ; and
continue your route until you reach the more elevated situation near Mr. Guesneau's estate. This
spot, being itself totally devoid of trees, presents
an uninterrupted prospect, for many miles round,

of hills and valleys, mornes and ravines, covered
with umbrageous forest trees and interspersed with
cane fields, coffee bushes, and gardens, in endless
variety. The *coup d'œil* is at once picturesque
and sublime. At this point the *Trace* com-
mences and runs along the summit of the mountain range, abruptly winding up and down through
a labyrinth of brushwood and broken trees. The
ridge in many places is so narrow as not to admit
of two persons riding abreast; and the passage or
track is extremely dangerous, being bounded on
either side by tremendous and unfathomable precipices. During the hurricane months the summit of this mountain is shrouded in mists ; and
the huge masses of rock which are seen projecting
on every side, held up by the roots of trees, shooting from their interstices, impart a wild and sombre
aspect to the scene. But the most remarkable
feature of this extraordinary mountain-pass is
the descent from the summit of Morne Barabara
to the valley of Mabouya. Here, while the traveller is panting for breath, he contemplates beneath him a declivity, 2000 feet in depth, and all
the way down a perpendicular track, shaped into
a corkscrew by the inequalities of the ground.
As he proceeds on his headlong course, hanging
over the horse's neck, both man and horse ap-

pear suspended from the side of the precipice,
as if supported by some invisible agency. In
proportion, however, to the danger of the descent is the precaution of the traveller, and
serious accidents are of unfrequent occurrence.
Some persons never dismount; others never do
otherwise : this may depend upon the state or
strength of a man's nerves. After a heavy fall
of rain the earth becomes detached and slippery, and then the danger is truly appalling. But
in general it is much safer and less fatiguing to
ride the whole way down than to lead your horse.
As the Trace is the only communication by land
between the windward and leeward districts (except by making the tour of the island) the people
have become accustomed to it. The creole horse,
too, from its hardy and tenacious character, is
wonderfully adapted to this description of road ;
and what to a stranger might appear totally impracticable, is daily accomplished with spirit and
agility by numerous *cavaliers* and pedestrians.

On reaching the foot of the Barabara the
traveller is agreeably relieved of the fatigue and
anxiety of the route, by the beautiful prospect un-
folded to his view in the rich, luxuriant valley of
Mabouya. The first object that attracts his notice
is the river of Dennery, rolling its pellucid waters

towards the Atlantic. For many miles along the serpentine course of this lovely little stream its banks are adorned with innumerable clusters of the bamboo, containing each about seventy reeds, most of them fifty feet high. These clusters are thrown together in the most fantastic forms, having their tops so thickly interwoven as to exclude the rays of the sun, whilst admitting a sufficiency of light and air. The space between their base is formed into compartments of every size and shape, opening into each other through doors and gateways, arcades, arches, and porticoes ; and the ground, or rather floor, is free from vegetation, or lightly strewed with the small yellow leaf of the reed. The " bamboos " are, in truth, an enchanting locality, and as a natural curiosity are only surpassed by the volcano, while the stillness and solitude of the spot, unbroken save by the soothing murmur of the pebbled stream, point to it as the chief attraction for the lovers of pic-nic and maroon parties.

There is nothing peculiarly remarkable in the nature of the road from Dennery to Vieux Fort. It is an up hill, down dale route of about twenty-five miles, terminating in a beautiful piece of road, three miles long—the only one that has ever been used as a carriage road in St. Lucia.

The road from Castries to Gros-ilet is the chief

communication between Morne Fortuné and Pigeon Island. It extends over a comparatively level country, and is generally in good condition.

Besides the roads already mentioned there are two others of a more inland direction. The one diverges from the Gros-ilet road, near Choc, and leads to the Marquis and Grand'Anse estates, passing over the steep hill called Paix-Bouche. The other, in an incomplete state, lies across the breadth of the island. It was commenced in 1839, under the auspices of Governor Everard and discontinued in 1841 for want of the requisite funds. The object of this road was, by opening a direct communication between the windward districts and the town of Soufriere, to establish a greater facility of intercourse than that afforded by the Barabara and the Trace. Towards the accomplishment of this desirable object the Legislative Council had voted the sum of £150 sterling, and £100 had already been expended, when it was discovered that nothing short of £600 would be sufficient to complete the work. A fresh application was made to the Board, but Honourable members were unwilling to appropriate any more money for that purpose. No sooner, however, was the scheme abandoned, than they proceeded to vote £450 for the construction of water-works

in the town of Castries. It would have been un-
profitable at the time to have indulged in speculations as to the practicability of these water-
works; and I have no doubt that the money votes
were well intended: but the result has now clearly
demonstrated that the £450 would have been
more usefully employed in completing the pro-
jected line of road across the island—an object of
paramount importance to the social and commercial interests of the community.

The public roads are placed under the controul
of certain Commissioners, appointed to superintend their construction and repairs. These Officers
are nominated annually and required to perform
the duty under a penalty of £50 sterling. The
appointment is generally conferred on the most
influential planters, two of whom are allotted to
each district or parish; but there is neither salary
nor emolument attached to the office. The duties
are defined by a local enactment, dated the 8th
September 1834, the principal provisions of which
are, that the roads and highways shall be repaired
twice a year; that the inhabitants of the rural
districts shall be called upon to give sixty hours'
labour, or an equivalent in money, at the rate of
four-pence sterling for every hour's labour; and
that all bridges and canals, for the advantage or

convenience of private parties, shall be kept in repair at their expense. In June 1841, on the assumption that this ordinance does not make adequate provision for the reparation of the roads, it was proposed to abolish the office of Road Commissioner, and substitute a Civil Engineer, with a suitable salary from the Colonial revenue. This change has not yet taken place ; and it is doubtful how far it may be calculated to remove the difficulties and abuses of the present system. Perhaps, upon the whole, those abuses and difficulties are less referable to any defect in the provisions of the law, than to the supineness of the Road Commissioners and proprietors of estates.

In consequence of the dangerous shoals in the bays to windward, and the prevalence of strong breezes from the Atlantic, communication by water with that division of the island is very unfrequent, and only carried on by means of Droghers : but on the leeward side it is established on a much more extensive scale than even the communication by land. The principal conveyance is a five-oared boat, called a *pirogue*, of which there are no less than a dozen belonging to the town of Soufriere alone. They ply every day, Sundays excepted, between Castries and Soufriere, and occasionally between the latter place and Vieux Fort. Sails are used during the voyage to

Soufriere, which is generally performed in three hours and a half—the pirogue starting in the afternoon and reaching the entrance to the bay about sun-set. Passing along the coast you are presented with a succession of cliffs and coves, producing a corresponding alternation of calms and currents of air. Strong gusts of wind rush down through the valleys with such violence, as to require a constant look out on the part of the boatmen, who are often compelled to throw the whole of their weight on the larboard side to keep the pirogue steady. Apart from this the admirer of tropical scenery may yield his soul to its favourite dream, as wrapt in admiration he contemplates the lovely prospect before him—the stupendous rocks, standing bare to view or scattered in detached masses at the base of the cliffs—the smooth expanse of ocean gilded by the rays of the setting sun, and the host of silvery clouds escorting the mighty monarch to the limits of the horizon : nor is there wanting either the silent serenity of the evening breeze, or the softening sadness of the creole boat-song, to breathe a halo over the solemn scene.

It takes five hours of hard rowing to accomplish the trip from Soufriere to Castries, and in order to avoid the risk of being carried adrift by the currents, the pirogue must be steered close to the shore. When the sea is agitated there is some danger in passing the shoals at the Grand Caille, about a mile distant from the bay of Soufriere. In fact, such is the feeling of awe by which the pirogue-men are impressed from the repeated accidents that have occurred at this spot, that they have caused an image of the Virgin Mary to be placed on the summit of the cliff, where it overhangs the dangerous shoal.

The communication with Vieux Fort is remarkable for the perilous pass, formed by the breakers at Balambouche. Here the sea, at a considerable distance from the land, rises up into mountains of foam, which succeed each other with great force and rapidity. The slightest contact with them is invariably attended with disastrous results ; and the presence of mind, courage, adroitness, and physical force of the boatmen are put in requisition, to effect a passage between two breakers, without touching the one or being overtaken by the other.

Communication by water with the northern division of the island only extends to the town of Gros-ilet. It is chiefly established for the accommodation of the troops at Pigeon Island ; and a sailing-boat, fitted out at the expense of the military department, is allotted to this particular service.

CHAPTER II.*

Early History—Caribs—First occupation by the British—Grant of St.
Lucia to the French West India Company—Sale to Houel and Dupar-
quet—Treaty with the Caribs—Rival pretensions of England and France
—Incursion of the Barbadians—Defeat of Bonnard—Peace of Breda—
Surrender of St. Lucia to the French—Attempt of the English to
re-capture it—Peace of Utrecht—Grant of St. Lucia to Marshal
d'Estrées—Grant to the Duke of Montague by George the First—
Wring's Expedition—Arrival of Champigny—St. Lucia evacuated by
the English and French troops—Its neutrality recognized—Progress of
Colonization—St. Lucia re-captured by the French—Treaty of Aix-la-
Chapelle—St. Lucia again declared neutral—Renewal of hostilities—
Surrender of St. Lucia to Rodney and Monkton—Treaty of Paris—St.
Lucia assigned to France—Its importance as a Military Post—Operations of Admiral Barrington and General Grant—Capture of the Vigie
and Morne Fortuné—French fleet under D'Estaing—Battle of the Vigie
—Surrender of St. Lucia to the British—St. Lucia invested by the French
fleet under De Grasse—Preparations of General St. Leger—Retreat of
the French—British fleet under Rodney—Victory of the 12th April 1782
—Peace of Versailles—Restitution of St. Lucia to the French—Administration of Baron de Laborie.

AT the period of its discovery, St. Lucia, like
the other Antilles, was occupied by the Caribs;
and no attempt at colonization appears to have
been made before 1635. In that year the King

* The details in this and the succeeding chapter are derived from
the "Annales du Conseil Souverain de la Martinique 1786"—The St.
Lucia Almanacs for 1778 and 1789—the Code de la Martinique—

of France made a grant to Messrs. Lotine and Duplessis of all the unoccupied lands in America ; but these persons having selected Martinique for their place of residence, the Caribs continued in the uninterrupted possession of St. Lucia until the arrival of some English settlers in 1639. In August of 1640 a vessel of that nation having attempted to carry off some Caribs who visited her while she lay becalmed before Dominica, the news of this outrage was sufficient to rouse all the natural jealousy of these savage tribes : they fell upon the English settlers, massacred many of them, and drove the rest from the Island.

In March 1642 the King of France, still assuming a right of sovereignty over St. Lucia, ceded it by Edict to the French West India Company, together with all his other possessions in America. This Company, chiefly composed of needy adventurers, soon found itself unable to provide for the profitable cultivation of the islands. Differences arose amongst the direc-

Edwards's History of the British West Indies—" Loix et Constitutions des Colonies Françaisesde l'Amerique sous le vent, 1784"—Southey's Chronological History—Labat—Du Fertre—Raynal—Life of Lord Rodney—Life of Sir John Moore—Continuation of Bryan Edwards—Sir G. Blane's Select Dissertations—Life of Sir Ralph Abercrombie—James' Naval History—Colonel David Stewart's Sketches—Report of Governor Nogues —Local Records, Official Reports, and other authentic sources.

tors ; the most influential began to dictate to the majority ; and at length, on the 22nd September 1650, it was resolved to get rid of the more troublesome shareholders by selling some of the islands to them. In this way St. Lucia, Grenada, and Martinique were disposed of to Messrs. Houel and Duparquet, for the sum of 41,500 livres, or £1,660 sterling. This sale was confirmed by Letters Patent in August 1651, and on the 22nd October following, Duparquet was invested with the administration of the Government of the three islands, subject to the supreme authority of the French Monarch. Duparquet appears to have been a person of a fanatical but enterprising spirit. He erected the first fort in St. Lucia, and formed a settlement of forty colonists under the command of one Rousselan, or Chousselan, who married a female Carib, and from this circumstance soon became as much an object of veneration amongst the natives, as, from his singular intrepidity, he had been an object of terror to the Caribs of the neighbouring islands. The death of this daring adventurer, which occurred in 1655, proved a heavy loss to the rising little Colony, and to add to their embarrassments it was followed by the death of Duparquet on the 3rd January 1657.

After the death of Rousselan the Colonists
were kept in a continual state of alarm by the
incursions of the Caribs from the neighbouring
islands.   In the space of three years the administration successively devolved upon Messrs.
La Riviére, Haquet, Le Breton, De Coutis, D'Aigremont, Lalande, and Bonnard.   But of these La
Riviére, Haquet, and D'Aigremont were murdered
by the Caribs ; Le Breton was forced to flee ; De
Coutis was recalled, and Lalande fell a victim to
the climate.   At length on the 31st March 1660
a general peace was concluded at St. Christopher's,
at the residence of the French Governor, M.
Longvilliers de Poincy, between the English and
French on the one hand, and the Caribs on the
other.   By this treaty the former entered into an
offensive and defensive alliance for the purpose of
preventing any further hostilities on the part of
the Caribs : and it was stipulated on behalf of the
latter that they would abandon all claim to the
lesser Antilles, on condition of being left in peaceable possession of St. Vincent and Dominica.

This peace, however, was not of long duration.
St. Lucia soon became a bone of contention
between the two rival nations — the English laying claim to it in right of priority of settlement,
and the French in virtue of length of occupation.

Thus in 1663 the inhabitants of Barbados formed
the design of taking possession of the island; but
their project soon came to the knowledge of the
authorities of Martinique, who sent a deputation
to Barbados to notify to the English Government
the title deeds of the Heirs Duparquet. In the
meantime orders were given to put St. Lucia in a
state of defence, and a line of fortifications was
constructed along Choc Bay. These measures had
the effect of giving a temporary check to the
ardour of the Barbadians; but in the following
year they renewed their plans of attack, and in a
close engagement with the French troops, under
Bonnard, they finally put them to rout and took
possession of the fort.

In the beginning of 1664, owing to the little
progress made by the West India Company towards the colonization of the islands, the King of
France became dissatisfied with their administration, and by an arrêt of the Council of State,
bearing date the 17th April in that year, His
Majesty revoked and cancelled all the grants
made to the Company, as well as the different
sales and transfers passed by them to private
parties. A new Company, with similar powers,
but upon a footing of greater respectability and
independence, was instituted by Edict on the 28th

May, and immediately invested with the direction of the West India affairs. St. Lucia, however, continued under British rule until October 1667, when Robert Faulk, the Governor, acting in accordance with the spirit of a treaty of peace, concluded at Breda on the 31st July, sent a deputation to M. de Chambré, the Company's Agent at Martinique, inviting him to come and take possession of the island. A deed of settlement was accordingly drawn up between the parties, before a Notary Public at Martinique, and Messrs. Chambré and Clodoré took over the island in the name of the French. From that period until 1674 the Colony remained under the peaceable management of the West India Company, which was finally dissolved by Edict of the King in December of that year, and the settlements in America were re-annexed to the domain of the Crown.

St. Lucia now became a dependency of Martinique under the general Government of Count de Blénac; and no attempt appears to have been made to dispute the preponderance of the French until 1686, when an English man-of-war of fifty guns came to take possession of the island on behalf of the King of England. But Count de Blénac, being apprised of these hostile proceedings, sent a body of troops to the relief of the inhabitants, and the English Captain was compelled to relinquish his project.

On the 13th July 1700, the Governor of Barbados intimated to the Marquis d'Amblimont, Commander-in-Chief of the French Antilles, that he had received orders from the King of England to expel the French settlers from St. Lucia; to which d'Amblimont replied that the King of England had no right whatsoever to the island; and that, if any attempt were made to molest the French, he would repel force by force. This threat put an end for a time to the projects of invasion of the Governor of Barbados.

Matters continued in this state for some years. After the peace of Utrecht on the 11th April 1713, a number of deserters, sailors as well as soldiers, having taken refuge in St. Lucia, Marshal Count d'Estrées was induced to apply to the Duke d'Orleans, Regent of France, for a grant of the island, which was made over to him by Letters Patent in August 1718. The Marshal took immediate measures to colonize his new possessions: he sent out a body of troops, some pieces of ordnance, and a number of cultivators; and placed the management of its internal affairs in the hands of a Commission, composed of Messrs. Thibault,

Thouzay, Ducheneteau, Petit, and Attorney-General d'Hauterive. But in December 1722 King George the First, by way of retaliation, made a grant of the island to John, Duke of Montague, who in his turn despatched Captain Nathaniel Wring, or Uring, with a strong party to take possession of it in his name. No less a sum than forty thousand pounds is said to have been laid out on this expedition: the settlers were liberally provided with stores, provisions, artillery, and every thing necessary for an infant colony; and useful artificers were induced to give their services by the certainty of an ample reward. As soon as intelligence of these proceedings reached Martinique, the Chevalier de Feuquières, Governor-General, sent two military officers in the name of the King of France to request Captain Wring to retire. On their arrival Wring assembled a Council of his adherents, who advised him not to surrender the island. When this determination was communicated to de Feuquières he immediately mustered a party of Martiniquians and Guadaloupians, about 2000 strong, and sent them over to St. Lucia under the command of the Marquis de Champigny, who landed without opposition in little Carénage bay on the night of the 15th January 1723. Next day the British Commander

deputed two of his officers to meet Champigny;
and on the 18th, to avoid the effusion of blood, a
treaty was concluded to the effect, that the English
should evacuate the island within seven days; that
the forts and batteries should be demolished; that
the French troops should withdraw, immediately
after the departure of the English; that the Island
should remain neutral until the decision of the
two Crowns on their respective pretensions ; and
finally, that in the meantime both nations should
be allowed to resort thither for wood and water.

St. Lucia, which appears to have made but
little progress during the incursions and quarrels
of the English and French, now began to wear an
appearance of prosperity. An impulse was given
to agriculture in the cultivation of coffee and
cocoa, and several colonists from Martinique were
induced to settle in the windward District, which
until then had been left wholly uncultivated. There
was, however, no regular government in the island.
The French, apprehensive of exciting the jealousy
of the British, had cautiously avoided making any
appointments. They nevertheless managed to
attach to their interests some of the principal inhabitants, who were instructed to watch over their
respective districts, and report their proceedings
to the authorities in Martinique. All litigious

points were referred to the Chief Judge of that Colony.

The next attempt of the French to regain possession of St. Lucia was made in 1744, when the Marquis de Caylus, Governor-General, took advantage of the declaration of war to send over a body of troops in the name of the French King. But M. Martin, their Commander, died soon after their arrival. In the following year M. de Longueville, a resident colonist, was invested by the authorities of Martinique with all the powers and jurisdiction of a Military Commandant, in which capacity he administered the government until the treaty of Aix-la-Chapelle in 1748, whereby the neutrality of St. Lucia was recognised by the contending parties. De Longueville appears nevertheless to have retained the authority of Civil Commandant.

On the renewal of hostilities in 1756 M. de Bompart, Governor-General, reinstated M. de Longueville in his military attributions, and sent him some troops to assist in putting the island in a state of defence. Governor de Longueville dying in 1759 was succeeded by his nephew, the Chevalier de Longueville, who administered the government until 1762. On the 26th February in that year the sister colony of Martinique having

already succumbed to the combined operations of
the sea and land forces under Admiral Rodney
and General Monkton, the Admiral detached a
reinforcement of his squadron, consisting of the
Dragon, Norwich, Penzance, Dover, Levant and
Basilisk, and despatched them to St. Lucia under
the command of Captain Harvey, with orders to
summon the Governor to surrender the island to
his Britannic Majesty. On the arrival of the
hostile forces de Longueville used every effort to
rouse the inhabitants in defence of the Colony;
but they refused to take up arms, and he was
compelled to surrender at discretion. The ships
immediately entered the harbour and took possession of all the forts and batteries, which had forty
pieces of cannon mounted, and were capable of
making a long defence. From this period the
Colony continued in the possession of the British
until the treaty of Paris on the 10th February
1763, when a division was made of the neutral
islands, and St. Lucia was definitively assigned to
France.

Being now secure in the possession of this long
disputed island, the French resolved to establish
the Government upon a scale of imposing
grandeur. They made it the seat of a general
administration, authorised to correspond directly

with the Government of the Parent State; and erected Courts of Justice with their attendant train of offices. The chief functionaries of the new establishment were the Chevalier de Jumillac, Governor-General, M. de Chardon, Intendant, and M. de Micoud, King's Lieutenant. But the Court of Versailles soon discovered that the resources of the Colony did not admit of such an expensive establishment; and by a Royal Ordinance of the 20th September 1768 it was re-annexed to Martinique under the general government of Count d'Ennery. De Jumillac was recalled and de Micoud left in charge of the Government, which continued in his hands until his departure for France in 1771. It was during this officer's administration that the principal fort, which had been erected on the Peninsula of the Vigie, was removed to Morne Fortuné; and the town which had been commenced at Little Carénage bay, on the right of the harbour, was transferred to its present more advantageous locality.

Governor de Micoud was succeeded by his nephew, the Chevalier de Micoud, who was superseded in 1773 by the appointment of M. de Karny. But the latter dying in Martinique in 1775, the Chevalier de Micoud resumed the provisional administration until the arrival of M. de

Courcy, appointed to succeed M. de Karny. In 1776 de Courcy having been promoted to another government, the administration of affairs in St. Lucia was confided to M. de Joubert, who fixed his residence in Martinique, and empowered the Chevalier de Micoud to act as his deputy.

Such was the position of affairs when in 1778 the war broke out between England and France. The conquest of St. Lucia had now become an object of ambition with the British. Its cession at the peace of 1763 was condemned as an unwise measure. The Earl of Chatham had positively refused in his previous negotiations with M. de Bussy to cede it to France; and Admiral Rodney had at all times been so sensible of its value and importance to Great Britain, that from his earliest acquaintance with the island he never ceased to urge and advise its retention. In a letter addressed to the Earl of Sandwich, in May 1778, that brave and enterprising officer thus forcibly impressed upon the Minister the necessity of securing possession of St. Lucia. " I had lately the honour to present to your Lordship a copy of a letter I thought it my duty to send to the King's Minister before the conclusion of the last war, pointing out the great consequence of retaining some of the conquered islands, par-

ticularly Martinique or St. Lucia; and though at
that time I preferred the retention of Martinique,
I am now fully convinced that St. Lucia is of
more consequence to Britain. Martinique, though
possessing four harbours, has none equal to the
Carénage of St. Lucia, or so secure and capable
of being defended, which alone is of the utmost
consequence to a maritime power. Besides, St.
Lucia having been greatly cleared and cultivated
since the last war, will render the conquest easier,
more healthy for the troops; and when possessed
by His Majesty, be such a check upon the French
commerce, as to render Martinique and the other
islands of little use, as His Majesty's squadrons,
stationed at that island, will have it in their power
not only to block up every port in Martinique; but
likewise the cruisers from St. Lucia can always
stretch to windward of all the other islands, and intercept any succours intended for them. Add to
this the infinite consequence of the harbour called
the Little Carénage, where the largest ships of war
can be careened, be secure during the hurricane
months, and always ready to afford a speedy
succour to His Majesty's other islands, and a
certain security to the southern islands of St.
Vincent, Grenada, &c., and which at present are
equally liable to depredations from St. Lucia and

Martinique. The former island being in our hands will put Martinique in the same predicament as Dominica is at present, viz., between two of the enemy's islands, and if attacked a speedy succour in a few hours might be sent from St. Lucia ; whereas at present, whatever assistance might be necessary to defend Dominica, if attacked, must come from Antigua, an island far to leeward ; and in all probability Dominica would fall before such assistance could arrive.

" The place for careening and refitting the British ships in those seas, and the station for the Admiral who commands them, being at Antigua, an island without wood or water, and whose harbour is small and incapable of receiving large ships of war, to leeward of all the enemy's islands, must be extremely detrimental to His Majesty's and the public service during a French war ; must give the enemy great advantage, and alone points out the necessity of taking either Martinique or St. Lucia.

" Pardon, my Lord, the trouble I give you in perusing this letter ; but the observations I made when I commanded in those seas, and my frequent reflections since on the infinite importance of St. Lucia or Martinique to a maritime power, have convinced me that either of these islands, in the hands of Great Britain, must, while she remains a great maritime power, make her sovereign of the West Indies."*

The Government of the day, adopting the suggestions of Admiral Rodney, issued orders to Sir Henry Clinton, then stationed at New York, to send a reinforcement to the British commanders in the West Indies, to be employed in the conquest of St. Lucia. " By a singular coincidence it happened that the French fleet, of twelve large ships of the line, under Count d'Estaing, sailed from Boston on the same day that the British fleet, greatly inferior in strength, sailed from Sandy Hook, and that for a part of their course they sailed in parallel and not distant lines towards the West Indies. A violent gale, during which Commodore Hotham kept his ships together, while those of d'Estaing were dispersed, at once saved the English vessels from falling in with their too powerful adversaries, and enabled them to reach the West Indies before d'Estaing, and to form a junction with Admiral Barrington. The squadron, however, even after the junction, consisted of only one seventy-four, one seventy, two sixty-fours, two fifties, and three frigates."†

* Life of Admiral Lord Rodney.

† Continuation of Bryan Edwards.—The St. Lucia Almanac for 1789 gravely asserts that the squadron under Admiral Barrington consisted of eighty sail.

On the 13th December 1778 these forces, together with twelve transports and about 5,000 men, under the command of Major-General Grant, entered the bay of Grand-cul-de-Sac; and in the evening a landing was effected by Briga-dier-Generals Meadows and Prescot. At this period the garrison at Morne Fortuné was composed of but 50 men, one Captain, one Lieutenant, one Ensign, one Engineer officer, one Artillery officer, and half a dozen Artillery men. These, together with two companies of Militia, which on the first intelligence of the rupture with Enggland, had been mustered amongst the free inhabitants, constituted the whole forces of the Colony. In this defenceless condition the Cheva-lier de Micoud was speedily driven from all the posts in the vicinity, among which were the Vigie and Morne Fortuné. On the morning of the 14th, as the British advanced in three columns, they carefully secured all the heights, and amply manned the batteries. General Meadows with thirteen hundred men occupied the peninsular position of the Vigie, at the extremity of the English line, while the principal part of the army, under General Grant, was stationed on the hills between the Carénage and the bay of Grand-cul-de-Sac. At nine o'clock the French forces under

Governor de Micoud withdrew to Morne Paix-Bouche, where they were soon joined by the Militia from all parts of the island. Here they rendezvoused in the hope of receiving succours from Martinique, whither M. de Micoud had despatched three vessels to apprise Count d'Estaing of the capture of St. Lucia. Only one of these, however, escaped the vigilance of the English fleet.

D'Estaing's forces, which appear to have been intended for the reduction of Grenada and St. Vincent, consisted of about 9,000 men, partly sent from France, and partly collected in the French islands; while in addition to his twelve men-of-war he was joined at Martinique by a number of transports, frigates, and privateers. Thus equipped he proceeded to the relief of St. Lucia, accompanied by the Marquis de Bouillé, Governor-General of the French West Indies. " Fortunately for his antagonists it was so late in the day when d'Estaing appeared off St. Lucia, that he thought it proper to wait till the following morning before he commenced his operations. Admiral Barrington availed himself of this delay to station the transports at the bottom of the Cul-de-Sac, and to moor his ships in a line at the entrance, flanked by two batteries, one on each

side of the harbour. Before morning his defensive preparations were completed. D'Estaing
was as yet ignorant that the Vigie which commands the Carénage was in the power of the
invaders, and therefore with the view of landing
his troops and erecting batteries on the heights
to drive the British from the Cul-de-Sac, he bent
his course towards the harbour of Carénage. He
was received there by a discharge of artillery,
which convinced him that nothing could be done
in that quarter. After some hesitation he bore
down upon the British squadron with ten sail of
the line, and commenced a vigorous attack, in
which however he was gallantly repulsed. At
four in the afternoon he renewed the engagement
with twelve sail, and continued it with more
perseverance and a heavier weight of fire, but
with no better success. He was finally driven
back in confusion, without having made the
smallest impression on his opponents. On the
next day he appeared disposed to return to the
combat; but at length, instructed by his two
defeats, he changed his mind, stood to windward,
anchored in Gros-ilet bay, and employed that
night and the following morning in disembarking
the troops. It was now the turn of the French
soldiery to try what they could achieve against

an enemy, by whom their naval armament had already been foiled.

" The plan of the French generals was to seize on the heights, which commanded the Cul-de-Sac, and by means of a bombardment to compel the British squadron to quit its anchorage. To their great disappointment, however, they found those heights so strongly occupied by General Grant, as to make it impossible for them to carry their plan into effect, without risking a battle on disadvantageous terms. This was a risk which they did not choose to encounter. As their first project had become impracticable, they determined to bend their efforts against General Meadows, whose position could receive no other support from the main body of the army, than what was given by the two batteries on the south side of the Carénage; and who, if overpowered, was without the means of retreat. It was thought that the cutting off of this division, an event which appeared highly probable, could not fail to decide the contest in favour of the French.

" Leaving about four thousand of his troops to prevent General Grant from detaching any part of his force to interrupt their operations, the French generals on the 18th February led five thousand men to storm the lines, which the

British had thrown up to cover the position of the Vigie. They advanced in three columns, the right headed by Count d'Estaing, the centre by Count de Lowendahl, the left by the Marquis de Bouillé. As the columns approached the position of General Meadows, they were enfiladed by the batteries on the other side of the Carénage, and suffered severely. They nevertheless rushed to the assault of the lines with impetuous bravery. The coolness and firmness of the defenders were, however, more than a match for the impetuosity of the assailants. Not a shot was fired by the British till the columns were at the foot of the entrenchments. One destructive volley was then poured in, and the French were received at the point of the bayonet. The struggle was long and terrible. At last the French were driven back with heavy slaughter : seventy of them are said to have fallen within the works at the very first onset. In spite of this fierce repulse they paused only to rally and recover breath; and then hurried back with undiminished fury. The second conflict was no less violent than the first: it terminated in the same manner. Though their ranks were sorely thinned by this double discomfiture, they were induced to make a third charge; but they had no longer that ardour which originally inspired them. They were speedily broken, overwhelmed, and scattered in complete and irretrievable disorder. Their dead and wounded even were left in the hands of the victors. The battle being over, however, Count d'Estaing entered into an agreement with General Meadows by which he was suffered to bury the slain and to carry away the wounded, on condition that the latter should be considered as prisoners of war.

" So great a slaughter has seldom taken place in so short a time. Its amount exceeded the number of the English troops. Four hundred men were slain on the spot; five hundred more were so desperately wounded as to be disabled from service, and six hundred more received wounds of a slighter kind. The loss of the victors was comparatively trifling, and not a single officer was among the killed. This blow seems to have had the effect of absolutely palsying all the faculties of Count d'Estaing. He was still far superior in naval and military strength to the British. He was master of the sea, with a French Colony, that of Martinique, close at hand, whence he could draw resources; and the Chevalier de Micoud still held a part of the posts in St. Lucia. Yet, M. d'Estaing could not rouse his courage to any further exertions. Without any apparent object, unless he imagined that his presence would do what his arms had failed to accomplish, he lingered ten days inactive on the island, and then embarked his troops and resigned it to its fate. The Chevalier de Micoud was now bereft of all hope, and accordingly, before the squadron of Count d'Estaing was out of sight, he surrendered the colony to the British commanders, from whom he obtained more favourable terms than in his defenceless situation he had any reason to expect."*

Although the French retired from the island, they did not relinquish all hope of finally wresting it from the hands of the British. To the distant reader it may appear incredible that two such nations as England and France should thus have exhausted their naval and military resources in contending for an island apparently so little worthy of their ambition. But the truth is, whatever little importance might have been attached to it in time of peace, it could not fail, from its advantageous position and numerous fine harbours, to become, in every war between the two nations, the theatre of their military operations in the West. At its northern extremity, and within the short

* Continuation of Bryan Edwards.

distance of three miles from each other, it possesses four of the largest and safest bays in the
West Indies, namely, Cul-de-Sac, Castries, Choc,
and Gros-ilet—all situated within view of Fort
Royal, the chief naval depôt of the French, and
all admirably protected by the batteries of Morne
Fortuné, the Vigie, and Pigeon Island. Deprived
of this post, the British commanders must have
been secluded within the remote and inconvenient
stations of Barbados, on the one hand, or Antigua,
on the other. Whereas, with St. Lucia in their
possession, they were enabled to command the
Archipelago : there they concentrated their forces
during the war, and thence, as from an impregna-
ble fastness, the British seaman, guided by the
dauntless spirit of a Rodney or a Hood, bore down
upon the enemy in every part of the Antilles,
French, Spanish, and Dutch—pursuing their
fleets, capturing their convoys, storming their
fortresses, blockading their ports.

In May 1781 the French commanders, having
received from Europe a naval reinforcement of
twenty-one sail of the line, resolved to strike a
decisive blow against St. Lucia ; and the more
effectually to accomplish this purpose they took
advantage of the temporary absence of Admiral
Rodney, while he was endeavouring to form a

junction to leeward with the fleet under Sir Samuel Hood. Accordingly, on the 12th May the whole French fleet of twenty-five sail of the line weighed from Fort Royal bay, under the command of the Count de Grasse, and proceeded at once to invest St. Lucia; while the Marquis de Bouillé, with a considerable body of troops, succeeded in effecting a landing and took possession of the village of Gros-ilet. Emboldened by this first exploit the Marquis sent to demand the instant surrender of Pigeon Island, under pain of every severity of war. "But his threats were received with the contempt they deserved, and he was soon convinced that his vanity was not likely to be gratified by the capture of that island, by the British opening from the batteries a heavy fire upon the enemy's fleet, which continued until seven of them were compelled to cut their cables and retreat to leeward. Intelligence of these proceedings was immediately communicated to Sir George Rodney, who detached several quick-sailing vessels to apprise Lieutenant Millar, R.N., commanding at St. Lucia, that he was hastening to his relief. Fortunately at this juncture His Majesty's ships Thetis, Sancta Monica, Sybil, and Scourge, arrived off the bay of Carénage, and by their

presence greatly contributed to the preservation
of the island. Captain Robert Linzee waited
upon General St. Leger, who commanded the
troops, and requested to know in what manner
the naval department could best assist him on
this occasion. The General was of opinion that
the ships should come into the Carénage immediately. In doing this the Thetis struck upon a
rock and was sunk and totally lost. It was
resolved that detachments of the seamen and
marines should be forthwith landed from the
ships. Part of these corps, under the command
of Captains Linzee, Rodney, Smith, and Hichens,
went to the assistance of the troops, posted on
Morne Fortuné. The cheerfulness and alacrity
with which these troops marched on this service
raised the spirits of all around them, and animated them to exert themselves in making an
obstinate resistance. The vigilance of General
St. Leger at this moment of difficulty and danger
was extremely conspicuous, and proved that he
was well qualified to discharge the important
duties he had to execute; and the ardour of the
troops could be equalled only by the same disposition which displayed itself in the officers
and seamen of His Majesty's ships. The
planters, the merchants, the masters of the

trading vessels and their sailors—all ascended the hills, and repaired with the greatest alacrity to the different posts assigned them.* The whole force seemed animated with one spirit, and the effects of this spirit the enemy would have experienced, if they had dared to put their threatened attack in execution: but contrary to the expectation of the garrison, instead of marching to assault the British works, they took the very opposite route, and moved silently off to the beach, where they re-embarked their troops in the night, and retired to the bay of Fort Royal in such a hurry, as prevented their taking on board all their baggage, a part of which, with a quantity of ammunition, they left on the Island."†

The inhabitants, though naturally partial to the domination of their countrymen, were so worn out and disheartened by the repeated aggressions of the two contending powers, that they gladly availed themselves of any opportunity to secure the blessings of peace. At that period there was a high price for colonial produce, and this circumstance, coupled with the encouragement which

* It is worthy of remark that while the French inhabitants of St. Lucia were actively employed in aiding the British authority to repel the attacks of their countrymen, some of the English settlers in Barbados were assisting the French to gain possession of that island.

† Life of Admiral Lord Rodney.

they received from the British merchants and capi-
talists, enabled them to resume the cultivation of
their estates with such activity, that in a few years,
and notwithstanding the disastrous effects of the
hurricane of 1780, the Colony attained an un-
precedented degree of prosperity.

On the 19th February 1782 Sir George Rodney, after an absence of some months in England,
resumed his command in the West Indies. On
this as on former occasions, Gros-ilet bay in St.
Lucia was selected for the rendezvous of the fleet,
and here in the early part of March Sir George
took up his station with thirty-six sail of the line.
At this time the French fleet, consisting of thirty-
three sail of the line, and two ships of fifty guns,
had assembled in the bay of Fort Royal, Martinique, under the orders of Count de Grasse.
The design of the enemy was to form a junction
with the forces under the Spanish Admiral off St.
Domingo, and attempt the reduction of Jamaica.
And when we consider the weighty interests in-
olved in the issue of a naval encounter with the
combined forces—the honour of the British flag ;
the preservation of our West India Islands ; our
pre-eminence as a maritime power; nay, our very
existence as an independent nation—it is no insignificant honour to St. Lucia, that by the

position which Admiral Rodney occupied in one
of its harbours, he was enabled to watch the
motions of the enemy's fleet, to pursue them at
an hour's notice, and finally, on the 12th April
1782, to achieve that glorious and decisive
victory over Count de Grasse, whereby the
mighty projects of the coalesced powers were
annihilated, and Britain's dominion on the ocean
secured.

This victory decided the fate of the war, and
the preliminaries of a general peace were signed
at Versailles on the 20th January 1783. As in
every war the first blow was struck at St. Lucia,
so in every treaty of peace the disposal thereof
formed an important subject of negotiation. In
this instance the British used every effort to
retain it; but having stipulated the restitution of
several of their more ancient colonies, which had
been wrested from them during the war, it was
finally agreed that St. Lucia should be restored
to France. The British, however, continued in
possession until 3rd January 1784, when Major
Chester delivered it up to Viscount de Damas,
the French Governor-General.

The island of Grenada having by the same
treaty of peace been restored to the British, its
French Governor, the Baron de Laborie, was

transferred to St. Lucia, where he arrived about the middle of January 1784. The Baron was an able and enterprising engineer officer, and proved a great benefactor to the Colony, as well from the numerous improvements which he introduced into every branch of the administration, as from the many works of public utility which his professional experience enabled him to accomplish. Some time previously to his arrival the island had been infested by the Maroon Negroes, who taking advantage of the defenceless situation of the planters, had committed the most wanton depredations on the different estates, and even cruelly murdered some of the inhabitants. But by the energetic measures of General Laborie they were soon reduced, and their incursions arrested. This officer restored confidence in the commercial transactions of the Colony, and re-established those privileges of free trade which had prevailed before the war. He encouraged its agriculture by the cultivation of several spices, which he took great pains to procure from Cayenne; and became the founder of a society for the establishment of a direct commercial intercourse with the French metropolis. He promoted by his example the zeal and activity of the other functionaries of government; caused the town of Castries to be paved and otherwise improved ; constructed mineral baths near the *Soufriere* for the use of invalids from the different islands, and commenced the erection of a fountain in the principal square. But the great work which will perpetuate the name of Laborie, as a benefactor of St. Lucia, is the formation of the public road which still bears his name, and to this day the only practicable road in the island.

In the various measures of his enlightened administration the Baron de Laborie was ably supported by Messrs. de Manoel and Mongiraud, the chief civil officers of his government, to whom he was indebted for many valuable suggestions respecting the internal affairs of the Colony. The inhabitants, however, were not long destined to reap the advantages of his paternal rule. His death, which occurred on the 14th April 1789, and the subsequent proceedings of the revolutionary faction, soon plunged the Colony into all the horrors of anarchy and bloodshed.

CHAPTER III.

THE revolution of the 10th August 1792 had over-
thrown the institutions of a thousand years. The cry
of "périssent les Colonies plutôt qu'un principe,"

had been re-echoed from the other side of the Atlantic; and the blood-stained tree of Liberty, trans-
planted to the wilds of the west, had been adopted
as a native of the soil. Foremost amongst the
islands that freely drank in the maddening enthusiasm of the times stood St. Lucia ; and to such a
pitch of extravagance did her deluded children
carry their revolutionary antics, that the National
Convention conferred upon her the distinguished
appellation of " *The faithful;*" and as a token of
its special favour authorised her to send a Deputy
to France to represent her interests in that body.
Early in the year 1791 Montdenoix and Linger,
two Republican Agents, came and hoisted the tri-
color-flag on Morne Fortuné, and compelled the
Governor, Colonel de Gimat, to seek safety in flight.

In the beginning of December 1792 the St.
Lucia patriots received a visit from Captain La
Crosse, Commander of the frigate *La Félicité*, entrusted with the delicate mission of circulating
the new philosophical doctrines amongst the
Antilles. In Martinique he had met with a
cold reception : from Dominica he had been ordered away by the English Governor ; but in St.
Lucia—" the faithful" St. Lucia—he was received
with open arms, and every demonstration of sympathy and support. The incendiary pamphlets

and proclamations which this crazy adventurer
caused to be circulated throughout the island,
contributed not a little to foster that unfortunate
partiality for the doctrines of the new school,
which had already but too strongly manifested
itself. The work of the estates was discontinued,
the plantations were deserted, and nothing prevailed but anarchy and terror, in the midst of
which the Negroes under arms were discussing
the " rights of man."

Having organised the St. Lucia patriots to his
satisfaction, La Crosse proceeded to Martinique
and Guadaloupe, where the seeds of dissension,
scattered amongst the inhabitants on a former
visit, had now sprung up into full maturity. The
authorities were forthwith expelled—the planters
and their families forced to seek refuge in Trinidad, and La Crosse left in the undisputed control
of the islands. Though successively invested
with the administration of affairs in St. Lucia,
Martinique, and Guadaloupe, he did not think it
prudent to fix his residence in any of them, but
acted as a sort of Governor-General for the whole,
with the assistance of their patriotic clubs and
committees of public safety. These honours, however, he was not long destined to enjoy; for, the
National Convention, in total ignorance of the

proceedings of their Agent, had appointed General Ricard to the Government of St. Lucia, General Rochambeau to that of Martinique, and General Collot to that of Guadaloupe. Of the administration of Ricard, who arrived in St. Lucia on the 3rd February 1793, the only act worth recording is the promulgation of the Decree of the 4th February 1794, for the Abolition of Slavery in the French Antilles.

On the first declaration of war by the French, the West Indies became again the scene of military operations. The British, however, took the lead in actual hostilities, and a fleet consisting of four ships of war and nine frigates, together with a body of troops, six thousand strong, was immediately put in readiness, and placed under the command of Vice-Admiral Sir John Jervis,* and Lieutenant-General Sir Charles Grey. These forces arrived at Barbados on the 6th January 1794, and on the 5th February proceeded to invest the island of Martinique. Owing to the natural and artificial strength of that island, the inhabitants were enabled to make a protracted defence, and it was not until the 20th March that General Rochambeau finally surrendered on capitulation.

* Afterwards Earl St. Vincent.

" Victory having thus far crowned the British arms, General Grey determined without loss of time to persevere in his career of glory. Wherefore, leaving five regiments under the command of General Prescott for the protection of Martinique, he and the brave Admiral proceeded on the morning of the 31st March to the attack of St. Lucia. This island had not the means of a formidable defence ; and on the 4th April His Royal Highness Prince Edward,* after a fatiguing march of fourteen hours from the landing place, hoisted the British Colours on its chief fortress, Morne Fortuné—the garrison, consisting of 300 men, having surrendered on the same terms of capitulation as those that had been granted to General Rochambeau. Ricard, the officer commanding, desired and obtained permission, as Rochambeau had done, to embark for North America ; but the garrisons both of St. Lucia and Martinique were sent to France immediately on their surrender."†

Having thus completed the conquest of St. Lucia, General Grey appointed Sir Charles Gordon Governor, and leaving the sixth and ninth

* Edward Augustus, Duke of Kent, father of Her Most Gracious Majesty Queen Victoria.

† Bryan Edwards.

regiments with detachments of Artillery and Engineers, as a garrison, he turned his attention to Guadaloupe. On the 10th April the British forces made their appearance before Pointe à Pître, and on the 21st Governor Collot, after an ineffectual attempt to rally his scattered elements of defence, surrendered the island and its dependencies to the King of Great Britain, on the same terms as those allowed to Ricard and Rochambeau.

St. Lucia though reduced was far from tranquil. The insurgent slaves had retired into the woods, where they were joined by a number of French soldiers, who had succeeded in making their escape : and these motley masses, organised and instigated by a few democratic whites, carried on a harassing war against the British until the commencement of 1795. To add to their misfortunes, the garrison, originally inadequate to the protection of the island, had been reduced by sickness to nearly one half of their numbers ; and the survivors were worn out by fatigue from the nature of the warfare they had to sustain over a rugged and mountainous country.

Such was the embarrassing situation of the British, when a new and implacable enemy presented himself in the person of " Citoyen " Victor

Hugues.   Towards the close of 1794 this notorious character, the worthy associate and *protégé*
of Robespierre, was appointed civil Commissary for
Gaudaloupe.   Early in 1795 he received supplies
and reinforcements from the Mother Country,
and immediately commenced operations against
the British Colonies.   Though his designs were
simultaneously carried on against all the islands,
yet the plan which was first matured appears to
have been that against St. Lucia.   Thither about
the middle of February he despatched Commissary
Goyrand with a considerable body of troops ; and
having prepared the way by a series of brutal and
sanguinary proclamations against the British, the
disaffected of every class and colour hastened to
swell the ranks of the Republicans. The garrison,
reduced and disheartened, offered but a feeble
resistance ; and in a few days the whole of the
Colony, with the exception of the two posts of
Castries and Morne Fortuné, was in the possession of the enemy.

   " Affairs remained in this situation till about
the middle of April, when Brigadier-General
Stewart resumed active operations in the hope of
recovering the lost ground. The enemy were
twice defeated, compelled to retire from Vieux
Fort, and to fall back upon Soufriere, which was

their chief hold. Resolved to follow up this blow General Stewart advanced against Soufriere. Undismayed, however, by their recent defeats the Republicans had collected together a very formidable force for the defence of their main position. They knew indeed that upon the retention of it every thing depended. On his march the British General was suddenly attacked by a division which had been placed in ambush; and it was not until after a severe struggle that the insurgents were driven back. On the 22nd April the troops reached the neighbourhood of Soufriere, and were led to the assault. The contest continued warmly for seven hours; and though every exertion was made by the British, they were finally compelled to retreat to Vieux Fort, with a loss in the two engagements of nearly two hundred men.* This repulse put an end to all hopes of doing more for the present than barely retaining a footing in the island, by means of the posts that were yet in their possession. The natural strength of Morne Fortuné justified the expectation that they might make a stand there till reinforcements could arrive.

---

* Amongst the British officers that distinguished themselves on this occasion was Lieutenant Lorenzo Moore—afterwards Major-General Sir Lorenzo Moore, and Governor of St. Lucia in 1828.

" Two months passed away without the occurrence of any event worthy of notice. Sickness,
in the mean time, was making great ravages
among the British, one half of whose force was
generally unfit for service. Desertion too is said
to have assisted in thinning their ranks. The
enemy, on the other hand, were daily gaining
fresh accessions of strength. To the climate
they were habituated; and besides, disease is less
fatal to the active and victorious than to the
inert and defeated. From Guadaloupe arms and
other supplies were frequently transmitted, and
though some of the vessels fell into the hands of
the British cruisers, many of them reached their
destination in safety.

" The Republicans now began to act decisively.
They first reduced Pigeon Island and several
other posts; and on the 17th June made themselves masters of the Vigie. By this means they
interrupted the communication with Castries,
and held as it were the keys of Morne Fortuné,
upon which they now prepared for a desperate
assault. As, in the weak condition of the garrison, it would have been imprudent to hazard the
consequences of the meditated attack, the General determined to withdraw his troops. This
determination was hastily carried into effect on

the evening of the 18th : the British, leaving behind them some women and children and a quantity of stores, withdrew undisturbed to the ships ; and thus the whole island reverted to the Republican controul. It is but justice to the enemy to state that the women and children were without delay allowed to pass over to Martinique in a flag of truce."*

The abandonment of St. Lucia at this critical juncture was attended with the most disastrous consequences. Not only were the Republicans left in the undisturbed possession of an important military post, but they were enabled to send reinforcements to their friends in the other Colonies, by means of which the revolters in St. Vincent, Grenada, and Martinique opposed a successful and not unfrequently a fatal resistance to the British arms. Thus in August 1795 a detachment from St. Lucia surprised the post of Owia in St. Vincent, killed about eighty of the garrison, and compelled the remainder to take refuge in some small vessels, leaving behind them their cannon and large quantities of provisions and stores. From St. Lucia, in the month of September, Victor Hugues despatched to the same island a military force, consisting of 500

* Continuation of Bryan Edwards.

men, which so completely turned the scale on the side of the Republicans, that the British were forced to abandon their principal positions and retreat in dismay to Kingstown. In October of the same year, two corvettes from St. Lucia contrived to land at Grenada 200 men and some supplies, the whole of which arrived without opposition in the rebel camp. This timely succour roused the drooping spirits of the insurgents : they attacked and carried the works on the hill above Charlotte Town, and Lieutenant-Colonel Shaw, who commanded in the town, was compelled to retire to St. George's, leaving behind him the women and the sick in the hospital. And finally, it was his position in St. Lucia that inspired Victor Hugues with the bold design of invading Martinique, then a British Colony. On the 7th December he secretly despatched thither about 160 men, together with four field pieces, 700 stand of arms, and a quantity of ammunition; and after a protracted struggle the colonists only owed their deliverance from the thrall of that execrable tyrant to the opportune arrival of a body of Militia from Dominica.

The failure of the military operations of 1795 became a fruitful subject of complaints and recriminations, both at home and in the Colonies

By some it was ascribed to the inadequacy of the resources brought into play for the protection of the islands : by others to a want of vigilance in those who were at the head of affairs, and a want of vigour in prosecuting the various operations of the campaign. In the case of St. Lucia, more especially, the latter complaint seems to be well founded. Lieutenant-General Sir John Vaughan, with a considerable body of sea and land forces at his disposal, continued an indifferent spectator at Martinique of the struggle going on in St. Lucia ; while the Colonists, left to fight their own battle under every possible disadvantage, were doomed to witness the annihilation of the British rule within twenty miles of their head-quarters. As regards the other Colonies the case was different : some steps appear to have been taken for the rescue of St. Vincent and Grenada ; and the reverses of the British in those quarters must have resulted in a great measure from that universal feeling of terror, whereby men's energies were prostrated at the very name of Victor Hugues.

Citoyen Goyrand had now, during a period of nearly fifteen months, held sovereign sway over Republican St. Lucia, when the British Government resolved to take decisive measures for the protection of their West Indian possessions. As usual, St. Lucia was signalled out as the primary object of attack; and accordingly, on the 26th April 1796, Lieutenant-General Sir Ralph Abercrombie arrived off the island with a body of troops, 12,000 strong, supported by a detachment of the squadron under the command of Rear-Admiral Sir Hugh Christian. Goyrand's forces at this period consisted of about 2,000 well-disciplined black soldiers, a number of less effective blacks, and some hundred whites. By the aid of French engineers he had skilfully fortified the whole range of mornes from Grosilet to Grand-cul-de-Sac, and he was abundantly supplied with artillery, ammunition, and stores. Morne Fortuné was, however, his main stronghold; and it was resolved that this position should be invested without delay. The nearest approaches were the bays of Castries and Grand-cul-de-Sac; but these being powerfully protected by the surrounding batteries, the British General directed a landing to be effected in three divisions at Longueville bay, Choc bay, and Anse Laraye. For these operations a corps of nineteen hundred men was placed under the orders of Major-General Campbell, a division of which, commanded by Brigadier-General John Moore,*

---

* Afterwards Lieutenant-General Sir John Moore.

made good its landing at Longueville bay. In executing this service the enemy's batteries at Pigeon Island attempted to arrest their progress, but they were speedily silenced by the fire of the ships under Admiral Christian. In the course of the evening General Campbell landed the other detachments and effected a junction with Moore. At three o'clock on the morning of the 27th they moved forward by moonlight to invest Morne Fortuné, and in their march fell in with a party of the enemy, about 500 strong, who had posted themselves on Augier's plantation. As the troops advanced the rebels fired, and then fled to Morne Chabot, leaving the British masters of the heights above Choc and of the batteries on the shore. Next morning the fleet stood in and anchored in Choc bay, and General Abercrombie, landing with the rest of the troops, proceeded to reconnoitre the ground. After a close inspection of the heights Sir Ralph became convinced of the necessity of dislodging the enemy from their commanding position on Morne Chabot; and for that purpose orders were given that two columns, consisting of a thousand men each, under the command of Brigadier-Generals Moore and Hope,* should march at midnight and attack the Morne on two

* Afterwards Earl of Hopetown.

opposite sides. This plan, so admirably concerted for annihilating the Republican force, was partly rendered abortive through a miscalculation of time. General Moore's division, consisting of seven companies of the 53rd Regiment, led by Colonel Abercrombie, 100 of Malcolm's Rangers, and 50 of Lowenstien's, commenced its march at midnight; but being misinformed by the guides, they fell in with the advanced picket of the enemy nearly two hours sooner than had been expected. General Moore, finding himself discovered, nobly resolved to fall on the rebels with his single division, and being supported in this gallant resolution by the troops, he pushed forward to the assault. The Republicans made a desperate resistance, but without avail, and they were finally driven from the Morne with considerable loss. The main body, however, succeeded in effecting their retreat, before the arrival of General Hope, who came up with his column at the appointed time, but too late to intercept the fugitives.

On the following day, 29th April, the two Generals, observing another commanding position in the rear of Morne Fortuné, called Morne Duchaseau, determined to seize upon it before the enemy could recover from their panic. They accordingly marched to the summit of the hill with a strong

detachment, and threw forward pickets to within
twelve hundred yards of the entrenchments on
Morne Fortuné. While they were engaged in this
quarter, Major-General Morshead with the third
division effected a disembarkation at Anse Laraye,
and advanced upon Morne Fortuné. This post
being thus completely invested, the enemy began
to prepare for a vigorous resistance. On the 1st
May they sallied forth upon the advanced post of
Colonel Macdonald's grenadiers ; but after a sharp
conflict they were repulsed with much slaughter—
not, however, without the loss of several officers
and grenadiers on the side of the British.

Hitherto the rebels had successfully protected
the entrance to the bay of Grand-cul-de-Sac by
means of batteries erected at the south side of the
base of Morne Fortuné. To open this bay to their
fleet was an object of great importance to the British, and Sir Ralph therefore resolved to make an
attempt against the batteries. General Morshead's
division was directed to advance in two columns,
on the left, and General Hope, on the right, was
to attack the battery *Sèche*, close to the works on
Morne Fortuné ; while a part of the squadron was
to lend its assistance by keeping up a cannonade
on the works of the enemy. Accordingly, at dawn
of day on the 2nd May, General Hope advanced

from Morne Chabot with five companies of the Highlanders, the light infantry of the 57th Regiment, under Colonel West, and a detachment of Malcolm's corps, supported by the 55th Regiment, which was posted at Ferrand's. This division promptly executed its part of the service, and drove the enemy from the battery. Not so Major-General Morshead's division. On the 1st May the General himself had been taken ill, and the command had devolved upon Brigadier-General Perryn and Colonel Riddle. The latter made himself master of the battery of Chapuis, on the left of the beach; but General Perryn, having met with some unforeseen obstruction, failed to accomplish his part of the service by passing the river at Cools. The consequence was that the victorious columns, being discovered at daylight in this insulated position, were furiously cannonaded from the fortress above, and were constrained to fall back upon their former station. In this encounter the British had to regret the loss of Colonel Malcolm, who fell at the head of his gallant Rangers, and of eleven other officers and privates, besides 56 wounded and 34 missing.

The Vigie was the next point that attracted the notice of General Abercrombie. This post, which commands the bay of Castries, was held by about

200 men. The attack was fixed to take place on the night of the 17th May, and the 31st Regiment was chosen for the purpose. The soldiers advanced with spirit and carried the first battery, consisting of three eighteen-pounders. The guns were spiked and thrown over the precipice : but a shower of grape-shot from the battery on the summit of the hill threw the troops into confusion, and they took to flight. The loss of the assailants was one Lieutenant killed, 114 officers and privates wounded, and 65 missing; and it might have been more severe, had the grenadiers not moved forward to cover their retreat.

Undaunted by these reverses, Sir Ralph Abercrombie pushed on the preparations for attacking the enemy's main position. This was a task of no small difficulty : the chain of investment was ten miles in extent; the guns had to be dragged across ravines and up the acclivities of the mountains and rocks ; and this could only be accomplished by the zeal and exertions of the seamen. " All the roads that were necessary were to be made ; of carriages there were none ; horses were scarce, and the Republicans had been industrious in availing themselves of all the natural obstacles to the progress of the troops, and in creating as many others as their ingenuity could contrive.

Yet, notwithstanding all this, the works against
Morne Fortuné were pushed forward with unremitting diligence. It was from the ridge of
Duchaseau, against the north side of the enemy's
entrenchments, that the principal attack was
carried on."*

The first battery, mounting eighteen pieces of
ordnance, was completed on the 16th May, and
on the 24th this battery and two others with
twenty-four pounders were opened upon Morne
Fortuné. ' In front there was an advanced out-
work, named a *Fléche*, full of troops. The guns
were directed against it, and after battering it for
some hours General Moore moved forward with
the grenadiers and light infantry of the 27th
regiment, and carried the work by storm. But
no sooner had he driven out the enemy than a
shower of grape-shot was poured upon him from
Morne Fortuné, only five hundred yards distant.
Having determined to keep possession of the
Flêche, he ordered the soldiers to reverse the
parapet and to raise a trench to cover the flanks
of the rest of the regiment, which came up to
their aid. While working with the spade and
pickaxe under a heavy cannonade, a numerous
body of the enemy sallied forth, who had the

* Continuation of Bryan Edwards.

means of covering themselves by some houses and by the inequalities of the ground, and their fire was dreadful. Moore ordered the flank companies to charge and drive them back. Colonel Drummond gallantly led them on. He engaged with his sword a French officer whom he killed, and the enemy were repulsed by the bayonet. But these brave troops in returning to the Flêche suffered much from grape-shot, fired from the batteries."

General Cotin, who commanded the Republicans, "seeing this advantage, reinforced his party and impelled them to make another sally with greater resolution. They advanced boldly close up to the British, who from the confined nature of the ground could present only a narrow front. The enemy's fire was consequently superior: officers and men were falling fast, and General Moore apprehended every instant that the regiment would give way. In this distress two companies were again ordered to charge, which was done daringly: but Major Wilson and Captain Dunlop fell wounded, and many valiant soldiers were killed in this assault. Yet the others, undismayed, drove the enemy before them at the point of the bayonet, and pursued them with great slaughter to the fort. They were then recalled, but when retreating were again exposed, as before, to the guns of the rampart. General Moore then commanded the houses in front to be set fire to, and the entrenching to be proceeded in. He rallied his few remaining soldiers, and prepared them to repel a third sally, which he momentarily expected. But the fire from the enemy's cannon had ceased, and when the smoke was dispersed, instead of an armed band of soldiers, there issued from the fortress a train of Negro bearers, carrying biers to collect and take in the wounded, who, moaning piteously and crying for help, were strewed among heaps of the dead."*

The Republicans, daunted by this defeat, sent a flag of truce to request a suspension of hostilities. A conference ensued and terminated in terms of capitulation. On the 26th May 2,000 men, chiefly Negroes and people of colour, laid down their arms, and marched out prisoners of war. Nearly a hundred cannon and mortars, large quantities of ammunition and stores, and ten vessels of every size, fell into the hands of the besiegers. General Moore then took possession of the fort, and planted the British colours on the ramparts.

* Life of Sir John Moore.

The loss of the Republicans in this engagement has not been ascertained. That of the British was two field-officers, three captains, five subalterns, and 184 non-commissioned officers and rank and file, killed; and four field-officers, twelve captains, fifteen subalterns, and 523 non-commissioned officers and rank and file, wounded or missing.*

Sir Ralph Abercrombie immediately appointed General Moore Governor of the island, and sailed on the 4th June, with the fleet under Sir Hugh Christian, for the reduction of St. Vincent and Grenada. And thus terminated one of the most bloody and obstinate conflicts recorded in colonial history—a conflict in which untiring perseverance and consummate bravery on the side of the British, under almost insuperable difficulties, were met, on the part of the Republicans, by the most heroic deeds of daring and a self-devotion worthy of a better cause.

Although the regular military operations ceased on the surrender of Morne Fortuné, the rest of the island remained unsubdued. In all previous contests for the sovereignty of the island the

* Amongst the officers that distinguished themselves during this campaign was Lieutenant David Stewart, "of Garth," who became Governor of St. Lucia in 1829.

slave population had either stood aloof or looked
on with indifference; and when the struggle was
over they quietly returned to their ordinary pursuits. But on the present occasion the school-
master of revolution had been abroad; the capti-
vating doctrines of liberty and independence had
been sedulously propagated amongst them; and
the growing mischief of years was not to be ex-
tirpated in one day. As in the great model
Republic, so even in the mimic one of St. Lucia,
the people were split into numerous factions.
There was the white faction, and the black faction—the pro-slavery faction, and the anti-slavery
faction—the Royalists and the Republicans—the
English and the French. The whole, however,
resolved themselves into two principal parties—
the friends of law and order, and the abettors of
anarchy and spoliation. On the side of the
former stood the industrious of every colour, all
partial to the British rule, as their sole guarantee
of peace and prosperity: these formed the great
majority of the inhabitants. On the other were
to be found the disaffected of every class—the
deluded slave asserting his freedom, the designing
demagogue seeking for a political scramble, and
the virulent Republican " hatching vain empires"
—all hostile to the British connexion as in-

volving the destruction of their cherished projects.
These constituted a formidable because un-
principled minority, and received the merited
appellation of " Brigands." On the news of the
capitulation, large numbers of them retired to the
woods, and taking possession of the natural fastnesses of the interior, resolved to hold out to the
last against the British authority. The more,
however, the contest had hitherto been natural in
its object, and creditable in its prosecution, the
more the subsequent warfare became atrocious in
both. The one was a war of principle and
independence ; the other of ferocity and extermi-
nation. The misguided Republicans fought like
men ; the emancipated Negroes like savages.

" The corporal frame and mental qualities of the
Negroes fit them peculiarly for desultory warfare.
They are stout, agile, expert in the use of arms,
and can endure patiently the scorching sun and
the torrents of rain of the tropical climate. They
can live on the roots which grow spontaneously
or with little culture in the fields ; and being
bold and cunning are ready to oppose their
enemies by force, or deceive them by stratagem."*
Never were these advantages turned to a more
melancholy account than on this occasion by

* Life of Sir John Moore.

the Negroes of St. Lucia. They made repeated excursions from their fastnesses; murdered the inhabitants without distinction of age or sex; plundered the houses; burned the plantations; and committed numerous deeds of cruelty.

The first measure of General Moore's administration was to issue a proclamation to the inhabitants, granting a free pardon to all who would come within the British lines and deliver up their arms. But this step having failed to produce any salutary effect, he resolved to make a personal inspection of the different out-quarters and ascertain the real state of affairs. Proceeding along the leeward coast he successively visited Soufriere, Choiseul, Laborie, and Vieux Fort. Nothing can be compared to the scenes of sorrow and devastation which presented themselves on every side. Scattered bands of marauders had overrun the country; all who refused to join them had been mercilessly put to death; and the terrified survivors were seeking shelter in the towns and villages. Governor Moore saw enough to be convinced that the defensive and pacific policy, so strongly recommended by Sir Ralph Abercrombie, would be thrown away upon the Brigands. He therefore resolved to pursue an opposite course and carry the war into the

enemy's camp. For that purpose he established
a line of posts for the protection of the estates ;
placed detachments along the coast to intercept
the supplies of arms and provisions, which Victor
Hugues frequently contrived to throw in by means
of small vessels ; and lastly, he acted offensively
by attacking the Brigands wherever he could find
them. "Some few known agitators were then
arrested, the principal of whom, Rupès Roche,
had been one of the Republican agents. He
possessed some property, was clever and ambitious, and had been active in stirring up the
Negroes. When sent for he protested that he
was innocent, and confiding in his eloquence for
his defence, he declaimed with theatrical gestures.
But certain information had been procured of his
communicating with the Brigands. He was told
that he should be tried, and was ordered into
confinement. Some others, whose turbulent conduct was notorious, were shipped off from the
island."*

Scarcely had General Moore rested from this
excursion, when, with that energy for which he
was distinguished, he determined to visit the
windward Districts. At almost every step he
was assailed by the Brigands, who rushed upon

* Life of Sir John Moore.

him from their inaccessible recesses, surprising and murdering several stragglers of his party. At Dauphin they set fire to the houses and fled. At Dennery, whilst his men were collecting cattle, they were attacked by the Brigands, and it was with difficulty that he succeeded in chasing them to the mountains. When passing the Troumassé river, accompanied by an escort of only twenty men, a party of the Brigands, about a hundred strong, pursued him with loud shouts, and his men became so alarmed that they could hardly be prevailed upon to charge. On this, as on almost every occasion, the General had to lead the assault, often trusting to his personal exertions for the preservation of his life.

In this unequal contest, however, the enemy were frequently repulsed with heavy loss. Altogether about three hundred of them were slain or hanged. " It was the wish of General Moore to have governed the Colony with mildness, but he was forced to adopt the most violent measures from the perverseness and bad composition of those he had to deal with."* And although his policy at first did not meet with the approbation of Sir Ralph Abercrombie, commanding in chief at Trinidad, there can be no doubt that it was the

* Life of Sir John Moore.

only wise and honourable policy under the circumstances. 1st, it was but common justice to
the peaceable inhabitants to afford them every
protection in his power. 2ndly, he considered
that exertion would be beneficial to the health of
the troops ; and on one occasion he had reason to
attribute to that cause the absence of disease in
certain regiments, more actively employed than
others. 3rdly, he kept the Brigands at a respect-
ful distance from Morne Fortuné, where, in the
event of a siege, he might have been subjected to
serious difficulties ; and lastly, by a constant display of activity he deterred Victor Hugues from
making a descent upon the island, which, with
the scanty force remaining for its defence, must
have fallen an easy conquest to the Republicans.
True, in one of these objects he was unsuccessful :
from some cause, or complication of causes, the
troops became unhealthy : every description of
fever prevailed amongst them, and they fell off so
rapidly in a few months, that he was obliged
to apply to Sir Ralph for reinforcements. At
the expiration of one year from their arrival,
the 31st Regiment, which landed in St. Lucia
915 strong, lost by disease and war twenty-two
officers and 841 men.

In this emergency General Moore resorted to

the expedient of destroying all the ground provisions within reach of the Brigands, in the hope
of starving them into submission; but even this
extreme measure failed of success. The enemy,
being in hourly expectation of succours from
Guadaloupe, continued to hold out; and these
succours they received soon after, to the great
mortification of General Moore. In truth, the
coast was too extensive and rugged to be effectually guarded at every point, and the windward
coast especially was left entirely open; while, on
the other hand, the activity and vigilance of
Hugues were so great, that no human foresight
could have counteracted his plans.

On the receipt of this painful news, General
Moore declared his intention of proceeding by
water to Vieux Fort; but such was the dishonesty
of those by whom he was surrounded on Morne
Fortuné, that intelligence of his movements was
immediately transmitted to the enemy. In total
ignorance of these treacherous doings he put to
sea in a six-oared boat, accompanied by Captain
Anderson, his Aid-de-Camp; and after proceeding
within a short distance of Soufriere, he suddenly
found himself invested by two boats, filled with
armed Brigands, who had lain concealed along
the coast. In this embarrassing situation, and

with certain death before his eyes, if he either advanced or retreated, General Moore directed the rowers to make for the neighbouring island of St. Vincent with all their might. A chase then commenced, which was kept up until sunset, when the pursuers slackened their speed and returned to the shore. Moore, being thus happily delivered from the clutches of the Brigands, shaped his course in a circuitous direction for Vieux Fort, where he arrived safely next morning.

The fatigue of these exertions induced an attack of fever, and it became necessary to have the General conveyed to Morne Fortuné. It was during this illness that he received intelligence from General Hunter, Governor of St. Vincent, that Marin Padre, the chief of the Brigands in that island, and a native of St. Lucia, had surrendered upon terms ; and General Moore thought it advisable to use this man's influence for bringing about a similar result with the Brigands of St. Lucia. Marin Padre, who owned some property in the latter island, which General Moore promised to restore to him, gladly accepted the proposition ; and in the beginning of December 1796 he was sent over to Fort Charlotte. He immediately put himself in communication with the Brigands ; but after a tedious correspondence, their chief, Lacroix,

"*Commandant l'armée Française dans les bois,*"
rejected the proposed terms, and the negotiation
was broken off. The failure of this business was
naturally attributed to a want of good faith on the
part of Marin Padre ; although, in reality, there
were no just grounds to doubt his sincerity.

In the beginning of January 1797 Sir Ralph
Abercrombie, being on a visit to Martinique, sent
for General Moore, and in consideration of his
valuable services offered him the government of
Grenada, which was then vacant. But Moore,
sooner than allow St. Lucia to fall into the hands
of the Republicans, declared his intention of returning to his government. On his arrival at
Morne Fortuné he learned that the Brigands, taking advantage of his absence, had surprised the
post at Praslin, and murdered the commanding
officer and most of the men. He immediately set
out with a party of troops, and scoured the country
from Marquis to Praslin, occasionally skirmishing
with the Brigands, and harassing them on every
side. This fresh call for exertion, however, brought
on a second attack of fever, which reduced him to
such an extremity, that he was conveyed insen-
sible on board of a vessel and transported to
Martinique, where Sir Ralph Abercrombie recommended his immediate return to England.

Thus ended the career in St. Lucia of Brigadier-General John Moore. Thus was the future hero of Corunna rescued from death, perhaps disgrace, for the glory of his country and the lustre of his name. How painful and humiliating it is to reflect, that one of the bravest officers Britain ever produced was thus left nearly twelve months to struggle, hand to hand, with Brigands and bush-fighters in the wilds of St. Lucia!

General Moore was succeeded in the command of the troops by Colonel James Drummond. This officer, wisely following out the plan of operations adopted by his predecessor, soon reduced the enemy to such straits that, before the end of the year 1797, the whole of the *"Armée Française dans les bois"* had laid down their arms and surrendered at discretion. The only stipulation they made was that, as they had borne arms for so long a period, and had enjoyed the immunities of freemen, under the sanction of the Republican laws, they should not be again reduced to slavery. The British authorities, glad to get rid of such troublesome "Citoyens" upon any condition, formed them into a regiment, which was sent to the coast of Africa. Colonel Drummond, now raised to the rank of Brigadier-General, continued in the peaceable management of affairs until the month of May 1798, when he was succeeded by Brigadier-General George Prevost.

General Prevost* has been deservedly commended for his mild and enlightened administration. Under his predecessors the effervescence of Republicanism had begun to subside, and the political firebrands had been removed; but there still glowed beneath the surface some scattered embers of disaffection, which required but a spark from the enemy without to set the whole in a blaze. To the abatement of these General Prevost applied the energies of his active mind; and although he encountered much negative opposition from some influential parties, his labours were ultimately crowned with success. The chief topic that received his attention was the disorganised state of the Courts of Law. Some of the officers had fled from the Colony; others had been murdered; and during a period of ten years the ordinary tribunals had been alternately superseded by martial law, on the one hand, and the law of brute force, on the other. To provide a remedy for this evil General Prevost, towards the close of the year 1799, submitted to the King's Government a plan for re-establishing the administration of justice as it prevailed before 1789, and subject to

* Afterwards Lieutenant-General Sir George Prevost, Bart.

the French laws in force at that period. This proposal having received the sanction of the Government, General Prevost proceeded on the 13th October 1800 to the installation of the new Courts and their respective officers. M. Jean Marie Aubert, who had given great satisfaction in the office of *Sénéchal* before the revolution, was appointed Procureur-General; M. Butel de Montgay, Sénéchal, and M. Antoine Marie Fayolle, President of the Court of Appeal. Having effected some other important reforms, and by his conciliatory proceedings won the esteem of the respectable inhabitants of all parties, General Prevost solicited from the Commander-in-Chief, and obtained in February 1801, leave of absence to return to England. As soon as this circumstance was communicated to the Court of Appeal (which exercised all the attributes of a financial body) they addressed a memorial to the King, praying, as a special token of His Majesty's bounty, that General Prevost might be invested with the authority of Civil Governor; and offering to provide him with a suitable salary from the colonial revenue. This arrangement having been acceded to by the Duke of Portland, General Prevost was prevailed upon to continue his services to the Colony: but his declining health soon com-

pelled him to adhere to his former resolution,
which he carried into effect in the month of
April 1802. On this occasion the members of
the Court of Appeal presented him with a
sword, to testify their grateful sense of his
paternal administration, and the numerous benefits which he had conferred on the Colony.
The address which accompanied this well-
merited compliment is signed by Messrs. William
Alexander, Devaux St. Philip, Pierre de Glapion,
Cornibert Duboulay, Thomas Naçaburn, the Marquis de Marsanges, Lamothe Hosten, Michel Levacher, Fs. de Monchy, Butel de Montgay, Robert
Ewing, Gerôme de Noroy, Ackey Lawrence, J.
M. Aubert, A. M. Fayolle, and E. Raphel.

On the retirement of General Prevost, Lieutenant General Trigge, the Commander-in-Chief,
appointed Brigadier-General George Henry Van-
sittart to the vacant post in St. Lucia. This
officer assumed the command in May 1802, just
as intelligence was received that the belligerent
powers had concluded a treaty of peace at Amiens
on the 25th March, whereby St. Lucia was once
more restored to France. He continued, however, in command until the 29th September,
when Admiral Villaret-Joyeuse, Captain-General
of the French Antilles, took over the island in

the name of First Consul Bonaparte. The
Admiral, whose attention was wholly engrossed
by the weighty interests of Martinique, deputed
Brigadier-General Jean François Xavier Noguès
to administer the government under his immediate
superintendence.

Noguès was a brave and intelligent officer—
one from whose experience and abilities the
Colony could not fail to derive every advantage,
had it continued under the French rule : but the
peace of Amiens was not destined to be of long
duration, and before the expiration of fifteen
months hostilities were renewed. The West
Indies became once more the scene of warlike
operations, and St. Lucia, as usual, the first object
of attack. On the 19th June 1803 a small
squadron, commanded by Commodore Samuel
Hood, and composed of the 74-gun ships Centaur
and Courageux, and some transports, sailed from
Barbados with a detachment of troops under
Lieutenant - General Grinfield. Although St.
Lucia was their immediate destination, they appear to have taken Dominica in their route ; and
General Prevost, then Governor of that island,
on being apprised that the object of the expedition was the re-capture of St. Lucia, tendered his
services to General Grinfield to assist in the

enterprise. On the 21st the squadron anchored in Choc bay; and in a few hours the whole of the troops were disembarked without opposition under the orders of Brigadier-General Robert Brereton. At their approach General Noguès, whose means of defence were somewhat scanty, retired with his forces to the strong post of Morne Fortuné, where he shut himself up to await the advance of the British. The Vigie and other out-posts offered but a feeble resistance, and at five P.M. the town of Castries was taken. Governor Noguès was then summoned to surrender; but he refused to listen to any terms, and General Grinfield therefore resolved to attempt an immediate assault. The storming took place at four o'clock in the morning of the 22nd, under the guidance of General Prevost, whose knowledge of the localities enabled him to lead the way. For some time the French made a desperate stand : at length, overpowered by the spirit and superior numbers of the besiegers, they began to give way. In less than an hour the whole of the works were carried at the point of the bayonet, and General Noguès surrendered on capitulation. The loss of the British was twenty-one officers and men killed, and one hundred and ten wounded. That of the French has not been ascertained; but the number of prisoners is stated at six hundred and forty.

On the 26th June General Grinfield appointed Brigadier-General Robert Brereton, Governor; since which period St. Lucia has continued without interruption under the British rule. And here terminated that struggle for dominion, which had lasted upwards of one hundred and sixty years.

CHAPTER IV.

THERE is no island in the Archipelago that has
obtained such depreciating notoriety in regard to
its climate, as St. Lucia. "It is considered,"
writes Dr. Evans, "one of the most unhealthy of
the West India islands, and there are parts of it
which most assuredly merit this unenviable cele-
brity, amongst which the town of Castries is one.
We see that it abounds in all the generally acknowledged sources of the tropical fevers—an
elevated temperature, imperfect ventilation, hu-

midity, and malaria from every attributable origin."*

Although a large amount of the mortality in St. Lucia, as in the other islands, may be traced to causes altogether foreign to the climate—the improvidence of Europeans, their intemperate habits, and disregard of local influences—yet it is undeniable that the climate is still very unhealthy. Throughout the year the thermometer ranges between 75° and 90° in the shade. The torridity of the heat and the mountainous formation of the island combine to generate heavy falls of rain during several months of the year. The rain produces swamps in certain localities, and a dank vegetation in the valleys : by this means the process of vegetable decomposition is established ; and as long as the swamps and valleys continue to send forth their poisonous miasmata, so long and in the same proportion will St. Lucia continue to merit its reputation for insalubrity. Dr. Evans thus describes the effect of the climate upon the newly-arrived stranger :—"The arterial system is excited ; the blood is determined to the surface of the body ; the skin is either preternaturally warm and dry, or covered with profuse perspiration. There is a desire for cool drink, which, when taken

* Tre.tise on the Endemic Fevers of the West Indies.

into the stomach, increases the perspiration, until
the clothes become saturated with moisture. The
skin then becomes irritable and covered with a
lichenous eruption, known by the name of 'prickly
heat.' The body seems to have acquired, if I
may use the term, an inflammatory diathesis, and
if blood be taken from a person under these circumstances it will be found to be of a brighter
colour than in Europe. It will separate completely
into its two parts, and the crassamentum will be
firm and tenacious."*

When with the causes that produce these results
is combined the deleterious principle called *malaria*,
so abundantly engendered by the fens and marshes
of St. Lucia, the effects are thus described by the
same author:—"An European, or a native after a
long residence in a temperate and healthy climate,
arriving in St. Lucia, complains of a feeling of
weight in the atmosphere—a something which
resists the wish for exertion or exercise. Both his
mind and body are oppressed; his intellect is
clouded; his spirits are low and desponding, and
all pre-existing love of enterprise vanishes. If his
residence be protracted, he has slight febrile
movements, which come on regularly or irregu-
larly, not sufficiently severe to prevent him

* Treatise on the Endemic Fevers of the West Indies.

pursuing his usual avocations, but which, nevertheless, are sufficient to induce him to throw
himself upon a sofa and require a powerful effort
of resolution to combat. In this manner his body
may gradually accommodate itself to the climate,
but he may consider himself fortunate if he escape
so easily. In general, if he be guilty of any im-
prudences he feels restless at night, and can only
sleep during the cool of the morning. He feels
out of sorts ; has pains in the back and extremi-
ties, as if from fatigue : he complains of head-ache,
sickness, and nausea ; and if these symptoms are
not attended to immediately, suffers what is vul-
garly called an attack of seasoning fever."*

The insalubrity of St. Lucia varies according to
the localities. In many places where the soil is
light and free from swamps, sickness prevails to
a less extent. Amongst these the quarter of Soufriere is pre-eminently distinguished. Even the
presence of the sulphureous mountain, instead of
imparting any deleterious quality to the atmosphere, is regarded as contributing to preserve it in
a healthy state. In this quarter the inhabitants
attain longevity, and both upon the estates and in
the town of Soufriere may be seen several persons,
chiefly females, upwards of eighty years of age,

* Treatise on the Endemic Fevers of the West Indies.

pursuing their daily avocations. But in places abounding in swamps and a deep alluvial soil, such as the valleys of Roseau and Dennery, and the town of Castries, insalubrity often prevails to a frightful extent, and every species of fever and disease follows in its train.

Of late years, however, the swamps have been partially filled up, and more attention is paid to the drainage of the valleys. There exists, too, a greater degree of ventilation, owing to the more regular visits of the trade winds: the temperature is in consequence somewhat lower: Castries is remarkable for a greater absence of disease; and whilst every Colony in the West Indies has been repeatedly visited by every malady peculiar to these regions, the climate of St. Lucia has been comparatively mild and temperate, and its inhabitants have enjoyed an unusual exemption from sickness and mortality. Even yellow fever, which in other islands has raged with all its former virulence, and proved so destructive to their populations, has only paid two brief visits to St. Lucia within the last twenty years. The first occurred in July 1839, and the second in August 1842. On the former occasion the number of deaths amongst the civilians was thirteen, and in 1842 only nine.

The situation occupied by the *Pavilion* or Government House, on the crest of Morne Fortuné, has been regarded as very unhealthy ; and if we might judge from the mortality which prevailed for some time amongst its occupants, there would be ample grounds for this unfavourable opinion. During a period of little more than four years, from November 1829 to January 1834, no less than four Governors died at the Pavilion ; namely, Major-General Stewart, Major-General Mackie, Colonel Mallet, and Major-General Farquharson. Even before the death of the last-named Governor, it was noted as an insalubrious locality, and its bad name in that respect was curiously illustrated by that officer himself in one of his eccentric moods. In 1832 the Bishop of the diocese, being on a tour amongst the islands, arrived at Castries, and immediately received a polite invitation to dinner from General Farquharson. The General was remarkable for his parsimonious habits in private life, and having left his family in England the establishment at Government House was conducted upon quasi-bachelor principles. He had made no preparation for the reception of the Bishop, except in the eating line ; and indeed, had he been disposed to do so, he must have had recourse to the offi-

cers of the garrison; for, his accommodation,
especially in the way of bedding, was very scanty.
Perceiving after dinner that the Bishop and his
suite showed no inclination to encounter the
fatigue of a ride to Castries during a dark night,
the wily General, being resolved to dislodge them
from their snug position, had recourse to a *ruse
de guerre.* " My Lord," said he, " perhaps this
is the first time you have visited Government
House: come with me and I'll show you the
apartments. I suppose your Lordship has heard
of the insalubrity of this place : every room in
the house has already witnessed the death of some
Governor ; but none of them has had the honour
of killing a Bishop: so, my Lord, you have only
to make your selection; I leave you to the
embarras du choix." The good Bishop, it is
reported, was so shocked at this strange recommendation of the Government House and its
hospitality, that he immediately ordered his horse
and rode down to town.

General Farquharson died in January 1834 ;
and since then, comprising a space of ten years,
the Pavilion has been successively occupied by
Colonel Carter, Sir Charles F. Smith, Sir Dudley
Hill, Colonel Bunbury, Colonel Mein, Colonel
Everard, Colonel Graydon and Colonel Clarke ;

and not only has there been no mortality, but not even the slightest sickness has made its appearance.

There was presented to both Houses of Parliament in 1838, under the authority of Captain Tulloch, a "Statistical Report" which contains some interesting particulars on the subject of the sickness and mortality among the troops in the West Indies, between the years 1817 and 1836. St. Lucia is, of course, included amongst the most unhealthy islands, particularly in regard to the white troops; and the diseases by which its climate is stated to be characterised are fevers and affections of the stomach and bowels : it is admitted, however, that "the climate seems to exert no marked influence on the black troops." The tables and statistical details in this Report appear to have been prepared with much care and ingenuity, and are, I have no doubt, in accordance with the data and materials with which the author was supplied : but the deductions and inferences, which he has formed from the "numerical results," are more curious than correct, more founded on figures than on facts.

After expressing his inability "to distinguish with certainty the essential causes of sickness and mortality," the author of the Report proceeds to

examine the various features, both of climate and
country, which are generally believed to be the
causes of insalubrity—reviewing in succession the
elevation and variableness of the temperature;
the extreme moisture and torrid heat ; the mountains, marshes, and miasmata ; the exuberance of
vegetation and want of ventilation; the rich soil
and dry seasons—and each in its turn is found
deficient of the requisite qualities to constitute an
essential and uniform cause of unhealthiness.
Elevation of temperature is rejected, because comparatively low temperatures are equally subject to
disease. The variableness of the seasons is found
wanting, because epidemic fever rages in all
seasons. Extreme moisture is a plausibility which
vanishes before the fact, that in certain dry localities sickness prevails to a greater extent than in
others of a more humid character. There is an
admission as to the influence of heat, but only
when it is combined with great moisture. The
insalubrity of swamps is a mere hypothesis :
otherwise British Guiana, a swamp from one
extremity to the other, would be more unhealthy
(which Captain Tulloch affirms it is not) than
other Colonies totally exempt from noxious exha-
lations. Again, the absence of ventilation, as an
essential cause of sickness, is at variance with the

"numerical results," inasmuch as other countries, in which ventilation is quite perfect, are not
less unhealthy than the West Indies : and finally,
as regards richness of soil and exuberance of
vegetation, they are the same in every year, while
sickness and mortality are extremely variable.
The author winds up his inferences by declaring
that he can point out no particular locality more
healthy than another—"no uniform or essential
cause of sickness."

Without discussing in detail the merit of these
deductions, it may be asked how any one, possessing Captain Tulloch's practical knowledge of
the subject, could have speculated upon such a
result as uniformity in the production of disease ?
Is it not obvious that no single feature of the
climate is sufficient of itself to produce a marked
degree of insalubrity ; and that where, as in the
West Indies, we have the simultaneous existence
or periodical reproduction of several agents, more
or less pregnant with insalubrity, we must look
for the uniformity and intensity of their action
in their various combinations, their counteracting influences, and the operation of concurrent
causes ?

But Captain Tulloch's deductions do not stop
here. In another part of the Report he investi-

gates what he terms "the doctrine of acclimatization;" and after submitting it to the test of his numerical results, he arrives at the conclusion, "that no length of residence, however protracted, is likely to be of any avail in diminishing the liability of the troops to the fatal diseases of this climate."* Again, with regard to intemperance, he hopes it may be inferred that those who hold the rank of non-commissioned officer are much less addicted to this vice than those under their command. The maintenance of discipline requires that the fault of drunkenness, on the part of sergeants and corporals, should be seldom pardoned. The consequence of detection is that they are immediately reduced to the ranks, and sober candidates for promotion appointed in their place. Thei nference, therefore, is, that sergeants and corporals are less intemperate than the mass of the troops; and as the mortality of these ranks, in the Windward and Leeward Command, is considerably higher than that of the privates, the final deduction formed by Captain Tulloch is, that intemperance cannot be regarded as producing a higher ratio of sickness and mortality.

These are indeed startling inferences—startling

* Statistical Report of the Sickness, Mortality, and Invaliding among the troops in the West Indies, 1838.

alike in their nature and tendency; and it is to
be regretted that they should have been deduced
from any investigation, based upon mere numerical results, in the absence of all knowledge of the
causes, essential or auxiliary, immediate or remote,
which may have contributed to the production of
disease. But admitting the results to be correct,
and that the mortality of the sergeants and corporals is higher than that of the privates ; yet,
the grounds upon which it is attempted to establish the superior sobriety of the former are in
many instances untenable. Of course, from the
dread of consequences, they are not so often
detected in a state of downright drunkenness, as
the privates : but their position presents them
with greater facilities for procuring spirituous
liquors, and their habitual intemperance, though
seldom amounting to actual inebriety, operates
more prejudicially upon the health than the occasional *escapade* of the private. The latter is
punished for his fault, and his grog is stopped for
a fortnight or three weeks ; whilst the sergeant
and corporal, revelling in the unrestrained enjoyment of superior sobriety, may indulge in liquor
to any extent short of actual intoxication.

The stimulating liquor, generally used by the
troops in St. Lucia, is a description of rum, not

inaptly called "white rum." When fresh from
the still it is of a most deleterious property. The
opportunities of procuring it are greater than can
be imagined : they find it at the canteens, and
purchase it during their occasional visits to
Castries ; but the chief supply is obtained through
their intercourse with a number of females, located on the crest of the hill, whose houses are
the resort of the troops, both black and white,
during their hours of rest and recreation. Indeed, the use of white rum and other strong
liquors is so common amongst the troops and
some of the lower classes of Europeans, that I
feel persuaded one-half of the amount of sickness (apart from epidemics) which prevails
amongst them, may be referred to that cause.
The relish for white rum increases in proportion
to the habit of drinking it, and the length of residence ; and hence the higher ratio of mortality
amongst the, so called, acclimated troops. The
same effect is produced upon the civilian : his
tastes and habitudes will induce him at first to
reject white rum as an unpalatable beverage ;
and whatever little he may indulge in will easily
comport with his strong European temperament :
but as he prolongs his residence, the effect becomes doubly injurious, from his gradually

increasing *goût* for this intoxicating drink, and the proportionably debilitated state of his constitution.

As far as my personal knowledge goes, I can safely affirm that, during a residence of thirteen years in St. Lucia, I have seen abundant evidence of the mischievous effects of intemperance upon all classes of the community. In July 1831 there were 142 European settlers in the island, 68 of whom, persons generally addicted to the use of ardent spirits, have been prematurely cut off—very few having attained the age of 35. The remaining 74, persons of temperate habits and steady demeanour, were living on the 15th July 1842 and in the enjoyment of excellent health. These facts are illustrated by the following table :—*

Number of Europeans residing in St. Lucia on the 15th July 1831.	Deaths between the 15th July 1831 and 15th July 1842.
British.............. 62 French.............. 80	British.............. 37 French.............. 31

By this it will further be seen that the rate of mortality amongst the British is considerably higher than that of the French; and as there was no advantage on either side in respect of

---

* It is hardly necessary to remark that these tables have reference exclusively to the male adult population.

acclimatization, (the average length of residence being nearly the same in both cases) this marked difference in favour of the French cannot fairly be attributed to any other cause than the superior sobriety for which they are distinguished.

The more the Colony progresses as a British settlement, the less inducement it will naturally hold out to foreigners as a field for speculation. The influx of French settlers has, therefore, been rather scanty of recent years. There is, however, a decided improvement in the rate of mortality amongst the British, which I have no hesitation in ascribing to the prevalence of sounder notions on the subject of intemperance, founded in a great measure on the examples that have been witnessed of its pernicious effects :—

Number of Europeans who settled in St. Lucia between the 15th July 1831 and the 15th July 1842.	Deaths during the same period.
British.............. 91 French.............. 37	British.............. 24 French.............. 10

During the period in question there were imported 52 Irish and Scotch immigrants, 29 Germans, and 23 Frenchmen and Savoyards. The Germans were located in one of the healthiest districts of the island, and being generally sober only two cases of mortality occurred amongst them. The Irish and Scotch were established in the insalubrious valley of Roseau and were all cut off. The French and Savoyards, on their arrival in January 1842, were removed to the equally unhealthy valley of Mabouya: five of them died in the course of a few months, and the others, becoming alarmed, retired from the district to seek employment elsewhere. In July 1831 there were no European labourers that might have been comprised in the first table. In order therefore to maintain the comparison between persons of the same class, similarly situated as to the localities, I have excluded the different European labourers from the second table. Moreover, the data supplied in their case would have afforded very unfair grounds for estimating the rate of mortality, where intemperance is considered as the chief auxiliary in the production of disease. For the same reason I have not included the number of deaths from yellow fever in 1839. Any observations on the ordinary causes of disease cannot apply to epidemics, whose visits extend to all regions, temperate as well as torrid, spreading death and desolation alike amongst soldiers and civilians, whether sober and steady, or drunken and debauched. My object is to show that the mortality in St. Lucia is as much the result of adventitious circumstances, as of the peculiar character of the climate ; and that mere numerical deductions, tending to disprove the advantages of sobriety and acclimatization, or to demonstrate that great heat and extreme humidity, variable seasons and noxious swamps, burning breezes and a heavy atmosphere, are not essential causes of insalubrity, ought to be rejected as opposed to common experience and common sense.

During the latter years of slavery no separate record was kept, as formerly, of the burials among the slave population ; and had it been otherwise, the entries would have afforded but an imperfect criterion for estimating the amount of mortality amongst that class. Even at the present day, whilst the marriages and baptisms of all classes are regularly minuted on the parish registers, the entries in cases of death only comprise certain burials. This difference arises from the circumstance, that marriages and baptisms cannot be administered without the assistance of a clergyman, who is bound by law to record all such occurrences : whereas burials frequently take place amongst the lower classes, at which the clergyman does not attend, and of which consequently he has no record to make. This happens whenever the parties are in indigent circumstances ;

for, in no case is the priest required to exercise his ministry gratuitously. I am not aware that the attention of the Government has ever been directed to this *lacune* in the existing law ; but there can be no doubt as to the impolicy of allowing it to continue without a remedy. All that is necessary might be accomplished by a short legislative enactment, directing that no burial should take place without the presence of a clergyman, and that all burials, whether paid for or not, should be carefully minuted in the parish registers. The Clergy are now liberally supported by the Colony, and they can well afford to bury the poor without making any charge, or, in their own language, *gratis pro Deo*.

So long as the law remains unaltered, it will be impossible to obtain any correct data as to the general mortality in St. Lucia. The following return, which I have compiled from the parish registers, comprises the whole of the deaths amongst the white and coloured classes ; and but a very small proportion of those that have occurred amongst the blacks :—

Years	1833	1834	1835	1836	1837	1838	1839	1840	1841	1842	1843
Burials	70	67	89	103	118	137	115	85	112	199	249

The increase in the number of burials is not ascribable to any increase in the rate of mortality, but to the increased notions of respectability amongst the Negroes. Many, who in the days of slavery could have left no means to pay for their interment, are now borne to the grave with all the honours of Christian burial, amidst a concourse of mourning friends.

The vicissitudes of the year are distinguished by two seasons—the dry season and the wet season. To the former the French have assigned the name of *Carême*—Lent being the principal period that marks its duration ; and to the latter, for a similar reason, that of *Hivernage*, which corresponds with our hurricane months. Carême embraces the months of February, March, and April ; and Hivernage those of July, August, September, and October. But it must not be supposed that the dry or wet seasons only extend to those months. Indeed, drought and rain are not confined to any particular period of the year, and three months of incessant " pouring" are as likely to be succeeded by three months of uninterrupted drought, as that any other atmospheric contingency should occur.

Various authors have variously divided the seasons in the Antilles : but many of such divi-

sions are more fanciful than founded in fact; or if
founded, are but modifications of the two principal seasons. Thus the months of November,
December and January partake of the dry season:
the prevalence of light breezes by day and of
heavy dews during the night imparts an unusual
degree of coolness to the atmosphere; the thermometer seldom rises higher than 80 of Fahren-
heit; the air is dry and invigorating; and with
its permanent advantages of climate and the
magic of its moonlight, this period of the year is
altogether a delightful relief from the rain and
rust of the hurricane months. It is, however,
chiefly acceptable to Europeans and natives of a
robust temperament; and often proves prejudicial
to the health of the Negroes, and of all those
whose constitution may have been impaired by
protracted exposure to the effects of a tropical
climate. It is the season of colds and catarrhs,
pleurisies, and pulmonary consumptions; and few
escape, especially amongst the old and young,
without receiving some impression more or less
transient from its otherwise healthful influence.

In like manner, the months of May and June
act as precursors to the hurricane months, which
they usher in with gradual manifestations of
humidity and heat. The English compute this

season from the 1st August to the 1st November,
and the French from the 15th July to the 15th
October. A more correct computation than
either is said to be that which fixes its duration
between the full moon of July and the full moon
of October. At times the heat and stillness of
the air are quite suffocating; the rain descends in
torrents: to say that it " pours" would convey
but an imperfect idea of the reality: it resembles
rather the spouting of cataracts than the spilling
of clouds. At other times, the atmosphere, big
with the strife of the elements, yields its burden
amid the broad blaze of lightning and the loud
burst of thunder: the vividness of the one and
the violence of the other are truly appalling.
Thunder storms, however, are never of long duration, and are usually accompanied by abundant
rains. During the hurricane months, as well as
the other less changeable season, the variations of
the barometer are scarcely perceptible, and as
indications of any change in the weather are un-
deserving of notice. This phenomenon Dr.
Levacher attributes to the extreme moisture of
the atmosphere, produced by evaporation, which
preserves the air in an almost invariable state of
rarefaction.*

* Guide Médical des Antilles.

One of the principal causes of the heavy rains
in St. Lucia is the mountainous formation of the
island. The clouds that are continually travelling
westward, instead of pursuing the course first
assigned them by the wind, are attracted by the
elevated mountains in the centre of the island.
As the mountains run from north to south, and
the uniform direction of the wind is from the east,
immense masses of these clouds are constantly
passing over the central districts, dispensing
abundant showers to the valleys in their immediate vicinity, and converting them into a series
of ponds and reservoirs; whilst the less favoured
localities to the north and the south, being totally
deprived of this advantage, present nothing but
parched tracts of sand and dust. This is particularly the case in the southern district of Vieux
Fort, which generally experiences a blighting
drought during nine months of the year. The
rain never makes its appearance until the hurricane months set in; and then, when it is too
late for the purposes of cultivation, this ill-fated
quarter is visited by a few clouds from the
superabundant, cast-off clothing of the central
mountains.

Amongst the disadvantages of the climate and
seasons must be classed the frequent occurrence

of storms and hurricanes. St. Lucia appears to
be situated within the range of these dreadful
visitations, and it has suffered more severely from
them than any other island within the tropics,
except perhaps Barbados.   There is no record of
any hurricane before 1756, but since that period
they have been of common occurrence, and have
occasioned terrific scenes of devastation and a
melancholy loss of human life.   So intense is the
feeling of awe with which the public mind is impressed by these phenomena, that the " miserere
mei, Deus" and other prayers are offered up in
the churches during the continuance of the hurricane months, and at the conclusion the " Te
Deum" is sung as a public thanksgiving.   From
1756 to 1831, a period of seventy-five years, St.
Lucia was laid waste by six hurricanes, the most
remarkable of which occurred on the 10th October 1780, 21st October 1817, and 11th August
1831.   The hurricane of 1780 was probably the
most destructive that has ever been experienced
in this hemisphere.   Its ravages extended over
the whole of the lesser Antilles ; but its main
force was spent upon the central islands of Barbados, St. Vincent, St. Lucia, and Martinique :
the loss of human life in these four islands has
been computed at twenty-two thousand souls.

The particulars of this hurricane, as observed at Barbados, were published in the " Gentleman's Magazine" and the " Annual Register" for 1780, and are quoted by Colonel Reid in his valuable " Essay on the Law of Storms," and also by the author of " Four Years' Residence in the West Indies." Some idea of its devastating effects may be formed from the following extract of a letter of Sir George Rodney to Lady Rodney, written from St. Lucia on the 10th December 1780.

" You may easily conceive my surprise, concern, and astonishment, when I saw the dreadful situation of that island (Barbados) and the destructive effects of the hurricane. The strongest buildings and the whole of the houses, most of which were of stone and remarkable for their solidity, gave way to the fury of the wind, and were torn up from their very foundations ; all the forts destroyed, and many of the heavy cannon carried upwards of a hundred feet from the forts.* Had I not been an eye-witness nothing could have induced me to have believed it. More than six thousand persons perished, and all the inhabitants are entirely ruined. Our friend, Sir P. Gibbs, has suffered severely. The hurricane proved fatal

---

* " On their carriages which had wheels," observes Colonel Reid.

to six of the ships of my squadron, amongst whom poor Jack Drummond perished on the back of the island of St. Lucia."*

I have not been able to collect any detailed information respecting the hurricane of 1817. At that period there was no newspaper published in St. Lucia, and the local records are silent on the subject. It was, however, a most calamitous visitation; and although the loss of human life was by no means so great as that caused by the hurricane of 1780, the injury done to the estates and other property, as well as to the shipping, was attended with grievous consequences to the agricultural and mercantile interests of the community. The most remarkable occurrence, as regards the loss of life, was the death of Major-General Seymour, who was buried in the ruins of Government House.

The hurricane of August 1831, which I had the melancholy gratification of witnessing in St. Lucia, confined its ravages chiefly to that island, Barbados, and St. Vincent. Of the three Barbados suffered most, St. Lucia least. Such was the violence of the wind, that in Bridgetown alone one-half of the houses and most of the public buildings were razed to the ground, and 1500

* Life of Admiral Lord Rodney.

persons lost their lives. In St. Lucia, on the day preceding the hurricane no very extraordinary appearance was noticed in the atmosphere. Towards the evening the sky assumed a somewhat heavy and lowering aspect, which at that season of the year did not attract any particular attention. At about four o'clock on the morning of the 11th a strong breeze set in from the north, accompanied by heavy rain. At five the increasing violence of the wind began to excite strong sensations of alarm. By this time it had completely veered to the east, and exhibited every indication of a most awful hurricane. At nine it was at its greatest height, and gradually subsiding dwindled into a perfect calm before two o'clock, P.M. The hurricane did not last altogether more than eight hours, and even its violence did not continue during the whole of that time, but manifested itself by sudden gusts, spreading dismay and devastation on every side. The number of persons that lost their lives did not exceed ten or twelve, and these chiefly belonged to the shipping; but considerable damage was sustained by the shipping itself, by the different estates, and the houses in the towns of Castries, Soufriere, and Vieux Fort. Nearly every anchored vessel within the harbour, drifted from her moorings: some were driven out to sea; others grounded in different parts of the bay; but these were set afloat again without serious injury.

It is horrible to contemplate what might have been the fate of the inhabitants, had the violence of the storm assumed a further degree of intensity. As it was, from the fury and frequency of the gusts of wind and the incessant pouring of the rain, there was no means of escape from the building to which you happened to cling for protection. I cannot conceive any situation that presents such a shocking picture of human misery, as that of a West Indian town during a violent hurricane. The ravages of fire, however frightful and destructive, are generally confined to property: the danger and devastation of an earthquake are all over in a few seconds: but, during a hurricane, the melancholy looks, the wailing and wild despair, exhibited in the gradual transitions from anxiety to fear, and from danger to inevitable destruction, are appalling in the highest degree. Who has not pictured to himself the heart-rending spectacle of a shipwreck—the vessel tossed about by the fury of the winds and waves—its imminent perils—the foaming billows opening up their insatiable bowels to ingulph the devoted victims, and then the disappearance and destruction of the vessel and crew? This is, on a limited scale, what occurs in the case of a hurricane. By the violence of the wind, as it veers from point to point, each house is transformed into a rocking vessel; shingles and tiles are fast swept away; the air is darkened with branches of trees and fragments of houses; the roofs once exposed begin to give way; the beams crack; the walls crumble down; crash succeeds crash; and in the space of a few hours not merely a ship's crew, but three, six, and sometimes eight thousand human beings lie buried in mutilated masses amongst the ruins of a whole city.

It is generally considered that the climate and geographical position of a country exercise but little influence in the production of earthquakes. However this may be, these phenomena are of frequent occurrence in St. Lucia. Their visits, formerly few and far between, have been repeated of late years to a truly frightful extent Time was when the only sign of alarm manifested was the " sign of the cross "—each one being content to ask his neighbour: " Avez vous senti le tremblement de terre?" But now the slightest shock drives the people into the streets—throwing the gentlemen out of their windows and their wits, and the ladies into holes and hysterics.

During the last five years the Antilles have been visited by three terrific and destructive earthquakes. The first took place at six o'clock on the morning of the 11th January 1839. It lasted about 40 seconds, and was felt in many of the islands, but its devastating effects were confined to St. Lucia and Martinique. Desolating indeed were the loss of life and destruction of property in the latter island. The town of Fort Royal, containing a population of 10,000 souls, was the principal scene of havoc. One half of the houses, including the churches and public buildings, were thrown down, and about two hundred others seriously damaged and rendered untenantable. Of about five hundred persons that were buried in the ruins, two hundred and sixty-one were dug out lifeless and horribly mutilated ; and the remainder sustained severe injuries. Fortunately there were no lives lost in St. Lucia ; but considerable damage was occasioned to the different estates and to the towns of Castries and Soufriere. Such was the violence of the oscillations in the former town, that the earth was fissured in several places : many of the stone-built houses were partially thrown down or dreadfully shattered, and none escaped uninjured. Amongst the buildings that suffered most were the Catholic church and the government offices ; and several private dwellings were so materially damaged that it became necessary to have them partially taken down and repaired.

The second earthquake occurred on the 7th May 1842, at half-past four o'clock P.M., and spread terror and devastation throughout the island of St. Domingo. The principal scene of its ravages was the town of Cape Haytian, once the capital of the island, but whose population had been reduced to about 9,000 souls. The shocks were repeated three different times in the space of a few minutes, and during their continuance the fissured earth vomited forth dark clouds of sulphureous steam. By this direful catastrophe the town was reduced to a heap of ruins, and upwards of three thousand human beings lost their lives. Immediately after the first shock the fallen timbers communicated with the fire of the kitchens, and the flames burst out on all sides, destroying much valuable property that had escaped the ravages of the earthquake.

The third earthquake, one of the most melancholy events in the annals of human misery, took place on the morning of the 8th February 1843.

It lasted altogether about three minutes, and was felt more or less sensibly throughout the Caribbean Archipelago ; but its direst ravages were destined for the devoted town of Pointe à Pître, in the French island of Guadaloupe. At the period of this dreadful visitation the town contained a population of 18,000 souls, and 2,500 houses, of which no more than 200 were built of wood. Though not the seat of government, it was, in point of fact, the capital of the island ; and for the elegance of its buildings, both public and private, and the extent of its mercantile relations, was justly considered one of the most flourishing cities in the West Indies.   On the night preceding the earthquake a grand ball had been given, and many were still reposing from the fatigue of the festive scene. The Court of Assize had assembled for the administration of human justice : the principal hotel was thronged with strangers and planters from the interior, discussing matters of business, or seated together at the "table d'hôte;" and on the quays and along the streets trade and traffic were proceeding with their wonted bustle and activity. At the fatal hour of 25 minutes to eleven there was heard a noise—a hollow, rolling, rumbling noise, as of distant unbroken thunder : the sea dashed tumultuously on the beach; the earth heaved convulsively, and opened up in several places, emitting dense columns of water. In an instant all the stone buildings had crumbled to the ground—a wide-spread heap of rubbish and ruins: and in that one instant—a dread, dreary, and destructive instant—five thousand human beings, torn from their families and friends, were ushered into the abyss of eternity. But the work of desolation did not stop here: scarcely had the earthquake ceased its ravages, when a fire broke out in several places at once; and such were the terror and confusion of the surviving inhabitants that not a single house was rescued from the flames. In another instant the pile was lit up—the devouring element was sweeping over the immense holocaust; and a loud and lugubrious shriek from the living, and a long and lingering groan from the dying, had told the tale and sealed the doom of Pointe à Pître, the pride of the West!

The scenes of horror that followed it would be difficult to describe. Fathers ran about in search of their children—children screamed aloud for their mothers—mothers for their husbands—husbands for their wives: and the wild and wailing multitude that wandered over the ruins, in search of a mother, a father, a husband, a child, a brother, a sister, or a friend, found nothing but headless trunks and severed limbs. Rich and poor, black and white, planter and peasant, master and slave—all lay confounded in one vast sepulchre—all were crushed, calcined, or consumed—all hushed in the shadow of death or the silence of despair.

The night that succeeded was a night of wretchedness and want—of sorrow and suffering. 12,000 inhabitants, without food, without raiment, without money, without means, without house, or home, or hope, had sought refuge under a temporary tent, erected in the open air. Who can depict, who imagine the visions of darkness and danger that haunted these widowed thousands, waking over the burning remains of the departed city? Three days did the devouring element, fed in its progress by a forest of projecting timbers, continue with unabated fury: three nights did the funeral pile send forth its lurid glare—a beacon to mariners, pointing to where Pointe à Pître now stood no more.

On the morning of the 9th the task of exploration began ; but to enable the workmen to proceed without danger, it became necessary to batter down several walls and portions of houses, whose shattered impending fragments threatened destruction on all sides. In the space of one week *six thousand* bodies were dug out of the ruins, fifteen hundred of which were still living, but mostly in a horrible state of mutilation. These were immediately removed to the town of Basseterre, and placed under medical care; yet, sad to say, not more than one-third of them recovered. With regard to the dead bodies, an attempt was made at first to have them buried in the public cemetery; but, as the exploration proceeded, so many were found that it was resolved to have them sunk in the sea. On this melancholy task hundreds of boats were employed for several days. At length the inconvenience of the floating corpses, many of which were washed ashore, compelled the authorities to resort to the expedient of burning them in heaps, and this proceeding continued until the whole were dug out and consumed.

What the ravages of the earthquake and the fire had left untouched, of population and property, was now exposed to the no less frightful scourges of pestilence and plunder. On the second day an attempt was made by some heartless depredators amongst the lower orders to ransack the Treasury and other buildings in search of the heaps of gold buried amongst the ruins; but owing to the energetic measures of Governor Gourbeyre,

who caused martial law to be proclaimed, five
of the ruffians were apprehended and placed in
irons. This example had the wholesome effect
of arresting the further progress of an evil, which,
had its contagious influence extended to the slaves
in the interior, might have plunged the Colony in
irreparable ruin. Epidemic disease, the consequence of a pestilential atmosphere, was another
source of serious apprehension. The stench,
however, which was intolerable for several days,
gradually disappeared; and when I visited the ruins
on the 23rd March (six weeks after the earthquake) there was not the slightest offensive smell
perceptible. It appears that some of the soldiers
employed in the exploration had gone mad; but
this was attributed to the harrowing impression
produced by the mangled appearance of so many
human bodies.*

I have but one more observation to make on the
subject of earthquakes. In 1780 the town of Pointe
à Pître, then chiefly built of wood, was destroyed
by fire, which induced the inhabitants to resort to

* The destruction of property in Fort Royal was estimated at 500,000*l.*
sterling; in Cape Haytian at 300,000*l.* sterling; and in Pointe à Pître at
4,000,000*l.* sterling. The apparent disproportion between the losses in
the two last cases is accounted for by the circumstance that, although the
population of Pointe à Pître was only double that of the Cape; yet, the
town itself was three times more extensive, and five times more opulent.

stone buildings. If ever the town is rebuilt, it is probable that the old fashion of constructing with wood will be again introduced. Indeed, after the calamitous experience of recent years, there can be no question as to the superior advantages of wooden houses. In a hurricane they are as safe as those built of stone or brick, and incomparably more so in an earthquake. The chief danger is from fire, but even that is confined to property. The fact is, between fires, and hurricanes, and earthquakes, the bewildered inhabitant of these islands scarcely knows where to go, or what to do; and yet, with all their disadvantages and all their dangers, he still fondly clings to the wild western rocks of his birth.

The soil of St. Lucia is advantageously distinguished for its depth and richness. The causes which operate so powerfully in the production of disease are equally pregnant with fertility, and hence the valleys of Roseau and Mabouya are remarkable for their great fecundity and exuberant vegetation. M. Beaucé affirms that in some places the soil is twelve times more productive than that of Europe—half an acre of land being sufficient to supply the wants of a man.* St. Lucia, in fact, may truly be said to possess the advantage

* Notice sur l'île Sainte Lucie.

of a virgin soil —" an advantage in almost all agriculture, but especially that of the tropics, which
no accumulation of capital and no improvement
in science and skill seem able to counterbalance."*

Although the island presents an inexhaustible
field for the study of geology, little has yet been
ascertained respecting the structure and composition of the soil. In the valleys and alluvial plains
it consists of a deep vegetable mould, mixed with
clay; and in the more elevated positions of red
earth. The substratum is a mixture of sand and
gravel. The mountains are composed of a "volcanic conglomerate."† Tufa, magnesia, lime, alum,
quartz, and iron and copper ores are to be found
in certain localities.‡ The quarters of Soufriere
and Gros-ilet present some beautiful petrifactions
and other mineral products : sea-shells and crys-
talizations abound.

The staple productions are sugar, coffee, and
cocoa. Maize is the only corn grown : it is
chiefly used as food for poultry. The principal
spices, dyeing stuffs, and medicinal plants are,
cinnamon, ginger, vanilla, cloves, pimento, nut-
meg, indigo, logwood, cassia, aloes, castor-oil,

---

* Merivale—Lectures on Colonization and the Colonies.
† Treatise on the Endemic Fevers of the West Indies.
‡ Guide Médical des Antilles.

quinquina, cactus, ipecacuanha, jalap, simaruba, sarsaparilla, and lignum vitæ. Yams, edoes, sweet potatoes, and cassada are produced in great abundance. The other leguminous plants and esculents are cabbages, cucumbers, peas, parsnips, beans, carrots, salads, radishes, egg-fruit, beet-root, celery, mountain-cabbage, sorrel, spinage, pumpkin, tomatoes, succory, ocros, and calalou.

All the delicious fruits of the West Indies and many valuable exotics grow to perfection in St. Lucia. The most attractive are the pine-apple, cocoa-nut, grape, melon, date, fig, sappodillo, orange, shaddock, lemon, lime, citron, guava, plantain, fig-banana, mango, star-apple, pomegra-nate, plum, cherry, mamee, grenadilla, water-lemon, avocado-pear, chestnut, tamarind, bread-fruit, cashew, papaw, bread-nut, custard-apple, golden-apple, sugar-apple, and soursop. The quarter of Soufriere in particular is justly famed for the great variety and exquisite savour of its fruits and vegetables. Its pine-apple, muscadine grape, melon, and fig are considered of a superior quality to those produced in any part of the West Indies.

St. Lucia is covered with forest trees of every form and of endless variety. They are, with few exceptions, indigenous to the soil. Many of them furnish valuable materials for building, and some, excellent specimens of fancy wood. The locust, or native mahogany, grows in great profusion. The other principal trees are the palm tree, trumpet tree, oak, white cedar, black cedar, bully tree, poplar, orange tree, cotton tree, sandbox, cinnamon tree, Indian fig tree, bamboo, sandal wood, cocoa-nut tree, satinwood, mango tree, tamarind tree, cashew tree, bread-fruit tree, calabash tree, citron tree, date tree, mamee tree, manchineel, soap tree, rosewood, avocado-pear tree, ironwood, guava tree, laurel, bois immortal, bois diable, sour-orange tree, willow, sea-side grape, simaruba, lignum vitæ, acacia, logwood, bois riviere, boistan, acoma, grigris, angelin, gommier, chatanier-grand' feuille, pois doux, bois violon, bois sept ans, bois pian, barabara, bois d' inde, bois flambeau, galba, mangrove, macata, rose mahaut, bois fourmi, fromager, balisier, latanier, paletuvier, and fougere.

The domesticated animals are the same as those of Europe, whence they were originally imported. Of the horse, ass, ox, mule, cow, hog, sheep, goat, duck, cock, hen, turkey, cat, dog, rabbit, goose, pigeon, and guinea bird, there are various species, and they all thrive admirably. The woods are inhabited by the wild ox, musk rat, wild hog, iguana, and agouti, which afford excellent sport to the native *chasseurs.*

The ornithology, although inferior to those of Demerara and Trinidad, comprises many interesting specimens of the feathered tribe ; and in the shooting season, from August to the end of November, the island is visited by a variety of excellent game. They are to be met with everywhere, but their frequented resorts are the flat districts of Gros-ilet and Vieux Fort. The most remarkable birds are the partridge, dove, wild pigeon, plover, parrot, snipe, banana bird, egret, thrush, humming-bird, quail, water hen, crabier, hawk, galding, ground dove, goat-sucker, swallow, cuckoo, wild duck, booby, frigate, trembler, white-throat, nightingale, woodcock, curlew, and yellow-legs. Some of these birds attain a wonderful size: the crabier, a native of the mountains, generally measures five feet six inches in height, and six feet from wing to wing.

The markets exhibit an abundance of fish of excellent quality : the rivers teem with it, and the sea coast, maugre the depredations of sharks and whales, is no less plentifully supplied. The choicest fishes are the sprat, cutlass, eel, dolphin, anchovy, herring, sole, flounder, mullet, ray, mackerel, doctor, flying fish, baracouta, captain, king-fish, parrot-fish, and snapper. Crabs, craw-fish, and lobsters are in great abundance and very delicate eating. There is no land-turtle ; but, *en revanche*, there is an amazing quantity of sea-turtle, which is much and deservedly prized. It is chiefly caught along the coast in the quarter of Vieux Fort. The fishermen are very expert in the pursuit, and such is their acquaintance with its favourite haunts, that a casual visitor in the district may be supplied with turtle soup for dinner at the shortest notice. Vieux Fort is also famed for its delicious little oysters.

St. Lucia is infested by countless reptiles and insects. Of the former the most dangerous is the yellow serpent—a genus peculiar to this island and Martinique. It measures between six and eight feet in length, and its bite is generally fatal. There are numerous other serpents of a smaller species and much less noxious. They all multiply amazingly—the female bringing forth from thirty to forty young ones at a birth—and every part of the island is more or less exposed to their fearful influence. In most cases, however, the bite, if immediately attended to, may be effectually cured: the planters and many of the Negroes are very skilful in the application of various specifics. The serpent subsists on birds, insects, and poultry. Its greatest enemy is the *cribo*, or black snake, an animal having the shape and appearance of the

serpent, but without its noxious power. A care-
less observer would be liable to mistake the one
for the other. In every encounter the Cribo is the
aggressor and generally comes off victorious. It
counteracts the mischievous effect of the bite of
the serpent by rolling itself on the leaves of a
plant, called *Pied-poule* (to be found in every part
of the island) and returns to the attack with
renovated strength. In this way the serpent is
ultimately overpowered, and then the Cribo gorges
the carcase, commencing with the head. When
(as is frequently the case) the body of the serpent
is longer and larger than that of the snake, the
latter retaining possession of its prey, feeds upon
it for several days, gradually sucking in such
portions of the carcase as may be sufficient to
satisfy the wants of the moment. The Cribo is
sometimes found with the lower part of the serpent protruding between its jaws, in this digusting
position.*

The most remarkable insects are the scorpion,
wood-slave, annulated lizard, locust, tarantula,
centipede, blacksmith, wasp, mosquito, bat, cockroach, fly, chigre, beetle, fire-fly, spider, wood-ant,

---

* The Cribo possesses some of the characteristics of the Boa-Constrictor,
of which there is a remarkable species in St. Lucia called the " Tête-
chien."

butterfly, bête-rouge, caterpillar, grasshopper, cricket, and bee.   Of these the scorpion and cen- tipede are the most dangerous, the ant and wood- ant the most destructive, the mosquito the most troublesome, and the cockroach the most repul- sive. The destruction caused by the ant is gene- rally confined to plants and flowers ; but the depredations of the wood-ant extend to the houses, furniture, and even clothes of the inhabit- ants ; and the mischief they occasion is no less incredible than the promptitude with which it is accomplished. The following humorous remarks, which appeared some years ago in the " Edinburgh Review " in reference to the insects of British Guiana, are strictly applicable to St. Lucia. " The bête-rouge lays the foundation of a tremendous ulcer.   In a moment you are covered with ticks : flies get entry into your mouth, into your eyes, into your nose : you eat flies, drink flies, and breathe flies.   Lizards, cockroaches, and snakes get into your bed : ants eat up the books : scorpions sting you on the foot.   Every thing bites, stings, or bruises : every second of your life you are wounded by some piece of animal life. An insect with eleven legs is swimming in your tea- cup : a nondescript with nine wings is struggling in the small beer, or a caterpillar with several dozen eyes in its belly is hastening over the bread and butter. All nature is alive and seems to be gathering her entomological hosts to eat you up, as you are standing, out of your coat, waistcoat, and breeches."

CHAPTER V.

THE population of St. Lucia is formed of the most heterogeneous elements, and comprises every caste and colour under the sun. The chief classification is that of whites, coloured people, and blacks. The whites are divided into creoles and Europeans : the creoles are subdivided into natives of the island and West Indians; and the Europeans into English and French. The English include Irish and Scotch, and the French—Germans, Italians, and Savoyards. The coloured population is no less confused and complicated, being composed of persons from every Colony in the West Indies, and of every grade and denomination from the Carib to the Quadroon. The blacks are natives of the island with a sprinkling of Africans and Martinique refugees.

The native white population consists of the descendants of several ancient and respectable French families, which had been the original owners of the soil.* Some of these families are

---

* I have met with several well-informed persons in St. Lucia, who entertain the conviction that Mademoiselle Tascher ·le la Pagerie, better known as the Empress Josephine, was born in that island, and not in Martinique, as is commonly supposed. Amongst others the late Sir John Jeremie appears to have been strongly impressed with that idea. The grounds of belief rest upon the following circumstances to which I find allusion is made in a St. Lucia newspaper of 1831 :—It is alleged that the de Taschers were amongst the French families that settled in St. Lucia after the peace of 1763 ; that they became located upon a small estate on the acclivity of Morne Paix-Bouche, where the future Empress first saw the light on the 23rd June of that year ; and that they continued to reside there until 1771, at which period the father was selected for the important office of Intendant of Martinique, whither he immediately returned with his family.

These circumstances are well known to many respectable families in St. Lucia : the late Madame Darlas Delomel and M. Martin Raphael were among the playmates of Mademoiselle Tascher at Morne Paix-Bouche. M. Raphael, being in France many years after, was induced to pay a visit to Malmaison on the strength of his former acquaintance, and met with a most gracious reception from the Empress-Queen Dowager.

still extant, and in comparative affluence ; others have retired to France or the French Colonies, and many have become extinct altogether. The native black population comprises the descendants of the Negroes, originally imported from Africa or the neighbouring Colonies. From the promiscuous intercourse of the white and black races have sprung the various classes of the coloured population. Of British settlers the Scotch are by far the most numerous, the English and Irish being limited to four or five.

The French inhabitants, other than the natives, are formed into two divisions ; namely, those who were domiciled in the island previously to its cession in 1814, and those who have settled there since that period. The former, as well as the natives of every colour and class, are regarded in the light of British subjects, and are entitled to a participation in all offices of trust and emolument. The latter are alone considered as aliens, and by a local enactment of 29th August 1826, are excluded from employment in the public service. This law, however, is seldom strictly enforced, and several aliens have been commissioned by the local Executive as medical practitioners, not a few as Justices of the Peace, and some even as members of the Council of Government.

The position of the aliens is nevertheless one of peculiar anomaly and embarrassment. If they are no longer subject to the limitations of the "droits d'aubaine," their naturalization, so indiscriminately conceded in former days, can now only be acquired by an Act of the Imperial Parliament. In short, of the various privileges enjoyed by foreigners in the early days of West Indian colonization, the sole vestige that now remains is the permission to hold landed property; and of this several Frenchmen have availed themselves by making purchases to a considerable extent. Now, mark the position of these parties, affected as they are by the simultaneous operation of four distinct and conflicting laws, viz., the Code Civil, the local law of St. Lucia, the ancient law of France, and the constitutional law of England. By one of the local ordinances the foreigner is debarred from all offices of trust and emolument. By another he is compelled, under a penalty of £50 sterling, to accept the offices of Justice of the Peace, Town Warden, and Road Commissioner. On the acceptance of any such office he forfeits his rights as a Frenchman, in accordance with the provisions of the Code Civil;* and although, by

* "La qualité de Français se perdra, 1° par la naturalisation acquise en pays étranger; 2° par l'acceptation non autorisée par le Roi de fonctions

virtue of the old French laws still in force in St.
Lucia, he may acquire property to any extent, yet
he is not bound by allegiance to the British Crown.
The law of St. Lucia says to him: "You have
fixed your abode in this island, and have purchased
property or established a commercial business;
you are therefore eligible to certain offices of trust:
but you must not aspire to those of Gaoler or Inspector of Police; these are offices of emolument
reserved for British subjects." On the other hand,
the constitutional law of England says to this
bewildered foreigner: "You may forfeit all your
privileges as a Frenchman; take as many oaths
of allegiance as you please; purchase the whole
island of St. Lucia, if you have the means of doing
so; become a member of Council, and as President of the Board assume the administration of
the Government: you are still, to all intents and
purposes, an unnaturalized alien—still a foreigner,
wholly unfettered by any ties of allegiance to the
British Crown."*

Much irritation and ill-will have prevailed
at different periods between the English and

publiques conférées par un Gouvernement étranger."—*Code Civil des
Français.*

* Legally speaking—of course the moral obligation would always
remain.

French inhabitants. On the side of the latter these feelings had their origin in the sense of humiliation produced by what they deemed the ill-advised and degrading cession of the Colony to the British Crown: and this humiliation acquired added intensity from the success of our arms at the close of the revolutionary wars. In such a state of things, the most trivial incident was calculated to rouse all the natural jealousy of the French settlers ; and every grievance, whether real or imaginary, was laid hold of as a subject of complaint against the British. On the side of the latter many circumstances had a tendency to foster a spirit of antagonism. Their bearing as conquerors, and their unguarded allusions to national points of difference, were not always marked by that moderation and deference, which prudence should have dictated and policy enjoined. The " amour propre" of the French— a sentiment which with them stood in lieu of *amor patriæ*—was thus unnecessarily wounded ; and for some time nothing prevailed but distrust on the one hand, and disaffection on the other. It appears that the local authorities, instead of adopting measures to allay these feelings, so unnatural between subjects of the same state, allowed the most unbounded scope for their gratification, until at length in 1819 matters had arrived at a state bordering on open hostility. Defiance and revenge were loudly talked of: several cartels were sent and accepted; and not content with private encounters, an arrangement was concluded that a general duel, or, rather, pitched battle, should be fought between the most violent partisans on both sides. The field selected for this absurd display was the promontory of Vieille Ville, famed for many a close conflict between the British and French, and saturated with the blood of the brave of both nations. The ground had already been measured —the pistols charged: five Britons and five Frenchmen stood frowning on each other in battle array; and the signal was about to be given for commencing the work of death, when M. Berté St. Ange, the Attorney-General, rode up between the combatants and put a stop to their intended engagement. From that period the mutual jealousy of parties began to subside, and it has now dwindled into mere discussions on the relative merits of the two nations—their wars in the reign of Louis XIV—those of the French Revolution—the battles of the Nile and Trafalgar, of Toulouse and Waterloo—with occasional disquisitions, scientific, literary, and poli-

tical, on Newton and Descartes, Shakspeare and
Corneille, Voltaire and Milton, Talma and Kean,
Cromwell and Bonaparte. The two nations have
been drubbing each other, on land and on sea,
for the last thousand years; and yet, according
to the English, the French have never gained a
victory, while if we credit the French, the English
must have lost every engagement but for the
timely intervention of traitors and turncoats.

The disappearance of their former rivalry and
their present fraternization are to be ascribed in
a great measure to their numerous intermarriages
of recent years. By this means the principal
merchants, planters, and public servants have
become connected with many of the old French
families; so that the best interests of the Colony
are now intimately wound up in the welfare alike
of English and French.

The following returns, compiled from authentic
sources, exhibit the relative numbers of the population at different periods:—

Years.	Whites.	Coloured.	Blacks.	Totals.
1772	2,018	663	12,795	15,476
1789	2,198	1,588	17,992	21,778
1810	1,210	1,878	14,397	17,485
1825	1,194	3,871	13,530	18,595
1843	1,039	5,287	14,368	20,694

We soc by these details that seventy years ago

the white population was nearly double that of the present day. It continued to increase until 1789, and then diminished by one-half under the devastating influence of the revolutionary principles of the day. Since that epoch it has remained almost stationary. The coloured population, which may not inaptly be termed the staple population of the Colonies, has rapidly progressed in numbers, wealth, and respectability. Independently of the natural increase amongst themselves, they are constantly receiving fresh accessions of strength through their intercourse with the whites and blacks, and the connexion of these races with each other. Few as yet have become owners of the soil to any considerable extent; but much of the property in houses and land, both in Castries and Soufriere, is possessed by them. Some are opulent merchants; others respectable shop-keepers; and many are industrious tradesmen. The advantages of education, too, begin to be more generally appreciated: not only are the clerkships in the public offices held by persons of colour; but the Medical Profession, the Press, the Bar, the Legislative Council, the offices of Crown Lawyer, Stipendiary Magistrate, Justice of the Peace, Deputy Registrar, Deputy Marshal, and Notary Public, are aspired to by candidates from amongst their ranks, and filled with credit and distinction. Although this result is mainly attributable to the good sense and steady deportment of the coloured classes themselves, it would be unjust to withhold from the whites our meed of praise for their liberal encouragement of their coloured brethren.

Amongst the blacks there has been much fluctuation. From 1772 to 1789, when the slave trade flourished in all its enormities, there was an increase of 5,197 persons. But the suppression of the traffic under the British, coupled with the decimation of the Negroes by famine and the sword during the revolution, reduced them in a few years to about 13,000. This class of the population has vastly improved in physical appearance—an improvement which, owing to the unrestricted controul of the parents over their offspring, and the increased leisure devoted by the mothers to the nursing and rearing of their children, cannot fail to become still more strikingly observable in the rising generation of blacks: but there is no corresponding augmentation in their numbers; nor is it likely the case will be otherwise, so long as the promiscuous intercourse of the sexes continues to be systematically persisted in by the great majority of thc people.

Dr. Levacher, a native of St. Lucia, and distinguished for his hatred of the British name, in a
work,* written expressly on the fevers of the West
Indies, has thought proper to introduce some unfounded observations on the tendency in St. Lucia
of what he is pleased to call the "domination
Anglaise." To that sole cause he attributes all the
wants and woes of the Colony, which he considers
to be fast retrograding towards a state of barbarism;
and in confirmation of this he refers to the fact
that the population in 1834 did not exceed 15,000
souls. Dr. Levacher's example has been followed
by M. A. J. Beaucé, a foreigner who settled in
St. Lucia in 1832, under the hospitality and protection of the British flag, and has since purchased
landed property in the island. In 1841 this person published in Paris a pamphlet† of fifty pages,
on the state of St. Lucia, wherein he misrepre-
sents almost every circumstance connected with
the Colony, and amongst other matters affirms
that " la population actuelle est d'environ 15,000
âmes, y compris les blancs, les gens de couleur,
et les négres." Now, Dr. Levacher might have
easily ascertained, and M. Beaucé must have
known, that according to the returns for 1834,
upon which they received their share of compen-

* Guide Médical des Antilles. † Notice sur l'île Sainte Lucie.

sation from the British Government, the slave population alone amounted to 13,348 souls; while the free population of every colour exceeded 6,000. But their object was to create an impression that the " domination Anglaise" is inimical to the prosperity of the Colonies, and thereby to foster the jealousy of the French Colonial aristocracy, and mislead the friends of the Negro in France.

The refugees from the foreign island of Martinique, commonly designated by the derisive appellation of *Passparterres*, constitute a characteristic ingredient in the population of St. Lucia. The origin of this *sobriquet* has never been satisfactorily ascertained. The most plausible supposition is that the early refugees, being unwilling to gratify the curiosity of the St. Lucians, respecting the means employed to effect their escape from slavery; and finding them incredulous as to the practicability of crossing the channel in an oared boat, had rallied their numerous inquiries by stating that they had " *come by land.*" And truly, when we consider the difficulties of escape—the vigilance of the authorities of Martinique—the system of espionage employed by the planters to check desertion amongst their slaves—the strict surveillance of the " guarda-costas," and the distance and dangers of the passage between the two islands, it is matter of surprise that so many of them should have succeeded in accomplishing their object. The distance from the place of embarkation in Martinique is in some instances upwards of forty miles, and the means of conveyance, the first boat or canoe that comes in their way. Still, it is no unusual occurrence to see twelve or fifteen men and women land on the coast of St. Lucia, from a canoe in which five persons could not sit at their ease. We know that numbers perish in the attempt, either from the roughness of the weather or the wretched condition of their boats; and that many, upon being closely pursued by the guarda-costas, plunge into the deep, never to rise again, preferring death and a watery grave to the life and labour of bondage.

Until 1831, desertion beyond the limits of the Colony was seldom resorted to by the slaves in Martinique. In the early part of that year an insurrection broke out amongst them, from the failure and results of which many were subsequently induced to seek refuge in the neighbouring British Colonies. I was residing in St. Pierre at the period of this occurrence, and am enabled to speak to the circumstances from personal observation.

The news of the " Revolution de Juillet " had excited various feelings amongst the colonial population. To the Republicans it was, in the words of the veteran Lafayette, " la meillure des republiques ;" to the friends of the tricolor flag, the signal of a return to conquest and glory; to the partisans of the old régime, the downfall and death-blow of legitimacy ; and to the victims of colonial power and prejudice, the dawn of a brighter, happier day. In the midst of these conflicting impressions, the ship " Glaneuse " laden with heroes from the streets of Paris, and bound for North America, arrived in the road-stead of St Pierre. It appears that the friends of Louis Philippe, finding their master firmly seated on the throne, began to examine the tools with which they had achieved the great revolution. Some, being quite worn out in the recent struggle, were put on the shelf ; others were mended and their tempers improved ; several were entirely remodelled ; while the greater number, having merely got rid of their rust, were found to have acquired both edge and polish. Amongst the last not a few possessed the advantage of cutting in opposite directions, and being at once the most useful and the most dangerous, it was proposed to compensate their services in depopulating the

" centre of civilization," by sending them to
people the wilds of Campeachy.   Such were the
turbulent spirits now let loose upon the population of St. Pierre ; and it was easy to perceive from
their airs and demeanour that the fermentation of
the " glorieuses journées " had not quite subsided
amongst them.   Being mostly artizans, " decrot-
teurs," and other humble orders of the French
populace, they were naturally shunned by all respectable inhabitants, and to make up for this
slight they formed an intimacy with the blacks.
The latter, as may be supposed, were delighted to
find themselves treated on terms of equality by
any class of white persons ; and for several days
nothing was seen but parties of Negroes and the
" heroes of July " parading the streets, arm in
arm, or carousing together in the beer shops.
The voyagers, excited by liquor, talked openly of
barricades and bloodshed ; expressing their surprise that slavery should still be found to prevail
under the tricolor flag, and recommending the
blacks to follow the example so nobly set them by
the heroes of the " Métropole." To crown the
whole, Casimir de la Vigne's celebrated song, of *La
Parisienne*, soon became the order of the day, and
the Negroes to make it tally with their position

and sentiments, parodied the " refrain " by substituting the word " colons " for " canons."

" En avant, marchons contre les *colons*."

The advice and suggestions of their new friends
being in accordance with their own pre-conceived
notions, the slaves soon formed the design of
setting fire to the plantations, and of murdering
the white inhabitants.   Secret meetings were
held ; a plot laid ; chiefs appointed ; parties
organized ; ramifications established ; arms and
ammunitions procured ; oaths and pledges ex-
changed ; and a day appointed for carrying the
scheme into execution. The outbreak was to have
taken place on the 24th December 1830 ; but
some unforeseen circumstance having occurred to
frustrate this plan, it was finally fixed for the 9th
February following. Before that time, however,
the attention of the white population had been
attracted by several incidents, which appeared to
announce an approaching explosion ; and they
had sent a deputation to Fort Royal to implore
the assistance and protection of the Executive.
Governor Dupotet ridiculed their fears, and to
convince them that there was nothing to be
apprehended from the blacks, he consented to
accompany them to St. Pierre, which, with its

population of 26,000 souls, was regarded as the focus of the insurrectionary movements. The blacks, who had all along looked up to Governor Dupotet as the legitimate representative of Revolution, and therefore favourable to their views, were now sorely disappointed to find that he was preparing to adopt measures against them; so that, in order to prevent the ruinous consequences of detection and defeat, the chiefs issued orders to arrest all proceedings for the time. These orders, however, were too late for the rural districts; for, at seven o'clock on the evening of the 9th February, just as the Governor disembarked at St. Pierre, eleven sugar plantations and three houses were seen on fire, forming one immense circle of flame in the outskirts of the town, and enveloping the horizon in dense clouds of smoke. In an instant the town was one scene of uproar and confusion: the regular troops, the gendarmes, the militia, horse and foot, the sailors of the merchant shipping, the inhabitants, white, black, and coloured, were seen running in every direction. I happened to be on a visit in the *mouillage* at the moment of the alarm, and had to traverse the town (a distance of three miles) to reach my apartments, which were within twenty yards of one of the houses on fire: and what with the sabring, discharging of fire arms, shutting of doors, beating of drums, ringing of bells, screaming of women and children, and gallopping of " Chasseurs à cheval "—a scene of greater terror and tumult it is scarce possible to imagine. The Negroes were up in arms on several estates; some were killed ; others were wounded ; the rest were easily overpowered ; and before five o'clock next morning this unnatural revolt, conceived in folly, brought forth in darkness, and strangled at its birth, had disappeared from the land. On the 10th martial law was proclaimed throughout the island ; and during that and the two following days no less than five hundred persons were arrested on suspicion. A Court of Assize was immediately appointed to try the prisoners ; but the greater number were set at liberty on the preliminary investigation, and only fifty-three were ultimately arraigned. The trial lasted fourteen days, and resulted in a sentence of death against twenty-two of the ringleaders.

On the 19th May—the day appointed for the execution, the town of St. Pierre presented one of the most melancholy and heart-rending spectacles ever exhibited in any country. Twenty-two human beings, having each a rope round his neck, were marched forth from the prison, near the

"Batterie Desnotz," escorted by soldiers, priests, and policemen, to the "Place Bertin," where a gibbet, sixty feet long, had been erected for their execution. Several were foaming at the mouth, and by their gestures, language, and looks, manifested the working of the evil passions within. But the greater number appeared resigned to their fate and were attentively listening to the exhortation of the clergy. Contrary to what takes place in Europe on similar occasions, the attendance of spectators was rather scanty ; but under the impression that an attempt might be made to rescue the prisoners, there was an extraordinary display of military force ; the *Place*, and every avenue leading to it were thronged with mounted gendarmes and troops of the line. On reaching the foot of the gallows the agitation of the wretched culprits assumed a frightful degree of intensity. The spell was now broken; the veil of delusion torn from their eyes: all their visions of glory had vanished; all their dreams of power and preponderance had dissolved; and nothing remained but the startling, shadowless reality of an ignominious death. The more violent ran about like maniacs ; and the flakes of foam that curled on their lips contrasted strangely

with the sable hue of their skin. The most remarkable actor in this tragic scene was a coloured
man, named Chéry, who had also been the chief
promoter of the insurrection. At the sight of
the gibbet he gave himself up to the wildest
despair, vomiting forth imprecations, both loud
and deep, against the white inhabitants, and
expressing his fervent hope " that the island of
Martinique might be swallowed up in the ocean
before another generation should pass away."
He had just commenced :

" En avant, marchons contre les *colons*,"

when the bourreau, shaking him by the rope that
dangled on his back, said, pointing to the gallows :
" Voila votre chemin." Chéry grinned and gnashed
his teeth: then tossing off his shoes in the air
(one of which struck a gendarme with great violence on the face) he ran up the ladder to the
head of the gallows, and in a few seconds was
seen hanging without a struggle or a sigh. The
others were then thrown off in succession, until the
whole twenty-two were left hanging together at
equal distances from each other. In an hour after,
the bodies were cut down ; and a long and lowering day closed on this lugubrious spectacle, just
as the twenty-two corpses, the destined food of

sharks, were dropped into the sea at some distance from the beach.*

I believe I was one of the last who retired from the scene of this horrible sacrifice to the rights and rigours of slavery; and as I passed along, it was easy to read in the strained resignation of the multitude, and the studied composure of their looks, the rage and rancour of the boiling spirit within.

From that period desertion became more frequent amongst the blacks in Martinique, and continued on the increase until the abolition of slavery in the British Colonies. Between Dominica, on the one hand, and St. Lucia, on the other, no less than 4,000 persons have effected their escape, including those that have perished in either channel. At first desertion was resorted to as a shelter from the punishment incurred under the outraged laws of the Colony; and the *Hue and Cry* against the early refugees comprised every possible offence, from the delinquency of "marronage" to the crime of murder. Had the representations of the owners been listened to, in almost every instance the fugitives should have been delivered up to the authorities of Marti-

* The late lamented M. de Maynard has glanced at these occurrences in his interesting Novel, "Outre-mer."

nique; but the Executive of St. Lucia, acting on the rule, that fugitive slaves from foreign Colonies become free the moment they set their foot on British soil, have uniformly refused to sanction their restitution, except in cases of murder, arson, and rape ; and then only on satisfactory *primâ facie* evidence being adduced before a British Magistrate, of the guilt of the party charged with the offence. The French have repeatedly remonstrated against this proceeding, as being at variance with the principles of international policy; nor, indeed, so long as Great Britain upheld slavery in her own dominions, could it be denied that their complaints had some colourable grounds to rest upon. But in the present relative position of the British and Foreign Colonies, this rule appears to be based on a due appreciation of the best interests of humanity and justice. In most cases the offences charged against the fugitives are either fictitious or unfounded; and their restitution would be followed by a prosecution for marronage—punishable with the utmost severity under the Martinique slave laws—and ultimately by their reduction to the most abject state of slavery. In fact, notwithstanding the numerous complaints of the slave owners of that Colony, and their reiteration of various crimes and misdemeanours against the refugees, the only case in which they have succeeded in bringing the charge home to the offender, is that of Sylvestre Pombarré, accused of murder, and he has been handed over to the authorities of Martinique, to be dealt with according to the laws of that Colony.

It cannot be denied, however, that amongst the refugees there are some who bring with them to St. Lucia the evil passions and fierce propensities, which may have marked their previous career in their native country. In their dealings with the St. Lucia Negro the slightest quarrel leads to a collision, and every collision to scenes of rancour and revenge: of this there is abundant evidence in the criminal annals of St. Lucia. But as a body they are well disposed and industrious; and their example has had the salutary effect of stimulating the somewhat indolent temperament of the native labourer.

The number of refugees never exceeded 800 at any time. In the days of the St. Lucia Militia they were formed into a company, called the "Alien Corps," and used to attend the parades in their *uniform* of white jackets, but without any of the pomp or pride of military attire. Until 1839 they enjoyed a monopoly of the advantages of free labour, and sedulously did they turn it to account : but on the abolition of slavery, having to compete with the awakened energies of 15,000 labourers, free like themselves, they were literally driven from the field, and many of them have emigrated to Demerara and Trinidad. Since that period also the arrivals have become less frequent, owing partly to the altered state of society in St. Lucia, partly to the increased vigilance of the authorities of Martinique, and partly to the prospect of approaching emancipation in the French Colonies.

I have thought it necessary to go into these details on the subject of the refugees, both on account of the close political connexion which existed in former days between Martinique and St. Lucia, and the intercourse and commercial relations that still subsist between the two communities. It is my firm persuasion that the " Passparterres " are but the fore-runners of other more numerous settlers from the same quarter ; and that when emancipation shall have been conceded to the French Colonies, the population of St. Lucia cannot fail to receive an important accession of industry and intelligence from the vast resources of Martinique.

The manners, customs, and language of the inhabitants partake in a great measure of the diversity and confusion which characterise the population itself; and in spite of the amalgamating influence of recent changes, the social habitudes of English and French, European and Creole, continue to display their various shades of dissimilarity. A great obstacle to improvement arises from a difference of opinion, as to whether strangers, on their arrival, should visit the residents, or receive that mark of politeness from them in the first instance. The former mode is insisted on by the French, as being comformable to the established usages of France ; and the latter is adhered to by the English, in accordance with the acknowledged ceremonial of English society. This vexed question was never worth half the wit and arguments that have been expended upon it ; and I am happy to observe that the French are giving way to what must be considered the more rational practice. A difference of language has contributed not a little to foster this difference of usage. It is but justice, however, to the ladies to state that whenever *they* can meet, on English or French ground, without the aid of an interpreter, a mutual disposition is evinced to waive all frivolous points of etiquette.

The want of social enjoyments, so generally observable in the West Indies, is sensibly felt in

St. Lucia ; less perhaps on account of the circum-
scribed circle of its society, than of the conflicting
elements of which that society is composed. Of
course, the divisions of colour, and class, and
language, and even political antagonism, have their
share in widening the breach ; but its principal
cause is the rage for devotional practices, which
of late years has taken possession of the whole
female population, both white and coloured.
Thus, in addition to the divisions of caste, we
now have a division of sex. The males and
females are severed, as it were, into two hostile
camps ; and while the gentlemen assemble in the
stores to discuss politics and pickles, the ladies
repair to their coteries to dilate on salvation and
scandal. In a word, dress and devotion are the
order of the day—the all-engrossing topics of
female society ; and both are so harmoniously
blended that the greatest *dévote* is often the
greatest coquette. As, however, with the exception of an occasional ball, the opportunities for
exhibiting their love of dress are limited to the
ceremonies of the Church ; so, on those occasions,
it is no unusual sight to see hundreds of fashion-
ably-attired females in the town of Castries, out of
a population of 4,000 souls. Never perhaps was
religion so emphatically the handmaid of com-

merce : never were the interests of the one so
strenuously promoted by the votaries of the
other.

French is the language commonly spoken. Its
continuance in all judicial proceedings, to the
exclusion of the language of the mother country,
was guaranteed to the inhabitants by the treaty of
cession; nor was it until the 1st January 1842
that it ceased altogether to be used in the courts
of law. The oversight, not to say impolicy, of
excluding the language of the Parent State, is so
clearly demonstrated by the experience of recent
times, that it is needless to enlarge upon it in
this place. In Canada and the Mauritius it has
produced neither contentment nor conciliation;
while, in the case of St. Lucia, not only has it
operated as a bar to the advancement of British
interests, but it has been fraught with illimitable
mischief to the French settlers themselves. As
might have been expected, all the young creoles
were sent to France for their education, either in
the fruitless hope that the French language would
never be superseded, or the still more fruitless
anticipation that the Colony might fall into the
hands of their compatriots. By this means every
anti-English feeling was encouraged; and when
after ten years of petitions and postponements,

the change of language was finally announced, only two members of the Bar were found possessed of a plausible knowledge of English to enable them to plead before the courts.

The Negro language is a jargon formed from the French, and composed of words, or rather sounds, adapted to the organs of speech in the black population. As a *patois* it is even more unintelligible than that spoken by the Negroes in the English Colonies. Its distinguishing feature consists in the suppression of the letter " *r* " in almost every word in which it should be used, and the addition of " *ki's* " and " *ka's* " to assist in the formation of the tenses. It is, in short, the French language, stripped of its manly and dignified ornaments, and travestied for the accommodation of children and toothless old women. I regret to add that it has now almost entirely superseded the use of the beautiful French language, even in some of the highest circles of colonial society. The prevalence of this jargon is one of the many disadvantages resulting from a want of educational institutions. It is the refuge of ignorance, and the less you know of French, the greater aptitude you have for talking Negro : a child three years old will speak it more fluently than a man of thirty. I can say for myself that, although possessing an extensive knowledge of the French language, acquired during a sojourn of five years in France, I have failed in obtaining anything like an adequate notion of this gibberish, during a residence of nearly fifteen years in St. Lucia and Martinique. Having remarked that I was laughed at by the Negroes whenever I attempted to use it in conversation, I have adopted the plan of addressing them in my best French, and now the laugh is all on my side. Nothing can be more amusing than the faces they put on to convince you that they are unable to understand French. " *Pas tan*" (*Je n'entends pas*) is the reply to every observation ; but the truth is, they often pretend ignorance in order to allure you into their own soft, silly dialect, whose accents are always flattering to their ears, however imperfectly it may be spoken.

Nor is this corruption of the language confined to mere words : it also extends to proper names ; so much so, indeed, that there are few persons in the island that are not designated by any name but their own. Some have the *sobriquets* of *Moncoq*, *Montout*, *Fanfan*, *Laguerre*. Others have their names mollified by means of certain dulcet, endearing terminations : thus, Anne becomes *Annzie*, Catherine *Catiche*, Besson *Besson-*

nette: whilst the greater number, dropping altogether the names given them at the baptismal font, have adopted others of more modern vogue. Jean Baptiste is supplanted by *Nelson;* François by *Francis;* Cyprien by *Camille;* and what is still more preposterous, not only are the christian names altered in this way, but the patronymics of many are entirely suppressed. M. Jean Marie Beaurégard considers *Jean Marie* too vulgar, and adopts the name of Alfred; and his friends consider *Beaurégard* too long, and omit it altogether in their dealings with him. By this process M. Jean Marie Beaurégard is. metamorphosed into plain M. *Alfred;* and his wife, if any he have, goes by the style and title of *Madame Alfred.* This confusion of names would be merely ludicrous, if it were not pregnant with mischief to the community. From being first sanctioned in the intercourse of every-day life, and introduced into family circles, the alterations and substitutions had gradually crept into the more serious relations of trade and litigation ; so that, when the Commissioners of Compensation were about to adjudicate upon the claims and counter claims from St. Lucia, scarcely a single individual was found to have invariably preserved his *proper* name in the different documents submitted on his behalf. Difficulty and delay were the result; and many persons only succeeded in establishing their identity and securing their fortunes, by obtaining affidavits, certificates of baptism, and notarial attestations, at considerable expense, from various parts of the world.

The higher class of creoles are distinguished for their courteous manner and cordial hospitality. Although few amongst them ever attain any eminence in literary or scientific pursuits, they are nevertheless generally intelligent and well-informed. The practice of duelling, so common in their "days of chivalry," has now almost totally disappeared. Impelled by a mistaken or exaggerated principle of honour, they were wont to seek reparation in single combat for the most trivial injuries; nor were they deterred from such exhibitions by the stringent laws of Louis XIV., then, as now, in force in St. Lucia. In those days no scion of colonial aristocracy was deemed qualified to enter on the business of life, until, in the phraseology of their code of honour, he had given proof in a duel of his daring and dexterity. To have shot his man and debauched his friend's wife were the surest recommendations to honour and distinction: without these he was held incompetent to assume the solemn duties of a hus-

band and a father; without these he was exposed
to the taunts and trials, the sneers and slander of
the self-styled brave. Now-a-days, however, this
digraceful practice is only resorted to in extreme
cases. The example of our neighbours of Martinique, by whom the fashion of duelling was once
regarded as the pink of gallantry, and the "ne plus
ultra" of social refinement, contributed in no small
degree to promote a bellicose disposition amongst
our friends in St. Lucia; and the abatement of
the evil in the "Faubourg St. Germain du Golfe
du Mexique"* has produced a kindred feeling
and corresponding results in the once sister
Colony of St. Lucia.

The creole women are a race apart; and, as
far as I am able to judge, are not inferior to those
of any country for elegance of form, gracefulness
of carriage, suavity of temper, and buoyancy of
disposition. To them may be truly applied Lord
Byron's description of the Italian woman :—

" Heart on her lips, and soul within her eyes,
    Soft as her clime, and sunny as her skies."

Dancing, with its train of airy and gaysome
evolutions, is the idol passion of the fair creole;
and in no place or position do her delicate beauty
and exquisite loveliness appear to greater advan-

* Martinique—thus described by M. de Maynard in " Outre-mer."

tage than amidst the attractions and superficial
excitement of the ball-room. Even the dance
itself is not with her what it is in the more extended circles of European society—a thing of
attitudes and gestures—a round of skimming and
shuffling. Here it is all gravity and decorum—
there nothing but flutter and frivolity. In France
it is the wild creation of fashionable extravagance ;
between the tropics a chastened and rational
exercise, which is often carried to the utmost
extent, without infringing any of the decencies of
life.

Amongst the lower orders the dance exercises a
still greater influence. Not satisfied with aping
those above them in finery and dress, the Negroes
carry their love of dancing to the most extravagant pitch—much too extravagant perhaps for
their means. True, the evil has its bright side in
the encouragement of trade and the promotion of
a spirit of emulation and industry amongst the
labouring classes ; but it must greatly impair their
physical energies, if it does not ultimately mar
their independence. The best that can be said of
it is, that it is inherent in, and common to, all
colonial populations of French origin ; and that
it is not to be put down either by preaching or
persecution. The spoiled children of artificial

enjoyment, French Negroes, like their betters, will have their feasts and festivals, their dressing and dancing. Let us hope that these recreations may long continue to preserve their primæval character of innocence and simplicity, nor, by contact with fashion and false refinement, become the vehicles of corruption and crime.

In order to gratify their propensity for dancing the Negroes have formed themselves into two divisions, or "societies," under the somewhat fantastic style of "Roses" and "Marguerites."* These "societies" exist by immemorial usage in the French colonies, and are still to be found in more or less activity in St. Lucia, Dominica, and Trinidad. The history of the Antilles is involved in such total obscurity in all that concerns the black population, that it would be impossible at the present time to trace the origin of the Roses and Marguerites. It appears that at one period they were invested with a political character; and their occasional allusions to English and French, Republicans and Bonapartists would seem to confirm this impression. Their connexion with politics must have ceased at the termination of the struggle between England and France, from which

* The Marguerites are also sometimes called " Wadeloes."

period their rivalry has been confined to dancing and other diversions.

These *societies*, which had remained almost in abeyance during the latter days of slavery, have been revived within the last five years with unusual *éclat* and solemnity. Although few persons, besides the labouring classes and domestic servants, take any active part in their proceedings, there is scarcely an individual in the island, from the Governor downwards, who is not enrolled amongst the partisans of one coterie or the other. The Roses are patronized by Saint Rose, and the flower of that name is their cherished emblem. The Marguerites are in the holy keeping of Saint Marguerite, and the *Marguerite*, or bachelor's button, is the flower they delight to honour. Each society has three kings and three queens, who are chosen by the suffrages of the members. The first, or senior, king and queen only make their appearance on solemn occasions, such as the anniversary of their coronation or the fête of the patron saint of the society: on all other emergencies they are represented by the kings and queens elect, who exercise a sort of vice-regal authority. The most important personage next to the sovereign is the *chanterelle*, or female singer, upon whom devolves the task of com-

posing their *Belairs*,* and of reciting them at
their public dances. Each society has a house
hired in Castries, in which it holds its periodical
meetings. Here the women, whose attendance
is much more regular than that of the men, assemble in the evening to rehearse some favourite
" belair" for their next dance, or to receive a
lecture from the king, who may be seen at one
end of the room, pacing up and down with an air
of dignity and importance suited to his station.
If any member has been guilty of improper conduct since their last meeting, the king takes
occasion to advert to it in terms of censure,
dwelling with peculiar emphasis upon the superior decorum observed by the rival society.
Gross misconduct is punished by expulsion from
their ranks.

The " belairs" turn generally on the praises of
the respective societies; the comparative value
of the Rose and the Marguerite; the good qualities, both physical and mental, of individual
members; the follies and foibles of the opposite
party, and of persons supposed to be connected
with or favourable to them. Nothing can sur-

* The *Belair* is a sort of pastoral in blank verse, adapted to a peculiar
tune or air. Many of these airs are of a plaintive and melancholy character, and some are exquisitely melodious.

pass the poetical fecundity of the chanterelles : almost every week produces a fresh effusion and a new belair. Some, indeed, are of a higher order than one would be entitled to look for from untutored Negroes: and it is but natural to suppose that they are assisted in these by their friends among the educated classes. Of this description are the following stanzas in praise of the Roses, which appeared in print in 1840:—

LES ROSES.

Venez, amis ; venez, dansons ;
De Sainte Rose c'est la fête :
Disons pour elle nos chansons,
Et que chacun de nous repète :
Chantons, amis ; rions, dansons.

C'est aujourd'hui jour d'allégresse ;
Nargue des soucis, des chagrins ;
A nous le plaisir et l'irresse,
A nous les vifs et gais refrains.
Venez, &c.

Des fleurs la *Rose* est la plus belle :
" Par mon parfum, par mes couleurs,
" Par mon éclat, je suis, dit-elle,
" Oui, je suis la reine des fleurs !"
Venez, &c.

Sur sa tige triste et flétrie
La *Marguerite* nait, périt ;
Mais la Rose, toujours fleurie,
Renait toujours et reverdit.

Venez, &c.

La Rose est la reine du monde,
Elle est aussi celle des amours !
Qu' à nos chansons chacun réponde
Vive la Rose pour toujours !

Venez, &c.

The occasions of festivity and dancing are ushered in with universal demonstrations of gaiety and joyousness. After assisting at a solemn service commemorative of the day, the Messieurs and Dames, decked out in their most costly dresses, proceed in groups to visit their friends amongst the higher classes, distributing cakes and flowers in honour of the fête. The costume of the men differs little from that commonly worn by gentlemen in England or France. The silk or beaver hat, the cloth coat, the swelled cravat, the sleek trowsers, the tassled cane—in short, the whole *tournure* and turn-out of the male exquisites, would do honour to Bond-street or the Palais Royal. But the dress of the women is quite another affair : although in many in-

stances the *Jupe** has given way to the regular
English gown ; yet, on fête days, the former re-
asserts its preponderance, as being more in harmony with the general costume.   First you have
the head-dress set off by the varied and brilliant
colours of the Madras handkerchief, erected into
a pyramid, a cone, or a castle, according to the
fancy of the wearer, and spangled over with costly
jewels ; next a huge pair of ear-rings of massive
gold ; then several gold and coral necklaces,
tastefully thrown over the dark shoulders ; then
the embroidered bodice trimmed with gold and
silver tinsel ; and lastly, the striped jupe of silk
or satin, unfolding its bright tints and broad train
to the breeze.   Add to these a profusion of
bracelets and bouquets, of *foulards* and favours,
and you will have a faint impression of this
bizarre yet brilliant, grotesque but gorgeous
costume.   Thus travestied the dancers proceed at
sunset to the place appointed for the *bamboula*.†
A circle is formed in the centre of some square

---

* The *Jupe* is a species of gown worn by the Negresses and some of
the coloured women in the French Antilles. Having neither sleeves nor
bodice, it presents the exact dimensions of a petticoat—hence the name.

† The Negro dances are of two kinds—the ball and the *bamboula*.
When conducted within doors it is always called a ball—when " sub dio "
a bamboula. The use of them varies according to the state of the weather ;
but there is a marked predilection for the out-door recreation.

or grass-plot. On one side appear four or five Negroes, quite naked down to the waist, and seated on their *tamtams*.* These, together with two or three timbrels, compose the orchestra. Flags and banners, richly emblazoned upon a red or blue ground, and bearing characteristic legends in gilt letters, are seen fluttering in the air : and as the groups of dancers advance in all directions, the darkness of the night disappears before the blaze of a thousand flambeaux. Now the *chanterelle*, placing herself in front of the orchestra, gives the signal with a flourish of her castanet : she then repeats a verse of the belair : the dancers take up the *refrain;* the tamtams and timbrels strike in unison ; and the scene is enlivened by a succession of songs and dances, to the delight and amusement of the assembled multitude.

To a superficial observer these exhibitions present somewhat of a profane and even heathenish appearance. In this light they were doubtless regarded by a reverend gentleman, who visited St. Lucia in October 1842, and on witnessing the dance exclaimed with a sapient shake of the head : " Juggernath ! Juggernath !" But the

---

* The *tamtam* is a small barrel, covered at one end with a strong skin. To this, placed between his legs, the Negro applies the open hand and fingers, beating time to the belair with the most astonishing precision.

truth is, there is no Juggernath at all in the
matter; and the Christian moralist, who takes the
trouble to examine and inquire, will find less to
censure in these primèval though fantastic diversions, than in the more civilised seductions of the
quadrille, the galopade, and the waltz.

The whole labouring population being divided
into Roses and Marguerites, it follows that, upon
the good understanding which subsists between
them, must mainly depend the peace and prosperity of the Colony. This good understanding,
however, is liable to be disturbed by the intrigues
of interested partisans, on the one hand, and
officious, would-be patrons, on the other: and
then their rivalry, habitually characterised by the
most friendly relations, will assume all the acer-
bity of a political feud. Thus in 1840, an attempt
was made by an unscrupulous planter to set one
society in opposition to the other, by pandering
to the worst passions of undisciplined humanity,
and exciting their emulation beyond its legitimate
sphere. The object was to allure the labourers
to his estates and get them to work on his own
terms: for this purpose he took one of the
societies under his special protection; had himself elected their king; purchased superb dresses
for the queens; and got up splendid fêtes for their

entertainment. Attracted by these dazzling fri-
volities hundreds of the labourers hastened to
range themselves under the banner of the " white
king." For some time all went on well, and the
planter had every cause to exult in the success of
his scheme; but when the day of reckoning came,
and the labourers discovered that all their wages
had been frittered away in gilded extravagance,
the prestige of the white king's popularity
speedily vanished, and his estates were deserted.

Another interruption of the general harmony
occurred in September 1841. At the instigation
of two or three individuals, in the assumed character of Patrons of the Roses, these foolish
people procured a blue flag (the colour peculiar to
the Marguerites)and paraded it in derision through
the streets. In the evening they gave a *bamboula*,
and the flag having been again exhibited, a party
of the Marguerites rushed into the ring, seized
the flag, and were carrying it off in triumph,
when the Attorney-General, who happened to be
present, ran forward, and by threats of vengeance
succeeded in wresting it from the discomfited
Marguerites, amidst the *vivats* and vociferations
of the Roses. The pretext for this proceeding
was the prevention of a breach of the peace; but
if such had really been the object, a more obvious

and efficacious means would have been, to have interdicted in the first instance the insulting display of the rival flag. In fact, the course pursued, instead of allaying the popular excitement, only fanned it into a flame; for when the dance was concluded, and the Roses were returning to their houses, they were assaulted by a numerous body of the Marguerites. A general melée ensued, in which the chief combatants were the women, and their chief weapons the flambeaux which they had brought away from the dance: and these they used with such indiscriminate fury against their opponents, that the respectable inhabitants were compelled to interfere to prevent the town from becoming a prey to the flames.

Amongst the numerous peculiarities of the Negro character, as it is moulded or modified by French society, is their constant aping of their superiors in rank. During slavery the most venial offence, the most innocent familiarity was regarded as an " insolence ;" and all the year round the din of " Je vous trouve bien insolent " resounded in the Negro's ear. From long habit this expression has now become a bye-word with the lower orders : it is, in fact, the staple of their abuse of each other, and the most opprobrious epithet in their Billingsgate vocabulary. *Canaille* is deemed too vulgar, and *négraille* too personal ; while " *in-so-lent* " carries with it a pungency and privilege, which receive added zest from the re-collections of the past.

But if to be deemed *insolent* is the lowest depth of degradation, to be held *respectable* is the highest step in the ladder of social distinctions. From Marigot to Mabouya, from Cape Maynard to the Mole-à-chiques, respectability is the aim and end of every pursuit. With the baker in his shop, as with the butcher in his stall, it is the one thing needful—the corner-stone of social existence ; and though it may not, like charity, cover a multitude of sins, it will screen a vast amount of meanness and misery. Nothing can be more amusing than to observe the talismanic effect of this word upon the lower orders : even the common street-criers take advantage of it in the disposal of their wares. Some time ago a female servant, being commissioned to sell a quantity of biscuits of inferior quality, hawked them about to the cry of " Mi* biscuits pour les dames respectables." As she passed along the street the conceited recommendation did not fail to attract the attention of those for whom it was thrown out. The hawker was stopped at every

---

* *Mi* is a negro word used instead of " voici " and " voila."

door, and so great was the anxiety of the Negresses to test the quality of her biscuits as a patent of respectability, that before she reached the end of the street, she had disburdened herself of the contents of her tray.

A still more striking illustration of the charm of respectability is presented in the following circumstances which occurred in August 1842. A dispute had arisen between the queen of the Roses and a coloured woman—a warm advocate for the Marguerites. During the altercation the parties came to blows, and the queen, being a strong, lusty woman, inflicted a pair of black eyes upon her antagonist. The matter soon reached the ears of the Attorney-General, and both combatants were brought up before Chief Justice Reddie in the Court of Police. As the quarrel had grown out of the previous dispute about the blue flag, the Court House was crowded to suffocation by the friends and supporters of the accused—each party anxiously expecting a verdict against its antagonist. This feature of the case did not escape the penetration of the Judge, who, resolving not to give either any cause of triumph, dismissed them both with a severe admonition, expressing his surprise that two such " respectable demoiselles" should have so far forgotten what was due to themselves, as to have assaulted each other in the public streets. The word "respectable" shot like electricity through the audience. A thrill of exultation seized every breast : the Marguerite looked at the Rose; the Rose smiled at the Marguerite; and as they retired from the Court, pleased with themselves and proud of the Judge, a murmur of applause ran from mouth to mouth. Since that period nothing but harmony has prevailed between the rival societies ; and it would now require no small amount of provocation to draw them down from the niche of respectability in which they are enshrined.

The Negro's pretensions to respectability are founded more upon the contrast between himself and the European labourer, than upon any positive good qualities that he can lay claim to. In some points there is a decided superiority on his side. His person and his hut, apart from the influence of climate, are cleaner than those of the white peasant ; his holiday dress more stylish, and his gait and attitudes less clumsy and clownish : but he is surpassed by the white man in the more solid advantages of industry and perseverance. A Negro espies his fellow at the end of the street, and rather than join him in a tête-à-tête, he will carry on a conversation with him for several

hours at the top of his voice, to the unspeakable
annoyance, perhaps the scandal, of all those who
may occupy the intermediate houses. Should
the wind blow off his hat and warn him to depart,
he will continue the conversation and let some
one else pick it up for him ; or if he condescend
to notice the occurrence, he turns round with an
air of offended dignity, puts his arms a-kimbo,
takes a quiet look at the hat as it rolls along,
shrugs up his left shoulder, and walks leisurely
after it until it meets with some natural obstruction.

The general character of the St. Lucia Negro,
physical, moral, and social, may be summed up
in a few words. His person is well-proportioned,
his movements are brisk, his carriage easy, without
stiffness or swagger. His disposition is uncom-
monly gay and good-humoured; he is always
singing or whistling when compatible with his
actual occupation. He is submissive, but never
obsequious; and though born and bred in slavery,
there is not a trace of servility in the outward
man. Unlike the European peasant, who seldom
presents himself before a clean coat without a
feeling of crawling obsequiousness and degradation, the St. Lucia Negro is polite to a point; he
can touch his hat to any one, but he will not

uncover himself in the open air, even for the
Governor of the Colony. He is docile, intelligent,
and sober ; active but not laborious ; superstitious but not religious ; addicted to thieving
without being a rogue ; averse to matrimony, yet
devoted to several wives ; and though faithful to
neither, he can scarcely be deemed debauched.
His friendship is sincere, his gratitude unbounded,
and his generosity to all about him only surpassed
by his affectionate attachment to his children.
In him the undisciplined character of the African
is tempered by the accident of his birth. He is,
in short, a compound of savageness and civilization—the rude production of the desert, .trans-
planted to a more genial soil, and polished off
externally by the decencies and humanizing contact of English and French society ; but without
that culture in religion and education, which alone
can impart either weight or moral dignity to the
social man.

CHAPTER VI.

Religion—Protestantism—Catholicism : its Exercise guaranteed by the
Treaty of Cession—Character of the Clergy—Bishop Macdonnell—
Bishop Smith—Conflict of Jurisdiction—Influence of the Clergy—
Parish Registers—When first confided to the Clergy—Number and
Composition of the Clergy—Superstition and Intolerance—The Abbé
Chevalier—His Removal from Martinique—Arrival in St. Lucia—Ser-
vices rendered to Catholicism—Sectarian Influences—His Hatred of the
French—His Intolerance of Protestants—The "Domine Salvum fac
Regem" Temporalities of the Church—Income of the Clergy—State
Provision—Opposition of Mr. Muter—Revenue of the Establishment—
"Droits de Fabrique"—Church Wardens—Parochial Assemblies—
Their Authority—Regulations of General Wood—Concessions of Colo-
nel Mein—Decision of the Royal Court—Consquences of Colonel
Mein's Interference—Intrigues and Influence of the Aliens—Case
of the Rev. Mr. Coyle.—Fees of the Catholic Clergy.

ALTHOUGH Protestantism became the dominant
religion in St. Lucia at the cession of 1814, it was
not until 1819 that measures were taken for the
location of a Clergyman of the Church of England. On the 13th May in that year, in compli-
ance with an order of the Prince Regent in Council,
a tax was imposed upon all the inhabitants, other
than the Roman Catholics, for the purpose of
providing for the maintenance of the Protestant

Establishment of the Colony. This mode of support continued in operation for some time ; but having been found inconvenient, inadequate, and precarious, recourse was had to the " Society for the Propagation of the Gospel in Foreign Parts," from whose funds the Clergyman's salary has since been supplied. Previously to 1824 the colonial Clergy was considered as being under the superintendence of the Bishop of London. By Letters Patent bearing date the 24th July in that year, St. Lucia, Barbados, Trinidad, Tobago, Grenada, St. Vincent, Dominica, Antigua, Montserrat, St· Christopher, Nevis, and the Virgin Islands, were created into the Diocese and See of a Bishop, called the "Bishopric of Barbados and the Leeward Islands," and a sum of £4,200 per Annum, was placed at the disposal of the Bishop for the appointment of Ministers, Catechists, and Schoolmasters, subject to the approbation of the Lords of the Treasury or the Secretary of State.*

The number of Protestants, including Presbyterians, is about four hundred. They have recently received an accession of strength by the introduction of labourers and overseers from Barbados. In 1842 the services of a second Clergyman were obtained for the parish of Soufriere. There is no

* Woodcock—" Laws and Constitution of the British Colonies."

Church as yet in that district, but it is in contemplation to have one erected. By the recent ecclesiastical division of these Colonies, St. Lucia is included in the Diocese of Barbados, under the jurisdiction of the Right Reverend Dr. Parry, Bishop of the Windward Islands.

The Roman Catholic religion is that professed by the great majority of the inhabitants. Its introduction is coeval with the first settlement of the French, under whose rule its economy and discipline were regulated by papal bulls and canonical enactments, open to the veto and revision of the Kings of France, in all matters affecting the liberty of the subject or the temporalities of the Church. By a fiction in geography St. Lucia was then regarded as an integral portion of the Diocese of Paris, and its chief Dignitary was a Prefect Apostolic, appointed by the Pope on the recommendation of the Archbishop of that Diocese. The Prefect held jurisdiction over the whole island, including the right of appointment and location of the inferior clergy, subject to the approval of the Governor.

This order of things prevailed until the commencement of the nineteenth century, when by an arrêté of Bonaparte, dated the 2nd July 1802, it was decreed that in future the Prefects

Apostolic should be nominated in the first instance by the consular authority—receiving their episcopal mission from the Pope, and their ordinary mission from the Archbishop of Paris. This arrêté also contained a prohibition to publish or put in force, without the previous sanction of the Governor, any bull, brief, edict, or mandate, emanating from the Pope, or from any other ecclesiastical authority; and it prescribed the following form of oath, to be taken by each priest before he entered on the duties of his ministry : " I promise and swear, before God and on His Holy Gospel, that I will bear allegiance and fidelity to the constitution of the French Republic : I also promise that I will not countenance any intrigue, assist at any meeting, or encourage any plot, either within this Colony or without, that may tend to disturb the public tranquillity ; and should I become aware of any conspiracy against the state, I will disclose it to the Government."

By the Treaty of Cession the unrestricted exercise of their religious worship was guaranteed to the inhabitants, and so far as the Government is concerned they have continued in the undisturbed enjoyment of that advantage. In all other respects, however, and especially as relates to the

internal economy and management of ecclesiastical matters, they have been visited, in common
with their co-religionists in some of the sister
Colonies, by all the elements of discord and dis-
turbance which have unhappily been rife for some
years. If their spiritual vessel is no longer at the
mercy of every political bubble or revolutionary
blast that may sway the helm of affairs in their
ci-devant Mother Country, it is still exposed to
be tossed about by the ruffled waves of domestic
jealousy and local prejudice. Dr. Macdonnell,
Vicar Apostolic, and Bishop of Olympus "*in
partibus infidelium*," has done much to allay the
prevailing discontent ; and he has been ably supported by his coadjutor, Dr. Smith, Bishop of
Agna. But neither has gone to the root of the
evil, which appears to me to grow out of the
peculiar composition of the sacerdotal body. It
is a notorious fact that, with comparatively few
exceptions, the Roman Catholic ecclesiastics in
the British West Indies are the refuse of the
French Colonies or of European countries ; and
until the Bishop turns his attention to the paramount advantage of combining ability with moral
worth, in the selection of the inferior clergy,
nothing but detriment to the cause of religion
and disgrace to the clerical order can be expected
to result.

Dr. Macdonnell is a prelate of truly patriarchal virtues, and his episcopal career has been alike distinguished for an enlightened piety and a frank and gentlemanly bearing in the relations of social life. But he is apt to misplace his confidence, and his estimate of the human heart is more in harmony with the rigid but righteous ways of primitive Christianity, than with the fashionable jugglery of modern times. He has been duped in his day by many a crafty and crawling pretender, and the worst of it is, he is always ready to be duped again. Until 1837 Dr. Macdonnell held undivided jurisdiction in the lesser Antilles, including some of the foreign islands. Towards the close of that year, under the impression that in this wide-spread and scattered diocese, one bishop was unequal to the task of regulating the affairs of the Church, he procured the appointment of a coadjutor bishop to assist him in the discharge of his episcopal functions; and this has been the radical error of his administration. Surely, if the alleged grounds for such a step had any foundation in reality, he should have divided the diocese, not his authority—erected two distinct and independent jurisdictions — not two co-ordinate and concurrent authorities in one district. He should, in fact, have known that two bishops can no more agree than two popes; and that when "the house is divided against itself," clashing and confusion are the natural consequences. Dr. Smith, on the other hand, is a prelate, cool, courtly, and conciliating—always ready to make allowance for the infirmities of our nature, and throw the veil of indulgence over the faults and follies of a brother clergyman. He is as prompt to heal, as Dr. Macdonnell is to wound. Not over fastidious in the means employed, his aim appears to be to serve a purpose rather than save a principle. To him belongs the charity that covers a multitude of sins : to his brother the fervour that finds faults and reproves them. Pride and popularity are to Agna what piety and prejudice are to Olympus; and the fading fortunes of Macdonnell are but the pedestal to the aspiring genius of Smith.

As a body the Catholic clergy have always possessed considerable influence in St. Lucia. Mediators during the days of slavery between the Negro and his task-master, their post was not unfrequently one of peculiar difficulty and importance. To the slave they had to vindicate and expound the laws of man—laws of circumstance, and expediency, and conventional policy: to the master the laws of God—laws of eternal justice and imprescriptible right. The one they were taught to regard as the licensed kidnapper of his kind; the other as the shackled and degraded image of the common Father of all: and although their sympathies, political as well as professional, were naturally enlisted on the side of the slave, there is scarcely an instance on record of any glaring abuse of their authority. No doubt, a large share of the influence of the clergy had its origin in the relation in which the master and slave stood towards each other, as members of the same Christian community; but its development and sustaining power resulted from the insulated position of the master, which, while it left him to his own resources in the hour of danger, rendered him inaccessible to the infidelity and religious antipathies of "La France régénéré." Both, master as well as slave, felt and acknowledged the influence of the priest; both looked up to him, though with different feelings—the master with mingled feelings of dread and distrust, as to one that might prove his greatest enemy—the slave with unalloyed sentiments of confidence and esteem, as to his main support under heaven.

The ascendant position thus occupied by the Catholic clergy in their sacerdotal character was not a little enhanced by the quasi-political func-

tions with which they were invested. Sole curators
of the parish registers under the ancient laws of
France, to them was assigned the duty of recording
the baptisms, marriages, and burials of the population : nor was this the least important function
of their office, when we consider how materially
the peace, the privileges, nay, the very existence
of families depended upon the faithful discharge
of that trust towards the community at large.

The scheme of a general registration of baptisms, marriages, and burials, to be confided to the
clergy, was first introduced into France in 1539.
It was afterwards improved by various ordinances
of the French monarchy, especially the ordinance
of Blois and that of 1667 : and it was uniformly
adhered to in France and her Colonies until the
early days of the revolution. With that memo-
rable epoch commenced a crusade against religion
and its ministers, which terminated in the over-
throw of all its institutions ; and by a decree of
the Constituent Assembly, dated the 20th September 1792, under the pretence of drawing a
line of demarcation between civil status and
religious credence, but in reality with a view to
gratify the national antipathy to the privileges
and preponderance of the clergy, the custody of
the parish registers was withdrawn from the

priests, and assigned to certain lay functionaries
styled " officiers de l'état civil." At a later
period this important modification of the law was
embodied in the Code Napoleon ; and it is now
the law of France and her transmarine possessions.
With regard to St. Lucia, it appears that notwithstanding her precarious position during the
revolutionary wars, and the unsettled state of her
relations with France, the authorities had succeeded in introducing this change ; but the former
practice was revived by the British at the capitulation of 1803. Finally, at the Restoration, while
continental France was adopting for herself the
Code Civil, together with the numerous modifications and improvements of her ancient laws,
effected during twenty-five years of revolution
and reform, the unqualified revival of those laws
was stipulated on behalf of her ceded Colony of
St. Lucia. By this means the custody of the parish
registry reverted to the clergy, and in their hands
it is now limited to baptisms, marriages, and
burials, instead of embracing births, marriages,
and deaths, without distinction of rich or poor.

For many years previously to 1838 there were
but three Catholic clergymen located in St. Lucia,
two of whom were established in Soufriere and
Vieux Fort, and the third in the parish of Cas-

tries, with the title and authority of Vicar-General.
In the altered state of society resulting from the
abolition of slavery, this number was deemed
inadequate to the wants of the population, and
the services of six other priests have since been
obtained.   Five of these are now located in Gros-
ilet, Dennery, Laborie, Anse Laraye, and Choiseul;
and the sixth is attached as curate to the extensive and populous parish of Castries.

Since the capitulation in 1803, almost every
Catholic country in Europe has contributed its
quota towards the composition of the St. Lucia
Clergy, and amongst them there have been Italians,
Spaniards, Germans, Irish, and French.   The
last still predominate on account of the language.
Considerable difficulty is experienced in securing
the services even of foreigners ; for although the
Colony presents an extensive field for the exercise
of the Christian ministry, the mere spiritual harvest, poor and unpromising as it is in a pecuniary
point of view, has but little attraction in this
age of clerical refinement.*   Every candidate for
church preferment is now a competitor for the
biggest loaf and the largest fish ; and amongst
modern missionaries the lamp of religious fervour

* The provision recently voted by the Legislative Council will have the
effect of removing these difficulties.

burns brightest "under a bushel" of gold, or in
the refulgent atmosphere of dollars and doubloons.
Mr. H. N. Coleridge, who visited St. Lucia in
1825, states that the "spirit of its ministers is
bigotted and intractable;"* and the author of
"Four Year's Residence in the West Indies,"
who says he *touched* there in 1828, affirms
that both the priests and the people are steeped
in "superstitious bigotry and pitiable ignorance."
Bigotry is to the peasant what intolerance is to the
priest; and as far as either has prevailed in St.
Lucia the evil is doubtless to be attributed to the
besetting sin of ignorance. These sweeping statements, however, should not be received without
due discrimination. Mr. Coleridge's visit only
lasted four hours, and his notions of the clergy
were imbibed over a cup of tea with Colonel
Blackwell at Government House. As to the other
traveller, he never put his foot in St. Lucia at all,
and the existence of the Captain Sullivan, from
whom he pretends he derived his information, had
no more foundation in reality than the position he
has assigned to the "Sugar Loaves," at the entrance of Gros-ilet bay— a distance of twenty-five
miles from their actual situation. Indeed, the
whole of this writer's observations bear internal

* Six Months in the West Indies.

evidence of having been borrowed from Mr. Coleridge and enlarged upon according to his own fancy. The truth is, the Catholic Clergy, with two or three exceptions, never had any just claim to enlightenment or zeal; but, notwithstanding a singular diversity of character and country, they have maintained a reputation for sobriety, morality, and moderation. The occasional display of intolerance, and departure from the rules of sobriety, and disregard of their vow of celibacy, which we have witnessed within the last twenty years, must be taken as exceptions to the general rule.

The late Abbé Chevalier, for many years Curé of Castries and Vicar-General of the Colony, presented in his person a strange combination of piety and intolerance. A priest as much by propensity as by practice, he possessed in a high degree many of the virtues that exalt the minister and adorn the man: but his religious principles were more selfish than secular, more suited to the narrow circle of cloisteral devotion than to the expansive field of Christian benevolence. He was, in truth, one of those (until late years a numerous section of the French Clergy) who considered Religion and Legitimacy as synonymous, and imagined they beheld the annihilation of Catholicism in the downfall of Charles X.

In October 1830, while the Abbé was employed
in one of the rural parishes of Martinique, the
accession of Louis Philippe to the throne of the
Bourbons was proclaimed in that island; and the
public functionaries, both civil and ecclesiastical,
were called upon to subscribe the usual oath
of allegiance to the new dynasty. It was given
out as a maxim of civil polity, as well as of
evangelical law, that princes and potentates,
from the moment they are seated on the throne
and recognised by the majority of the people, are
entitled to exact obedience and fidelity throughout their dominions; and that, whether they
wade to that throne through revolution and
bloodshed, or grasp it by usurpation, or ascend
it by popular election, or claim it by hereditary
right, they are all equally entitled to " Cæsar's
due." This maxim was somewhat reluctantly
acknowledged by the clergy of Martinique, and
among the most refractory were the Abbé Chevalier and the Abbé Carrand. The latter then filled
the important post of Prefect Apostolic, and from
his great abilities and enlightened piety was justly
esteemed by all classes. Opposition to the secular
power from a person of his rank and consideration was totally unlooked for: by some it was
assigned to conscientious scrupulosity, and by

others to infatuation ; but those who knew him best thought they could discover in the course he pursued, a latent desire of personal aggrandisement, founded upon the supposed instability of Louis Philippe's dynasty, and the consequent prospect of a rich bishopric in France, as a reward for his faithful adherence to the cause of the fallen Bourbons. But if there was no infatuation in the mind of the Prefect, there was nothing else in that of the Abbé, who had no bishopric to win and had every thing to lose. At length, after many fruitless remonstrances on the part of the Governor to bring the two ecclesiastics to a sense of duty, orders were given to have them put under arrest ; and the following day, " sans autre forme de procès," they were handed over to the master of a small schooner and conveyed to the British Colony of Trinidad. Immediately on his arrival the Abbé Carrand took his departure for France, and the Abbé Chevalier, after a vain attempt to gain admittance into Martinique, came and settled in St. Lucia.

The sympathy which the Abbé Chevalier met with in this island enabled him to accomplish much good. Indeed, no priest before his time ever laboured with such perseverance and success in the cause of morality and the advancement of religion. At the period of his arrival, the place resorted to for divine worship was a decayed wooden building, which had been originally used as a publican's shop. His first care was to have a suitable edifice erected, and in the attainment of that object he exhausted both his private pecuniary resources and his health. He it was who introduced order and decency in the Church service—regulated the fêtes and processions—organized a body of choristers, and established the different *confreries* and associations, which continue to bear evidence of his untiring exertions in the cause of Catholicism. Yet, as a drawback upon all this, there was at the bottom of his more exalted aspirations a narrow-minded, sectarian impulse—a spirit of enthusiasm and illiberality, which tainted even his most meritorious actions. He hated the French as a nation with all the characteristic hatred of a German* (for such he considered himself), always speaking with contempt of the "gochons de Vranzais:" and his intolerance of Protestants was as unseemly in a German Catholic, as it was unseasonable in a British Colony. During a conversation with him in 1836 I happened to express surprise that a man of his exclusive doctrines could pray

* The Abbé was a native of Bernardswiller in the Lower Rhine.

for the Protestant monarch of Great Britain, which he did every time he sang the "*Domine, salvum fac Regem.*" "Oh," said the Abbé, "we of course pray for our own king, not for yours." —"What," said I, "pray for Louis Philippe? I imagined he was the last man your Carlist principles would permit you to pray for."— "True enough; I could never bring my mind to pray for that 'crosse pête,' but thank God he is not the only king: have we not our own Charles Dix to pray for?"—"But you seem to forget that Charles Dix has abdicated in favor of the Duke of Bordeaux, and therefore the 'Domine, salvum fac Regem' cannot properly apply to one who refuses to be recognised any longer as king."— "Well, never mind; we pray for Henri Cinq— for the royal family, for any one, in short, but a Protestant monarch."—Upon this the Abbé began to wax impatient; and I suffered him to have his own way, convinced that nothing but a remonstrance from the Bishop would induce a sense of decency. Before, however, this could be accomplished a change took place in the person of the sovereign, and the present illustrious Queen ascended the throne. During the reign of William the Fourth, the Abbé had ostensibly adopted the prayer in question; and no one, unacquainted with his intentions, could discover its misapplication ; but now there was a female sovereign on the throne, the pious fraud could no longer be practised without detection. The propriety of adopting the prayer to the new order of things suggested itself at once to every man, possessed of a grain of sense or a scintilla of charity : but from the ascetic and intractable disposition of the Abbé, I felt persuaded that he would not deviate from the old formula : and this impression was confirmed on my next visit to the church, when the " Domine, salvum fac Regem" was chaunted forth with the usual solemnity. In 1838, however, during a pastoral visit from the Bishop of Agna, this abuse was corrected, and the unequivocal prayer of " Domine, salvam fac Reginam nostram Victoriam" has since been uniformly used.

The temporalities of the Catholic Church are derived from two principal sources, viz.: 1st, the fees and voluntary contributions received by the clergy for the divers offices of their ministry, and appropriated to their personal use; and 2nd, the landed property and other sources of revenue belonging to the establishment in its corporate capacity. The fees are regulated by a tariff,* and

* See Appendix to this Chapter.

the ministrations for which they are receivable are baptisms, burials, marriages, and masses. At baptisms and marriages the parties and their friends contribute according to their means and generosity : of course, nothing less than the fee fixed by the tariff can be received. But burials and masses are generally paid for according to the nature of the mass or the class of the burial. There are three sorts of mass—high mass, ordinary mass, and "messe de requiem," or mass for the dead ; and there are three classes of burial, distinguished not by any classification as to the colour or respectability of the deceased, but by the pomp and solemnity displayed on the occasion, and paid for accordingly. The meanest Negro, if his friends choose to pay for it, may arrogate all the honours of a first-rate interment; and the wealthiest white man, should his friends not deem it derogatory, may be lowered into the grave in the plain, unostentatious gear of the third class.

The income of the clergy varies according to the population of each parish and the extent of voluntary support contributed by its inhabitants. The living of Castries is by far the most valuable, yielding an average annual revenue of £600 sterling, inclusive of all perquisites. But some of the rural parishes do not produce more than

£200, which is considered inadequate to the decent maintenance of an ecclesiastic in a Colony where even the necessaries of life are very expensive. Until a recent period the parishioners of Vieux Fort allowed their Curé a fixed salary of £120 sterling, payable by contributions, levied under the authority of their vestries or parochial meetings, with the approbation of the local Government. The public Treasurer was charged with the collection of the tax, and the clergyman's salary was paid upon the order of the churchwarden. Subsequently this practice was resorted to by all the other parishes, with the exception of Castries; but the interference or sanction of the Executive was no longer deemed indispensable. Much irregularity, however, attended the collection of the tax ; and in some cases not more than half the amount could be made available.

To obviate this inconvenience and upon grounds of public policy, it was proposed to make a suitable provision for the clergy from the general revenue of the Colony. This scheme originated with Dr. Smith in 1838, and it subsequently received encouragement both from Lord John Russell and Lord Stanley, on the express understanding that the recipients of the salary should be priests of British birth or connexions.

After some opposition from the Honourable Mr. Muter, an influential member of the Legislative Council, this measure was finally passed in July 1842; and the sum of £1,200 sterling is now annually appropriated as a provision for the clergy; viz., £200 for each of the two Protestant clergymen and £100 for each of eight Catholic priests. There were some cogent reasons in support of this plan, and there were others no less weighty against it. The principal argument in its favour was, that the clergy were in want of the salary, and that it would materially enhance their usefulness and respectability. The chief ground against its adoption was, that the Catholic ecclesiastics in St. Lucia, being all foreigners, were not only disqualified by the conditions attached to the provision; but also by the local enactment reserving all offices of trust and emolument for British subjects. In addition to this it was argued that the St. Lucia labourers, being uninstructed in the principles of Christianity and totally ignorant of the Latin language, could not be regarded as professing the Roman Catholic religion; and that therefore it was unnecessary to make any provision for the clergy of that persuasion. Now, whatever may be said on the score of instruction (and it cannot be denied that the peasantry are

in a sad state of mental as well as moral destitution) the argument about the Latin language is at
best an idle fallacy : Latin may be necessary for
the clerical aspirant : indeed " a priest that lacks
Latin" is like a lawyer that lacks law ; but Latin
in the multitude of believers would be " knowledge ill-inhabited, worse than Jove in a thatched
house."

The revenue of the Church is principally derived from the rents of the pews. Like that of
the clergy, it varies in amount according to the
extent and population of each parish. In Castries
there is the additional income arising from certain lots of land, called the lands of the "fabrique,"
lying contiguous to that on which the church is
built, and comprising about three acres. The
whole yields an average annual income of £800
sterling, the administration of which is confided
to a Marguillier, or churchwarden, who is elected
annually and required to keep accounts, subject to
examination and audit by two notable parishioners.
A certain proportion of this fund is applicable to
the reparation and embellishment of the sacred
edifices, and to various items of expenditure, connected with the performance of divine worship.*

* In the early days of Christianity one-fourth of all church revenue was
set apart for the reparation of the *ecclesiastica fabrica :* hence the origin

The most useful purposes to which it has recently been applied are the construction of a bridge over the Castries river, at the foot of the public cemetery—the acquisition of the lot occupied by the parsonage—the repair of the building itself, and the purchase of the requisite furniture.

The churchwardens exercise their authority under the control of the parochial assembly. This institution is another remnant of the old régime, and its privileges and responsibility are defined by various Edicts, Letters Patent, and Declarations of the French monarchy. It appoints the churchwardens, audits their accounts, and co-operates in the installation of the clergy ; but its most important function consists in levying contributions for parochial purposes, and regulating the disposal of the funds. With a view to obviate the abuses that might result from the existence of this "imperium in imperio," in a Colony circumstanced like St. Lucia, a law was enacted on the 1st July 1809, under the administration of General Wood, directing that no parochial meeting should be held without the previous permission of the Executive, solicited

of the "droits de fabrique." Although in St Lucia the practice of exacting fees under that head still prevails, the funds are no longer appropriated to their original destination, but form part of the perquisites of the clergy.

and obtained in writing, upon a statement of the different matters to be submitted for discussion ; and that no resolutions or proceedings of any meeting should be carried into execution without the express sanction of the Governor. This law was scrupulously observed until the month of April 1838, when, on the occasion of a meeting convened by Dr. Smith, Colonel Mein, then administering the government, was pleased to dispense with the usual formalities. This proceeding was hailed at the time as one of sound and liberal policy ; but upon a closer examination of the various interests involved, and after six years' experience of its practical results, it must be confessed that it is open to very serious objections.

Dr. Smith lost no time in taking advantage of the ground thus conceded by Colonel Mein ; and in a series of representations, addressed to the Colonial Minister, he succeeded in obtaining the sanction of Her Majesty's Government to the repeal of the law. A despatch was accordingly received in July 1841, directing that a Proclamation should be issued to that effect; but the Attorney-General of St. Lucia gave it as his opinion that the Ordinance in question, being a legislative enactment, could only be rescinded by another legislative enactment—a Proclamation being insufficient for that purpose :* and the Solicitor-General of Barbados having concurred in this view, the question was again referred to the Secretary of State, from whom, I believe, no further decision has yet been received. Meanwhile, much irregularity and confusion prevailed: some parishes adhered to the provisions of the Ordinance; others, chiefly that of Castries, availing themselves of Colonel Mein's permission, continued their proceedings without the slightest regard for the law. Delays and discussions arose; cabals and conflicts ensued; individual rights were compromised; public order menaced; and after a vain attempt on the part of the Executive to re-assert its authority, the question was submitted to the civil tribunals in a series of actions, instituted by some of the parties aggrieved. On the 6th December 1842 the Chief Justice delivered the judgment of the Court, which bears in substance that British Governors, as the Represen-

---

* This may be true in regard to the chartered Colonies; but in a conquered or ceded country (St. Lucia is both) the authority of the Crown is paramount; and although it might be irregular and even unlawful for the Governor to initiate by a Proclamation the repeal of any existing law; yet, a Proclamation, emanating from the Sovereign, or from the Governor under instructions from the Sovereign, must be held to be sufficient for such a purpose.

tatives of a Protestant monarch, have no right to interfere with the Roman Catholic religion or its temporalities; that the French kings only interfered with them in the assumed capacity of Heads of the Church in their dominions; and that it would be unconstitutional for a Protestant Government to arrogate any such character or jurisdiction.

Dr. Smith's object in seeking the repeal of the Ordinance, appears to have been to sever all undue connexion with, and dependence upon, the Government; in other words, to withdraw his Church and its concerns from under the control of the civil authority. But it may be asked: where is the improper dependence; where the objectionable connexion ? I confess I can see nothing in the Ordinance but a wise police regulation, whose scope is to enable the secular power to arrest *in limine* the waywardness and irregularities of the parochial meetings ; to protect the people against vexatious and unnecessary taxation; to prevent the improper application of the funds; in short, to exercise that salutary guardianship in reference to the temporalities of the Church, which every well-regulated state should possess over the management and disposal of corporate property. In effect, nothing can be more inconsistent than the course pursued by Dr. Smith. He first solicits

the repeal of General Wood's Ordinance, with
the ostensible design of rendering his Church
independent of the civil Government; and in the
same breath he solicits from that Government a
state provision for his clergy—the natural consequence of which is the annihilation of the privileges of his Church as an independent community.
" Aussi long-tems que le prêtre recevra le salaire
de l'état, aussi long-tems il demeurera, et la religion avec lui, complétement dans la dépendance
de l'autorité civile".*

The views entertained by the Secretary of State
and the Governor-General, as to the expediency
of repealing the law, were chiefly formed upon the
ex parte statements transmitted through the
Governor of St. Lucia; but it may be doubted
whether Sir Evan Mac Gregor and Lord John
Russell would have adopted those views had the
whole circumstances been laid before them. One
thing is certain, they never intended to sanction
the abrogation of the law, without a full knowledge of the grounds upon which it was originally
established, and of its bearings on the actual
state of the community. Doubtless, it would be
unconstitutional for the Protestant sovereign of
Great Britian to exercise the prerogatives or

* De la Mennais, Affaires de Rome.

jurisdiction of head of the Roman Catholic Church : but it would be equally so, I imagine, for even a Catholic sovereign. In truth, no king of France or of any other country ever was, or assumed to be, the head of the Roman Catholic Church : such a pretension could only have been set up by a madman. We know that the king of France prided himself on his title of "fils aîné de l'Eglise," and that, as a great continental monarch, he not unfrequently lent the weight of the secular power to uphold the institutions and discipline of the Church ; but we also know that the "haut et puissant prince" was never lost sight of in the "fils aîné," and that numerous police regulations were enacted from time to time to restrain ecclesiastics within the bounds of order and good government. For this purpose the sovereign reserved to himself a veto in reference to certain clerical appointments, and a right of revision on all questions affecting the liberty of the subject or the temporalities of the Church. Now, temporalities are one thing and tenets another : to meddle with the tenets might be unconstitutional, but to watch over the temporalities is quite the reverse. The French kings always did so without the slightest infringement of ecclesiastical privileges, and there is no reason why the sovereigns of Great Britain, or their representatives in St. Lucia, may not lawfully continue the same policy. To adopt the contrary doctrine would be for the State to abdicate its proper privilege of protecting its subjects against the arbitrary or vexatious measures of a few influential demagogues. If we are to have a change, let us abolish altogether the power of the parochial assembly to levy taxes and contributions, as was done in France in 1803 ; but if the old machinery is to be preserved, we must be careful to hedge it round with those salutary provisions and securities, whereby its abuses may be prevented, and itself rendered ineffectual for the ends of mischief.

Since the period of Colonel Mein's inopportune and ill-advised concessions, the parishioners of Castries have continued to meet without the permission of the Executive ; and some of their proceedings afford a striking illustration of the sinister purposes to which the parochial assembly may be induced to lend its influence. I shall mention one instance : in 1840 the health of the Abbé Chevalier having been much impaired by exertion and fatigue, the Rev. Thomas Coyle was appointed to take charge of the parish, conjointly with him. Mr. Coyle presented himself in the (to the St. Lucians) novel character of a British

clergyman ; and this, coupled with the circumstance of his being the bearer of instructions from
the Bishop, for the correction of abuses connected with funeral processions, soon rendered
him obnoxious to the anti-English party (chiefly
composed of aliens) as well as to the more numerous sticklers for tinsel and trumpery amongst
the bigoted section of the community. A formidable array of hostility was soon opposed to
the prosecution of his plans of reform ; and to
avert the disorder and scandal of the gathering
storm, he retired to the neighbouring island of St.
Vincent. Dr. Macdonnell, however, on being
informed of what had taken place, ordered Mr.
Coyle, under pain of interdiction, to return immediately to his post in St. Lucia.

On Mr. Coyle's arrival in Castries the aliens
resumed their hostile attitude ; and although he
communicated to the principal parties the impera-
tive orders of his superior, a meeting was got up
to oppose his admittance as Curé of the parish.
The pretext for this proceeding was the frivolous
one, that he had departed from the island without
apprising the parishioners of his intentions. The
meeting convened for the purpose was composed
of twenty-four persons, from a population of
7,000 souls. The churchwarden who called it

was an alien : the person who presided over it
was an alien : of the twenty-four members that
composed it nine were aliens, and six others did
not possess the requisite legal qualifications to
enable them to vote.　And lastly, the resolutions
adopted were, that Mr. Coyle should be considered
as a stranger ; that the parishioners should have
nothing to do with him ; and that he should be
interdicted the exercise of his ministry, and all
access to the books and vestments of the church.
After posting up these resolutions for the information of the other 7,000 parishioners, this self-
styled parochial meeting had the unparalleled
effrontery to report their proceedings to Dr. Macdonnell at Trinidad ; and the good-natured Bishop,
to humour their antipathies, appointed Mr. Coyle
to the rectorship of St. George's in Grenada.
Thus, in the year 1840, was a British ecclesiastic,
in the British Colony of St. Lucia, declared a
stranger by an illegal assembly of strangers ; and
subjected to the intolerable degradation of being
expelled from his own country by the intrigues
and influence of an alien cabal.*

---

* I would not be understood as giving to the term, *alien*, any strained
or unwarranted interpretation. The persons here alluded to are foreigners,
who have settled in St. Lucia since the treaty of peace, and are permitted
to reside during good behaviour.

APPENDIX TO CHAPTER VI.

TABLE OF FEES PAYABLE TO THE CATHOLIC CLERGY IN ST. LUCIA.

	STERLING.		
	£	s.	d.
A Baptism	0	8	0
An ordinary Mass	0	4	0
A marriage	1	12	0
A Mass of Thanksgiving	3	4	0

FIRST CLASS BURIAL.

	£	s.	d.
To the officiating Priest	6	6	0
" Droits de Fabrique "	3	4	10
To the Chief Chorister	1	6	5
To the Sacristan	1	1	7
To the Acolytes, &c.	1	5	2
	£13	4	0

SECOND CLASS BURIAL.

	£	s.	d.
To the officiating Priest	2	10	4
" Droits de Fabrique "	1	8	10
To the Chief Chorister	0	10	10
To the Sacristan	0	7	2
To the Acolytes, &c.	0	10	10
	£5	8	0

THIRD CLASS BURIAL.

	STERLING.		
	£	s.	d.
To the officiating Priest	-	6	4
" Droits de Fabrique "	0	14	5
To the Chief Chorister	0	7	2
To the Sacristan	0	4	10
To the Acolytes, &c.	0	4	10
	£2	17	7

HIGH MASS FOR THE DEAD.

To the officiating Priest	1	8	10
To the Chief Chorister	0	7	2
To the Sacristan	0	3	7
To the Acolytes, &c.	0	3	7
	£2	3	2

CHAPTER VII.

MORALITY has made but little progress in St.
Lucia. Any improvement that has taken place
is more in the tone than in the temper—more in
the shadow than in the substance. Amongst the
higher classes there is a greater regard for the
decencies of civilized life, and marriage as a
sacrament is somewhat more frequent : whilst the
newly-arrived European, instead of taking unto
himself a concubine in the guise of a housekeeper,
as was the practice in former days, will give himself up to a prostitute in the garb of a servant.

In short, with the exception of three or four inveterate and incorrigible sinners, public concubinage is now exploded by the *respectable* portion of the community ; and some have even gone the length of repudiating altogether the mothers of their illegitimate offspring, to be at liberty to contract marriage with other parties.

If a steady increase in the number of marriages and baptisms may be taken as evidence of progressive amelioration, the annexed return, compiled from the registers of the different parishes, exhibits the most gratifying results :—

Years	1833	1834	1835	1836	1837	1838	1839	1840	1841	1842	1843
Marriages..	18	21	24	36	27	43	35	66	76	102	171
Baptisms ..	142	266	467	480	561	566	598	557	641	577	769

My conviction is, however, that this increase affords but imperfect grounds for inferring the existence of a healthier state of moral feeling in the public mind. Independently of the proportionate increase, resulting from an increase in the population, much, as regards the peasantry, is ascribable to fashion and a wish to ape their superiors in rank ; and more still to that universal rage for respectability, which is naturally enhanced by the associations of the marriage state. Moreover, these marriages mostly occur between persons who have long cohabited together, and wish to take advantage of the *lex loci* to have their children legitimated; whereas the younger people still commonly cling to concubinage, or yield themselves unreservedly to a promiscuous intercourse. And yet, public prostitution can scarcely be said to prevail beyond the extent to which it is an inherent evil in all communities, whether savage or civilized. There is none of that cold, calculating spirit, by which its seductions are spread out in the capitals and provincial towns of Europe. It seldom makes its appearance in an undisguised and marketable garb, and few resort to it as an exclusive means of subsistence. The only exception to this occurred after final emancipation in 1838, when the females made an experiment of prostitution, as of everything else, to test the extent and security of their newly-acquired rights. Numbers of them quitted the estates for that purpose, and for several months the streets of Castries were frequented by crowds of deluded creatures, who had mistaken the libertinage of their superiors for the more solid advantages of rational freedom.

I have here spoken of morality as opposed to

the unauthorised and irregular indulgence of the fiercest of our natural propensities. In this sense an evil of enormous magnitude will long exist in the prevailing system of quasi marriages: the Negro calls his concubine "his wife," and appears indifferent to every other consideration. So far, however, as the term, *morality*, may imply an observance of the general duties of life, founded upon obedience to the law, St. Lucia has no cause to complain of the deportment of her people, and her criminal annals present a favourable contrast with those of other more civilized countries. In corroboration of this I may here subjoin a statement of the convictions had at the Court of Assize during a period of twelve years—a period of unusual excitement in the history of these islands :—

Years.	Murder.	Assault with intent to Murder.	Manslaughter.	Rape.	Arson.	Burglary.	Riot.	Robbery.	Resistance to Legal Process.	Common Assault.	Total for each Year.
1832	··	··	··	··	1	3	··	7	2	5	18
1833	··	··	··	1	1	2	··	7	1	2	14
1834	1	··	··	··	··	3	··	5	··	7	16
1835	··	··	1	··	··	3	··	10	··	8	22
1836	1	··	1	1	··	4	··	19	··	9	35
1837	··	··	··	··	··	1	··	12	1	6	20
1838	··	1	··	··	1	3	··	12	··	10	27
1839	··	1	··	1	··	3	··	3	··	6	14
1840	2	··	··	1	1	1	··	8	··	4	17
1841	··	··	··	··	··	1	··	4	··	7	12
1842	1	··	··	··	1	4	3	11	··	6	26
1843	··	1	1	1	··	··	··	14	··	3	20

These tables exhibit an average of twenty crimes in each year. Now, computing the average annual amount of the population during the twelve years at 20,000, we find the amount of crime to be in the proportion of one criminal to every thousand persons. As regards the offences tried before the Court of Police, mostly larcenies and trivial assaults or breaches of the peace, the following return shows the total number of convictions during the period already specified :—

Years......	1832	1833	1836*	1837	1838	1839	1840	1841	1842	1843
Larcenies ..	20	8	45	36	24	35	27	32	23	17
Assaults....	46	42	3	26	18	8	22	28	26	31

Thus the larcenies in each year are in the proportion of one to 754 persons, and the trivial assaults of one to 800. But the true test of popular depravity and demoralization is the prevalence of crimes of a more heinous and aggravated character, such as murder, rape, arson, and burglary; and in this respect the tables before us present upon the whole a satisfactory result. This result has been ascribed partly to the

* Owing to some misapprehension as to the extent of the Jurisdiction vested in the Court of Police, the cases of larceny and assault, that should have been tried by that Court in 1834 and 1835, were sent before the Justices of the Peace.

paucity of the population, and partly to the absence of distress and other exciting causes; but if we consider that the paucity, or rather the scattered position, of the population only affords a wider scope and greater chance of impunity for the perpetration of offences; that, in the absence of distress, there are other no less powerful incentives to crime; and that, moreover, the mass of the people are nurtured in the grossest ignorance, we should be disposed to attribute these results, such as they are, rather to the naturally inoffensive character of the population than to any other assignable cause.

The infrequency of infanticide is another circumstance that deserves particular notice. During the last twenty years there has been but one prosecution for this crime, and even in that instance the accused was acquitted. To the good-natured disposition of the Negro women some portion of this may be fairly attributed—to moral restraint none. The other causes that contribute to its production are the facility of rearing children, and the want of inducement to commit infanticide in a community where the illicit intercourse of the sexes is morally regarded with a degree of indifference akin to brutish sensuality.

The punishments commonly used are imprisonment, fine, whipping, pillory, solitary confinement, imprisonment with hard labour, tread-mill, transportation, and death. The following is a state- of those awarded by the Supreme Court of Criminal Jurisdiction from the 1st January 1832 to the 1st January 1844 :—

Sentenced to Death.	Banishment from the Colony.	Hard Labour for Life.	Hard Labour for periods not exceeding ten Years.	Pillory.
6	4	8	126	15

Whipping, with or without Imprisonment.	Imprisonment without hard labour.	Tread-mill.	Solitary confinement for limited periods	Fines varying from 1s. to £100 sterling.
52	23	14	10	22

The pillory was discontinued in 1837 and the tread-mill in 1839. Of the six sentenced to death only five have been executed. In three instances the punishment of expulsion from the Colony was left to the discretion and convenience of the Executive, and was not carried into effect : in the fourth, the case of a foreigner convicted of a rape, it was strictly enforced. Of the eight persons condemned to hard labour for life, the prerogative of mercy has been exercised in favour of four, their sentences having been either wholly or partially remitted. A mitigation of punishment has also been extended to many convicts sentenced to hard labour for limited periods. Whipping, the punishment of *villains*, is now seldom resorted to, and only for offences of an infamatory nature ; while the practice of working in irons, a characteristic feature of the chain-gang in bye-gone days, appears to have been totally discontinued, or reserved for refractory and unmanageable convicts.

In the generality of cases local labour and imprisonment are employed with comparative advantage ; but in the instance of an incorrigible offender they do not carry with them a sufficient degree of stringency, either as a correction to the offender himself, or as an example to his accomplices and followers in crime. I see no better means of providing against the inadequacy of this mode of punishment than the formation of a penal settlement for convicts from the different Colonies, a scheme which Her Majesty's Government appear to have had in contemplation for some years. Of course, in practice a necessity would seldom arise for resorting to transportation. Its chief advantage would consist, not so much in punishing vice, as in effecting the removal of evil example—a powerful agent in the dissemina-

tion of vicious habits in a small community.
Had this punishment been available, Edmond
Teague and Louis Hepburn, two notorious rogues,
would have long since been banished from the
Colony, and a check put to the robberies
daily committed through the influence of their
example. .These two Negroes make a trade of
imprisonment ; for, no sooner do they atone for
one offence by months and even years of hard
labour, than they perpetrate a fresh crime to be
again supported at the public expense. During
the last twelve years they have not spent six
months consecutively out of prison ; and neither
hard labour, nor gaol discipline, nor the iron
chain, nor even the whip has any terrors for
them. Still the callousness or incorrigibility of
two thieves is a matter of little consequence
compared with the pernicious tendency of their
example, constantly obtruding on the public
notice. If such an example, exhibiting as it does
a systematic mockery of justice and a reckless
disregard of all punishment, be productive of
evil in a populous European country, what a prolific source of mischief must it not prove in a
West Indian community, where the influence of
moral restraint is as yet scarcely acknowledged !

In presence of the withering effects of ignorance

and sorcery, it were vain indeed to attempt to trace any portion of the good we may discover to religious instruction or the diffusion of knowledge : the latter has hitherto been limited to children, as yet strangers to the ways of crime : and as for religious instruction, it is only made available to those that can supply the want of it—the educated classes, who can purchase and read religious books ; while it is almost totally beyond the reach of the poor, unlettered Negro. Some of the priests are zealous and attentive ; but their zeal and attention are confined within the walls of the church. They catechise and instruct on the week-days, but the Negro cannot quit his work. They preach on the Sundays and holydays, but then the church is crowded, and the devotee who has a seat and understands French may profit by the sermon, while the peasant, who stands at the door, either does not hear one word, or, if he hears, does not understand. What prevents the clergy from visiting the estates during the hours of cessation from work, and conversing with the labourers in their own dialect ? In former times the Christian missionary was to be seen travelling in every direction in search of spiritual patients, and he deemed it not derogatory to his calling to court acquaintance with the lowest haunts of

ignorance and vice : but in these days of selfishness and sound, he is castled up in towns and
cities, surrounded by the fashionable follies of
the rich, inaccessible to the vulgar vices of the
poor.

In nothing is the want of religious instruction
so conspicuous as in the addiction of the peasantry
to the practice of sorcery. This popular infatuation, known in St. Lucia by the name of *Kembois*,
still prevails to an incredible extent amongst the
uneducated classes. " Kembois" is another name
for Obeah, with certain Caribbean diableries and
incongruities engrafted upon it. It does not always imply a direct intercourse with diabolical
agents, nor indeed with any supernatural power ;
and its appliances are brought into play alike for
beneficent and for evil purposes. The adepts have
formed a sort of masonic brotherhood, and they
occasionally meet to discuss the pursuits and progress of the art : but all faith in its efficacy, like
the belief in *Zombies,* or spirits, is confined to
the ignorant and uninitiated, whose minds the
more crafty and intelligent pretenders hold in a
state of moral bondage, infinitely more degrading
and deeply rooted than that other sort of slavery
from which they have been disenthralled. This
want of faith amongst the professors may bc in-

ferred, both from the failure of their experiments, and their occasional recourse to poisoning and other criminal expedients, to realise their predictions.

It would be a waste of time to expatiate upon the absurdity of witchcraft and the numerous vulgar delusions connected with it in former days. These are now happily exploded by the more philosophical views of our own times. What I would call attention to are the disgusting impostures practised—the palpable crimes perpetrated, by an ignorant population, under colour of sorcery; and the necessity of adopting remedial measures to arrest its baneful influence. Indeed, of late years it appears to have assumed a more formidable character; and while its operations extend to the common dealings of life, there is no species of *maléfice* that is not put in requisition by the dabbler in spells and potions. So long as the art was limited to the conferring of invulnerability upon a duellist, or the enthralling of a reluctant lover; and it was sought to accomplish such ends by means of broken bottles and bits of bone, the professors of *Kembois* might have been laughed at as hypochondriacs, or pitied as fools ; but now they have extended their speculations to the mutilation of male children and other revolting practices ; and it is to the eradication of *Kembois*, as the nursery of such monstrosities, that the labours of the political philosopher and the moralist should be directed.

The prevalence of this mania, and the flagitious purposes with which it is associated, received a marked and melancholy illustration in a recent trial before the Court of Assize. In the wild and thinly inhabited district of Mabouya, there resided in 1841 a coloured female, named Eucharisse, who followed the business of a huckster. Being a stranger in that part of the island, which had long been noted for the lawless character of its inhabitants, Eucharisse placed herself under the protection of a Negro, named Louis Elie, in whose house she hired a room. This house was divided into two apartments, separated by a wattled partition, six feet high : Elie occupied the one and Eucharisse the other. There were a door and a window to each, but the only communication between them was over the wattled partition. Soon after the arrival of Eucharisse in Mabouya, a young man of colour, named Aurelien Martelly, conceived a violent love for her, and tried all the arts of seduction to gain her over to his desires, but his overtures were contemptuously rejected. He then had recourse to her protector, and with the assistance of another coloured man, named Alphonse Guis, a notorious professor of sorcery, he obtained the consent of Elie to be allowed access to her room. The night of the 29th December 1841 was fixed for the execution of this nefarious scheme; and Elie, in the delusive hope of impunity through the incantations of Guis, assisted Martelly over the wattled partition, while Guis himself stood outside to keep watch. Martelly having thus taken the girl by surprise, as she lay fast asleep, succeeded after a violent struggle in effecting his purpose. He was then about to retire, when Eucharisse stood up, and, upbraiding him in an accent of despair, threatened to denounce his brutal conduct to the public prosecutor. At this Martelly became exasperated, and to wreak his vengeance upon her, he repeated the assault with such savage violence, that the poor girl, struggling in the defence of her honour, was actually strangled in the ruffian's grasp, and fell a corpse on the floor.

On the first news of the murder of Eucharisse, suspicion naturally attached to Louis Elie, who, although assured by Guis that he was perfectly safe, was arrested and committed to gaol. A preliminary investigation then took place; but sufficient evidence could not be elicited to bring the charge home to him, and he was accordingly released—a circumstance which had the untoward effect of strengthening his belief in the efficacy of Guis' incantations. After a lapse of some months a clue was at length obtained to the guilty parties, and Martelly, Elie, and Guis were committed to take their trial on a charge of murder. Still the only evidence that could be adduced was of a circumstantial nature; for, although the particulars were well known to every inhabitant of Mabouya, such was the prevailing dread of sorcery, wound up as it was with the whole affair, that no one had the moral courage to come forward and substantiate the charge. The Attorney-General was compelled to proceed with the trial, his main chance of success resting on the hope that Elie might be induced to turn evidence on behalf of the Crown; but the latter persevered in his design to save the other prisoners. At the trial little was elicited beyond what had transpired at the preliminary inquiry; and it ended in a verdict of acquittal in favor of Guis and Martelly, and of *guilty* against Elie.*

When Elie heard the verdict of the Court he

* The three Judges, relying on the force and fulness of the circumstantial evidence, found all the prisoners guilty; but the three Assessors only concurred so far as Elie was concerned.

became dreadfully agitated, and appeared as if anxious to make some disclosure; but at that moment Martelly, who stood near him in the dock, whispered in his ear : " don't be afraid ; they can do you no harm ;" and the miserable dupe suffered sentence of death to be recorded against him with apparent unconcern.

From the intense interest that pervaded the public mind, and which this case was so eminently calculated to excite, I was induced to watch the convict through every stage of the proceedings. His delusions, unbroken by the sifting ordeal of the judicial investigation, accompanied him back from the crowd of the Court House to the solitude of his prison cell. On the following day, however, haunted by a vague misgiving of his impending fate, he sent for his counsel and disclosed the different circumstances of the murder—still pertinaciously clinging to a hope of deliverance through the interposition of Guis ; nor was the spell wholly dissolved until he beheld the formidable array for his execution. On the 22nd October 1842 he was led forth amidst the wailing and lamentations of the populace, and though his firmness and assurance remained unaltered to the last moment, " the big round tears" that glistened in his eye, as he approached the fatal gibbet, plainly showed that all confidence in the protecting power of *Kembois* had now vanished, exhibiting to the gaze of the sympathising multitude nothing but the wretched victim of sorcery and superstition.

Another trait that strongly indicates the absence of religious instruction in the St. Lucia Negro, is his total ignorance or wanton disregard of the obligations of an oath. The air of nonchalance, and even irreverence, with which he presents himself before a Court of Justice, is only surpassed by the barefaced assurance with which he can pronounce a falsehood or pervert a fact. It is unnecessary to quote instances : suffice it to say that, having received the depositions upon oath of some thousands of Negro witnesses, during a period of twelve years, I have had frequent and painful proof of the utter want of principle by which their evidence is characterised. They never scruple to conceal the truth, if they have any motive of interest or bias of friendship to induce them to do so : or, if ever, under such circumstances, they are made to " speak out," they do it more from the danger of detection and the dread of consequences, than from any innate love of truth, or any acquired notions of the heavy responsibility of an oath. Indeed, it may well be said that, in their estimation,

" Oaths are but words, and words but wind."

The St. Lucia peasant swears by holding up his hand, a practice still adhered to in France and other countries, and unobjectionable where the mass of the population entertain an adequate sense of the importance of an oath; but in a country like St. Lucia, where the people are characterised by an absolute prostration of conscience, it may be doubted whether any idea of duty, social or moral, is associated in their mind with the formula of an oath. The usage of swearing on the Bible would be a desirable substitute for the present practice, and materially conduce to the ends of truth and justice; but, of course, this change cannot be beneficially introduced until the peasantry shall have imbibed some idea of the character and contents of the sacred volume. This is a consummation only to be compassed by means of religious instruction, and its attainment would be greatly promoted, if a portion of the valuable time, now devoted by the ministers of religion to the exposition of the loftier principles and pursuits of Christianity, were employed in inculcating its elementary truths

truths and the more homely maxims of every-day life.

In connexion with crime I shall advert to the subject of destitution. During slavery all those who were incapacitated for labour, whether from extreme youth, bodily infirmities, or advanced age, received support and medical attendance upon the estates to which they were respectively attached. As there is no sublunar blessing without its alloy of evil, one of the disadvantages resulting from Emancipation was to throw upon public charity a number of persons, who had ceased to have any claim upon their former masters, and were unable to derive adequate support from their own resources or those of their friends. To meet this emergency an Ordinance was enacted on the 27th July 1838, making temporary provision for the "destitute poor," at the rate of sixteen shillings sterling per month for adult paupers, and six shillings and five-pence per month for orphans. All applications for relief were to be investigated and determined by two or more Justices of the Peace, and the amount of alimentary provision became payable by orders on the Colonial Treasury. The evils and abuses, engendered by the highly improvident, because unavoidably indiscriminate, adoption of this system, were soon felt and deplored. At first the relief was limited to the aged and infirm, who were permitted by the planters to retain the use of their huts ; but ere long a number of pretended paupers gradually swelled the list of applicants ; and the relief afforded, besides inflicting a heavy pecuniary loss on the public, operated as a premium on idleness and vagabondage. Indeed, the waste of the revenue was an evil of insignificant import, compared with the mischief entailed on the Colony, at a juncture when plunder and pauperism, advancing *pari passu*, threatened to overwhelm the planter with irreparable ruin.

From August 1838 to January 1839 the amount paid to the poor was £105 7s. 2d. sterling. In 1839 it was £983 11s. sterling ; and in 1840 £1,342 11s. 2d. This amount was enormously disproportioned to the numbers and necessities of the *really* destitute, who never, at any time, exceeded sixty for the whole island. In December 1840 the attention of the Legislature was directed to this growing evil, and a remedy was proposed in the formation of an asylum for the destitute of both sexes, combined with out-door relief on a limited scale. On the 10th January 1841 the establishment was opened for the reception of paupers, and has since continued in operation ;

but, although it still bears the name of asylum or poor-house, it has, in point of fact, been transformed into an hospital. The truth is, the wants of the Negro are but few, and those are easily supplied. He may be lazy enough to recur for his maintenance to private benevolence or even public charity; but he is little disposed to shut himself up in a poor-house, until driven to it by decrepitude or disease. Nor can it well be otherwise in a country where, owing to the great demand for labour and the high rate of wages, the able-bodied (such with very few exceptions are the native labourers) can readily find employment on the estates and thereby secure an adequate subsistence.

The annexed statement will exhibit the particulars relating to the asylum and the out-door paupers since 1840:—

Years.	Inmates of Asylum.	Died.	Retired.	Expense of Asylum.	Recipients of Out-door Relief.	Expense incurred for Out-door Relief.
1841	73*	31†	20	£718 1 5	98	£497 2 8
1842	50	18	9	570 5 3	104	523 18 2
1843	62	19	33	504 17 4	129	602 19 6

* The males and females are in nearly equal proportions in every particular.

† In many instances the deaths occurred whilst the paupers were being

Upon the whole the poor-house has proved an effective check upon idleness and vagrancy, and that, too, without any aid from the work-house system. To the institution, such as it is, the Negroes have taken a violent dislike, and even the sick and infirm seldom resort to it until they are in the last stage of disease; while those who get cured request as a favour to be discharged. At this moment there are no beggars and but few paupers in the island. Indeed, pauperism, as it exists in Europe, the curse and canker of the social body, is totally unknown, and must continue so for ages yet to come.

The greatest drawback on the social improvement of St. Lucia is the want of educational institutions. As matters stood fifty years ago, so do they stand at the present day. Now, as then, all those who may be desirous of imparting to their children the advantages of education, are compelled to resort to the schools and colleges either in Martinique, Barbados, England, or France—an evil which is the more grievously felt, as there are but few parents in a condition to defray the

conveyed to the asylum, or immediately after their removal thither. These were considered inmates of the establishment from the date of the warrant for their admittance, and are carried as such in the foregoing table.

heavy expense of maintaining their children at a distance from their homes. In this respect St. Lucia is far behind many of her sister Colonies. Hitherto every attempt at the formation of a respectable school has totally failed, either through the negligence of the teachers or the apathy of the people. At present there are but two private schools in the island, and even these have restricted their sphere of usefulness to primary instruction.

With regard to the humbler classes matters are scarcely in a better condition. A "Bishop's school" was set on foot in July 1828, under the superintendence of Dr. Coleridge, and supported partly from funds placed at his Lordship's disposal, and partly from local contributions. This school was regarded with a feeling of sectarian jealousy by the clergy, and some of the influential inhabitants; so that the number of pupils in attendance never exceeded thirty-five It was supplanted by the Mico schools in May 1838. In the infancy of the latter institution much good had been augured from its peculiar system of education—combining, as it was emphatically expressed, the threefold advantage of intellectual, physical, and moral training. But these glowing anticipations, I regret to say, have been but partially realised. At the same time it is but justice to the teachers to state that they have had great difficulties to contend with, especially in the paralyzing prevalence of the Negro language amongst the vast majority of their pupils. In proportion to the extent of this difficulty has been the success of their exertions, the most sensible result of which is the all but universal adoption of the English language by the children of the present day. In passing along the streets it is impossible not to be struck with the favourable change effected in this respect—a change in itself amply remunerative for any trouble or treasures that may have been expended in its attainment. To the removal of this obstacle and the dissemination of some valuable elementary principles have the labours of the institution been hitherto confined; nor, under the discouraging prospect of its proximate suppression, is there any likelihood that much further benefit can be derived from it by the inhabitants of St. Lucia.

A stimulus has, however, been given to the intellectual exertions of the rising generation; and it will be for the authorities to take heed that this advantage shall not be periled through any laxity or supineness on the part of the public. On the labourers themselves much will necessarily depend. That they possess the means of making a proper provision for the education of their children, there is daily evidence before our eyes in their profuse expenditure upon dress : nor will it be readily forgotten that in 1841 the Castrians alone laid out in one week no less a sum than £700 sterling, on the occasion of a visit from an itinerant company of equestrians. Should the Negroes, however, not appear to be sufficiently impressed with the paramount importance of education, and refuse to contribute their assistance, then the Government should interpose its parental authority, and devise some scheme of taxation to meet the necessary outlay. There is no labouring population in these islands that has more pecuniary resources at its disposal than that of St. Lucia ; and there is no more legitimate object to which those resources could be applied, under present circumstances, than the all-important one of providing for the moral and intellectual improvement of their children.

In the absence of educational establishments the best criterion for estimating the social advances of a small community will probably be found in the character and conduct of its press, the variety and respectability of its places of public resort and amusement, its theatres, its clubs, its libraries, its literary tastes and pursuits; and here again we find St. Lucia far behind many of the sister Colonies.

The first newspaper having any pretensions to be considered more than a channel for the communication of official matter, was set on foot on the 4th March 1820, under the somewhat ambitious title of the "*Courrier des Antilles.*" There was no editor's name affixed; but the printing department was under the joint responsibility of Messrs. Bertrand and Allard, Government printers. The "Courrier" was published in the French language and obtained a rather extensive circulation, especially in the French Colonies, where, as at the present day, the local press was subjected to the most odious censorship. But it was chiefly distinguished as a vehicle for the squibs and ribaldry of certain facetious lawyers, who amused themselves by propounding intricate questions of law, and exercising their legal acumen in splitting hairs at the expense of their *confrères.* The "Courrier" continued to be published until 1823, when it dwindled into a mere Government organ. It was succeeded in the course of that year by the "*Impartial,*" which pursued the same course and met with a similar fate.

On the 31st January 1831 a fresh newspaper was started under the title of the " *St. Lucia Gazette and Public Advertiser.*" Of this paper, as of its predecessors, the primary object was the publication of notices, emanating from the Executive ; and like the former it made its appearance under the auspices of the Government printer, who received for his trouble a salary of £450 sterling. At this period the situation of official printer was filled by Messrs. J. and R. B . . . . . ., whose father (a personage of multifarious honours and distinctions) combined with his office of Colonial Secretary, or as he was wont to style himself, " Chief Secretary," the important functions of Clerk of Council, Colonel of the Militia, Aide-de-Camp to the Governor, and Chief Commissary Commandant of the Colony. To no less a personage than this were the fortunes of the press now confided, and from his acknowledged ability as a man of business, and his previous connexion with newspapers, the public were led to augur favourably of the "Gazette." Of course, encomiums were unsparingly lavished on the activity and talents of the " Chief Secretary," in his various walks of official duty ; and every week saw blazoned forth in glowing colours his many deeds of public

utility and private benevolence—his dinners, his
speeches, his devotions, and even his puns.
With these, however, whether real or assumed,
the public had little concern and less sympathy;
and had the praise been bestowed upon things
commendable or merely indifferent, Mr. B......
might have run an uninterrupted course of self-
laudation and innocent amusement. But such
was the infatuation of the man, and so inordinate
his thirst for vulgar notoriety, that, when he had
exhausted the catalogue of his public virtues, he
turned to eulogize his private vices. A singular
instance of this occurred in July 1831, accompanied by circumstances of so disgusting a
nature (all minutely detailed in the Government
" Gazette") that the respectable inhabitants were
compelled to address a memorial on the subject
to Viscount Goderich, which ultimately occasioned Mr. B.'s dismissal.

This event, coupled as it was with the licen-
tious tone of the press, naturally led to restric-
tions on the " Gazette;" and orders were issued
that the printing work should in future be put
up to public competition, and the "Gazette" confined to the publication of official matter, to the
exclusion of all political or other discussion.
This measure, situated as the Colony was at that

period, without any other printing materials than what belonged to the Government, had the untoward effect of stifling the voice of the press : and for a space of nearly five years St. Lucia was the only island in the West Indies, that did not possess a single organ for the expression of public opinion.

In the month of September 1836 Mr. Charles Wells, then the contractor for the Government printing-work, availing himself of the materials at his disposal, commenced a weekly publication entitled " *The News*," and intended " to comprise the leading topics, political, literary, and scientific, of the four quarters of the globe, denoted by its component characters—n-e-w-s —north, east, west, south. " " The News" flourished during little more than a year ; and although it may not have realised the sanguine anticipations of the editor or the public, yet it afforded evidence of industry and abilities, and an earnest of future success under more encouraging circumstances. It was the first example of a divorce from the official printing, and a laudable attempt to get rid of those shackles which continued in the British Colony to crush down the energies of the press to the level of its servile condition in the reign of Louis XVI.

The next attempt to supply the want of a free press was made in June 1838. Mr. Wells was again the promoter of the undertaking, and through his perseverance was established the "*Palladium*" newspaper, which has since continued with little interruption. For some time before this, political divisions had been rife in the community, and Mr. Wells now proposed to steer a "juste milieu" course, between the Scylla and Charybdis of contending coteries; but he soon found out that it was easier to contradict than disprove the poet's position that,

> "The man who dwells where party spirit reigns,
> May feel its triumphs, but must wear its chains;
> He must the friends and foes of party take
> For his; and suffer for his honour's sake."

From the broad road of impartiality Mr. Wells gradually deviated into the more seductive but slippery bye-ways of vituperation; and the disin_terested narrator of passing events was soon merged in the virulent censor of men and measures. At first his adversaries appeared determined to oppose to the disparaging comments of the " Palladium," what they deemed a manly and contemptuous silence, unbroken save by an occasional retort in a Barbados newspaper. They soon, however, became sensible of the superior advantages of their antagonist, in having at his disposal a ready means of retaliation on the spot; and the consequence was the establishment, in September 1839, of an opposition paper, under the title of the " *Independent Press.*" The appearance of the latter was the signal for a renewal of hostilities, and from that moment the two newspapers have teemed with nothing but foul personalities and vulgar abuse. It would be an ungrateful task to go into the details of their numerous feuds. Suffice it to say that almost every respectable man in the Colony has been assailed by one or the other, if not by both. The rule appears to be: " qui non est pro me est contra me ;" the aim, rabid and indiscriminate censure ; the object, the gratification of a morbid spirit of malignity ; the weapon, the foulest engine that was ever wielded for the perversion of truth—an unbridled press in the hands of irresponsible agents. And while each is perpetually toiling to drag into the vortex of its troubled waters the greatest number of unsuspecting victims, the innocent are confounded with the guilty, the upright with the dishonest, the generous with the base. Governor, Judge, Colonial Secretary, Attorney-General, each is alternately patronized and pelted, lauded and lampooned ; and the man

who would abjure all connexion with either, but
more effectually incurs the rancour and ribaldry
of both.   In respect of editorial management and
general industry in catering for the information
and amusement of its readers, the "Palladium"
enjoys an undisputed superiority ; but until the
public appetite shows a craving for sounder mental nourishment, it is not to be expected that
either newspaper will soar above the depressing
atmosphere of scurrility and slander, and take its
stand on the loftier ground of public decency and
public good.

St. Lucia that boasts the possession of a Royal
Court and a Royal Gaol, also enjoyed at one time
the advantage of a Theatre Royal.   It was first
established in December 1832 by some English
and French amateurs, aided by a company of
artistes from Martinique, under the direction of
Mons. Charvet.   Performances were given two
or three times a week, and continued during a
period of six months, to the unspeakable delight
and amusement of the Castrians.   The piece
represented was generally one of Scribe's vaude-
villes or Beaumarchais' comedies, with an occasional attempt in some of the higher walks of the
drama.   Certes, it was a spectacle at once novel
and pleasing to behold the same audience suc-

cessively applauding the representation, on the
same stage and in different languages, of "Othello"
and the " Médecin malgré lui." In 1834 M. Charvet and his company paid a second visit, on which
occasion the corps dramatique (a host in themselves) received an accession of strength from the
excellent band and amateur performers of the 1st
or Royal Regiment, then stationed at Morne Fortuné. Since that time a feeling of apathy appears
to have seized the votaries of the histrionic art ;
nor has any attempt been made to revive a source
of public entertainment so eminently calculated
to foster sentiments of social harmony, and stimu-
late the intellectual exertions of all classes of the
people.

In June 1842 Mr. and Mrs. Hutchings, accompanied by " Master Hutchings, the Infant
Prodigy," made their appearance in St. Lucia,
having previously visited some of the neighbouring
islands, where the efforts of the juvenile Roscius
had attracted crowded houses. During the first
representation and while the audience were im-
patiently looking out for the little lion of the
evening, Mr. Hutchings, senior, presenting himself on the stage, proposed to sing what he
announced as " one of Mr. Braham's celebrated

songs;" but he had scarcely commenced the second verse, when some fastidious critic set up a groan of disapprobation, which soon spread all over the audience. The St. Lucians are rather remarkable for an acute sensibility to the "concord of sweet sounds." In this instance, however, their estimate of the performance was founded more on the presumed discernment of the critic in question, than upon any judgment of their own ; and while some hissed "for the fun of it," and others for the mischief of it, the greater number appeared to vie with each other in exhibiting what they mistook for fashionable criticism. After several unsuccessful attempts to resume his song, Mr. Hutchings, looking indignantly in the direction whence the hissing first proceeded, threatened "to teach the fellow better manners : he had sung the song in all parts of the world and had never been hissed before." This angry flash called forth a corresponding burst from the audience, and the discomfited vocalist was finally compelled to retreat. A similar entertainment was announced for the following night ; but this time the hissing began even before the rising of the curtain : and after a second ineffectual effort to propitiate the offended genius of Negro *virtu*, the Hutchingses took their

departure, carrying with them the conviction that
the poet who said or sang :—

"Music hath charms to soothe the savage breast,"

had never tried the effect of his vocal powers upon
the " savages" of St. Lucia.

There is neither public library nor literary institution of any kind in this island. A reading
room was established in 1830 and continued in
existence for about a year. A circulating library
was instituted in 1836, and lasted about the same
space of time. An attempt to get up a reading
room was again made in 1839 and failed, and
again in 1842, but met with no better success.
Indeed, reading is altogether at a sad discount.
With the French gentlemen it is chiefly confined
to the novels of Balzac and Paul de Kock ; with
the English to a few newspapers and magazines ;
and with the ladies to religious books. The
scanty support given to the *West India Magazine*
(a monthly periodical commenced in Barbados
in May 1840, and discontinued in November of
the same year) has been referred to as evidence
of a want of disposition to encourage a taste for
polite literature. Upon the whole, however, it
would hardly be fair to admit this test. The
Magazine possessed the natural advantage of local

interest on many colonial topics; but, independently of the inartistic style in which it was got up, it gave very little promise in a literary point of view, its pages being generally characterised by bombast, triviality, " bad grammar" (as the Editor used to term it) and worse taste. Perhaps the *prestige* of a name—the harbinger of all that is witty in thought, eloquent in language, and transcendant in genius—contributed more to relax the Editor's exertions, than any positive disadvantage under which he might have laboured.

CHAPTER VIII.

St. Lucia appears to have remained wholly uncultivated until about the middle of the seventeenth century. The settlers in those days, few in number, and moderate in their wants, sought their means of support in the pursuits of fishing and the chase. In the year 1651, as the population began to increase, the cultivation of tobacco, ginger, and cotton was introduced. These continued to be the chief resources of the colonist until the commencement of the eighteenth century, when they were almost entirely displaced by the more lucrative commodities of coffee and cocoa. At this period agricultural enterprise was confined to the leeward side of the island, and it was not until 1736 that some adventurers from Martinique, allured by the surpassing fertility of the soil, came and settled in the windward Districts. Even then, however, the tenure by which property was held was so precarious and insecure, that few were disposed to extend their agricultural speculations.

The first grant of land was made by Governor de Longueville in 1745—a measure which was soon followed by the apportionment of large tracts amongst the more influential settlers. This policy had the effect of strengthening the confidence of all classes; and the Colony soon rose to such a degree of prosperity that the inhabitants of Martinique, actuated by that spirit of commercial jealousy for which they have ever been distinguished, procured the passing of an ordinance whereby it was enacted, " that any ship or vessel, found within three miles of the coast of St. Lucia, should be held liable to seizure and confiscation." But, as may be supposed, the monstrous injustice of such a scheme of monopoly acted as an impediment to its practical operation.

From Grenada and St Vincent, on their restitution to the British at the peace of 1763, several respectable French planters emigrated with their families to St. Lucia. By this means a considerable amount of capital, independently of the usual accompaniment of slaves, was introduced, and an impulse given to trade and agriculture. In every part of the island plantations were extended, large uncultivated tracts reclaimed, establishments formed, and the cultivation of cotton, until then of little importance, soon spread all over the island.

The first sugar establishment was commenced in the quarter of Vieux Fort on the 15th April 1765, under the auspices of Messrs. Levacher and Le Blond. Another was formed a year or two after, by Madame Dubuc Roche in the quarter of Praslin. In fact, such was the rapid progress made at this period in the formation and extension of sugar plantations, that no less than thirty of them had been actually established, and upwards of twenty others were in an advanced state, when in 1780 a tremendous hurricane destroyed most of the estates' works, and threw a damp upon industry and enterprise, from which, followed as it was soon after by the still more discouraging effects of the Revolution, the inhabitants were unable to recover for a series of years.

After the capitulation in 1803 the people returned to their former occupations; but the slave trade, that once mighty lever of colonial enterprise, having been checked under the British, the pursuits of agriculture continued to make but little progress. Alternately harrassed by dissension and anarchy from within, and by hostile incursions from without, the remnant of the local aristocracy, now reduced to a state of ruin, were compelled to have recourse to the British merchants both in St. Lucia and the mother country, for the means of resuming the cultivation of the estates. In this way large sums were advanced at interest, and secured on the properties. The planter raised the crop, manufactured the produce, and consigned it to his correspondent; while the latter supplied the food and clothing of the slaves, and all the other wants of the estate—absorbing by his exorbitant profits the better proportion of the product. Thus reduced to the degrading condition of a trustee or manager of his own property, the planter, unmindful of the past and regardless of the future, appeared solicitous but to satisfy the present wants of himself and his family. His device was: " Après nous la fin du

monde;" and his object to prevent the estate
from passing into other hands during his lifetime.
There were some exceptions to this system, as
the Augiers and de Brettes attest to this day;
but the great majority appeared to vie with each
other in swelling the list of their incumbrances.
At this period there was no law to authorise the
seizure of real property, nor any office for the
registration of mortgages and privileged claims;
and under cover of this advantage to the planter,
but disadvantage to the merchant, a system of
fraud and double-dealing, on the one hand, and of
usurious charges and profits, on the other, was
carried on to an extent unparalleled in colonial
history. Unable to satisfy at the same time the
mortgagee in England, and the more clamorous
creditor on the spot, the planter had recourse to
every species of deception. To the one he promised a cask of sugar; to the other two casks;
but he frequently disappointed both, and gave the
whole to a third party, offering to supply the
wants of the moment: and in this way he kept
shifting from store to store until every merchant
and even shopkeeper in the island had obtained a
lien upon his estate. Exasperated by delay and
disappointment, the merchant in his turn resorted
to the expedient of sending a bailiff on the estate

to seize whatever manufactured produce might be found: and here again he was met by another system of double-dealing. The planter, constantly on the *qui vive* to avoid being taken by surprise, generally managed at the approach of the enemy either to secrete the produce, or to exhibit a fictitious sale of it to some conniving creditor: and when both these expedients failed, he perchance succeeded in bribing the bailiff to rest satisfied with a few casks, as the full extent of what he had found. It sometimes happened that two or three levies were made at the same time, or in close succession to each other; and then the planter had the mortification to witness the fruit of his toil carried off in parcels by the harpies of the law, and disposed of at a low price in the local market, to cover the expenses—first, of the levy; secondly, of the removal; thirdly, of the sale; and lastly, of the litigation between the seizing creditors concerning their respective claims to priority. It is easy to conceive what a ruinous system this must have proved to all parties. The crop was divided, as it were, into three lots. One of these the planter succeeded in placing beyond the grasp of his creditors, to enable him to procure a little ready money, besides clothing and supplies for his family. The second fell into the clutches of the merchant, and was carried to the credit of *compound interest* account; and the third was frittered away in law expenses, incurred in contending for the other two portions. Whoever lost, the lawyer was sure to gain; while the planter with an encumbered estate was running his course of drudgery and degradation, and the merchant, without capital or credit, was daily sinking into bankruptcy and ruin.

The confusion resulting from such a state of things had reached its height, when in the year 1825 arrived Mr. John Jeremie, appointed to the office of First President of the Court of Appeal. The canker of the social body did not long escape the penetration and tact of that able judge and enlightened philanthropist, who set himself to work with characteristic energy, and by introducing a series of salutary and well-timed reforms, gradually infused a current of vitality into the commercial relations of the Colony. Amongst the many devices adopted by the planter to defeat the pursuit of his creditors was that of selling his slaves apart from the soil, or removing them to some unencumbered estate; thereby depriving the creditor of that security, upon the faith and continuance of which he had been induced to make the advances. To counteract the consequences of this dishonest practice Mr. Jeremie procured the enactment of a law, declaring that all slaves, employed on an encumbered estate, should be held *glebæ adscripti*, or attached to the soil, and prohibiting the sale or removal thereof under the pains of " stellionat."

The second reform effected by Mr. Jeremie was the substitution of English commercial law for the confused, illiberal, and antiquated code, which had theretofore been allowed to prevail. On the surrender of the island to the British on the 26th May 1796, it was stipulated that all questions relating to trade should be determined by the law of England, in conformity with a regulation to be framed for that purpose. A period of thirty years, however, had been suffered to elapse, during which, this preliminary formality not having been fulfilled, the wise intentions of the Government failed to receive any practical effect. Mr. Jeremie's attention was immediately directed to the supplying of this omission, and on the 5th March 1827 he drew up a statement, setting forth in juxta-position the commercial law of France, as then observed, and the English law about to be substituted in its place. This regulation contains a clear and comprehensive exposition of the law on the following points :—

1. Property in shipping.
2. The building, repairing, and supplying of shipping.

3 The duties and powers of owners and masters of ships.

4. The qualifications of masters and seamen.

5. The duties of seamen.

6. The wages of seamen.

7. Freights, whether by charter party or bills of lading—and all questions relating to the conveyance of merchandize in shipping, including demurrage.

8. Stoppage in transitu.

9. Salvage.

10. Marine insurances and averages.

11. Bottomry bonds.

12. Bills of exchange and notes or bills to order or bearer.

13. The relative rights and duties of merchant and factor.

14. Commercial co-partnerships.

The next abuse that occupied Mr. Jeremie's attention was the loose and irregular mode of preserving mortgages and titles to property. To remedy this evil he recommended the establishment of an office for the registration of deeds and " hypothéques," to be regulated by the law of France and modelled, as far as practicable, on the plan of similar institutions in the French Colonies. By this important reform, which came into operation on the 7th July 1829, a stop was put to that illimitable system of credit, which had proved so detrimental to the trading interests of the Colony. The planter could now contemplate all the horrors of his position in the " tableau" of his debts, and the merchant measure the extent of his embarrassment in the list of his claims. Liabilities began to be incurred with more caution, advances to be made with greater security; while the transfers of property, until then inefficient and undefined, received the sanction and stringency of legal contracts. A term of eighteen months was allowed for the registration of all mortgages then in existence, and it was enacted that every mortgage, enrolled within that period, should retain its original priority and privileged character: but that otherwise it should only take rank and precedence from the date of the enrolment. Nothing can more forcibly illustrate the crippled condition of the Colony than the data furnished by these registrations. Perhaps few persons out of St. Lucia may be disposed to credit the startling fact, that before the expiration of the eighteen months, the number of mortgages produced to the Registrar, was one thousand nine hundred and eighteen, exhibiting the debts and liabilities of the proprietary body at the enormous sum of £59,498,249 17*s.* 6*d.*, late colonial currency, or *one million one hundred and eighty-nine thousand nine hundred and sixty-five pounds sterling.*

There was but one possible means of rescuing the colonists from this state of unmitigated bankruptcy—the enactment of a law to authorize the seizure and sale (saisie réelle) of immoveable property—and in preparing the Government and the country for the application of this panacea, Mr. Jeremie exerted himself with such perseverance and success, that before his departure in May 1831, he had the satisfaction to know that his views on this important subject had received the sanction of the Minister of the Crown—although it was not until January 1833 that measures were taken to give them the force and effect of a legal enactment. Soon after the promulgation of this law several estates were levied upon and brought to the hammer, and the same process has continued until almost every estate in the island has now been disposed of by judicial sale.* This course, pregnant in appearance with so much misery and impoverishment, was attended in reality with little hardship to any party. There were but few whose condition could have been aggravated by being dispossessed of property, of which they had but the nominal ownership; and fewer still, whose private means were absolutely restricted to the resources of the soil : while, on the other hand, the sale of the estates produced the highly advantageous results of enabling the

* See Appendix No. 1 to this Chapter.

planter to liquidate his affairs, and of throwing the estates into the hands of persons, possessed of ample means to provide for their cultivation on a footing of respectability and independence.

It was now that Mr. Jeremie's forecast began to be felt and appreciated. In the space of a few years the sale of the estates and other property brought into circulation no less a sum than £170,000 sterling, which, but for the opportune institution of the mortgage registry, must have lain in the marshal's coffers to this day. The estates might have been levied upon and sold ; but there could have been no marshalling of the creditors—no distribution of the proceeds. Nor was this the only benefit derived from the establishment of the mortgage office. By that were the Commissioners of compensation aided in unravelling the system of craft and confusion which had been carried on for better than half a century; by that were they enabled to adjudicate upon the claims of contending creditors, and ultimately to distribute with such general satisfaction the portion of the twenty millions accruing to St. Lucia (£335,627 16s. sterling). But above all it was the creation of the mortgage office that, by facilitating the sale of real property, enabled the Colony to assume an attitude of independence

on the advent of final emancipation. This por-
tentous change—a change fraught with embarrassment under the most favourable aspect—found
the greater proportion of the estates in the hands
of persons in easy and even affluent circumstances,
instead of finding them in the possession of a
generation of bankrupts, planters of the old school,
whose passions and prejudices, fostered rather by
the folly of the system than the fault of the men,
had long since unfitted them for the management
of willing slaves, and could have awakened but
little sympathy for the intercourse of free cultivators.

It would be idle, however, to institute any
comparison between the prosperity of St. Lucia
and that of other more favoured islands. If, on
the one hand, it cannot be expected to compete
with the more extensive colonies of Trinidad and
Guadaloupe, or with the more densely peopled
settlements of Martinique, Barbados, and Antigua; on the other, it has reason to be proud of
the industry and peaceable demeanour of its peasantry, its great facilities for trade, and the pro-
ductiveness of its virgin soil. And although its
progress has been retarded by a thousand vicissitudes—fires, and hurricanes, and intestine divisions, and maroon wars, and massacres, and

foreign invasion, and political broils, and financial difficulties, and even bankruptcy; yet there is no colony that has passed through the ordeal of Emancipation with less detriment to the interests of agriculture or of public order.

It has been much the fashion to run down the trade and agriculture of this Colony by contrasting its present situation and prospects with those which it had attained under the French. "Here," says the one, "formerly stood an extensive sugar estate—splendid works—superb establishment! but alas! where are they now? I really know not what will become of us if this state of things is allowed to continue!" "You see that large uncultivated tract," says another; "would you believe that in the time of the French all that was under cultivation? Beautiful cotton plantations in every direction! Indeed, I wish we had the French back again; nothing but that can save the Colony." "What a sad falling off we have here," exclaims a third: "the town of . . . . once possessed a white population of one hundred and ten persons, and now there are only two whites in the whole parish! Poor St. Lucia! the English will neither people it themselves, nor allow others to people it." By these and similar fallacies the cursory observer persuades himself, and would fain induce a belief in the minds of others, that the Colony is really undergoing deterioration and decay : and even the Lieutenant-Governor in making his tour of the island is sometimes imposed upon in this way, reporting to the Colonial Minister as the result of his personal experience, that " the Colony has remained stationary, if it has not retrograded, since its cession to the British in 1814."

The truth is, for one estate that has been abandoned, three others have been brought under cultivation, nay, actually called into existence. These escape the observation of the political grumbler, while his distempered eye never fails to dwell with sympathetic fondness amongst the ruins of the past—the faded glories of other days. Again, while admitting that large portions of land, formerly devoted to the cultivation of cotton, when cotton was the staple of the Colony, have long since been restored to their native wilds, we must not forget that other extensive tracts have been reclaimed from the wilderness for the production of sugar, the present more profitable staple. And lastly, what did the French do for St. Lucia ? In the early days of its colonization, instead of making it a field for the encouragement and reward of native skill and enterprise, they made it a dependency of Mar-

tinique. They permitted the jealous monopolists
of that island to crush or control every exertion
of the St. Lucia colonist, and sanctioned a commercial code whereby it was declared a crime to
be found trading within three miles of the coast.
The natural result of this unnatural policy was
that, while the more respectable settlers kept
aloof, the island was overrun by a swarm of
needy and profligate adventurers, who, being
destitute of the necessary capital for the formation
of extensive establishments, were restricted to
such branches of production as required but little
labour and expense.   These disappeared with the
" reign of terror ;" and the surrender of the
Colony to the British has since operated as a
discouragement to the introduction of persons of
a similar class. So far, it must be confessed, a
palpable diminution has taken place ; and if the
Colony's prosperity were to be measured by the
number of white faces amongst its population,
wretched, indeed, would be its prospects at the
present day. But we have yet to learn that the
coloured classes, which have succeeded the *petits
blancs** of former times, do not possess in a higher

---

* *Petit blanc* is a term employed by the French to designate that class
of whites, who from their habits and menial pursuits are placed on a footing
of social inferiority with the labouring population. The " petit blanc " of
the French islands resembles the " red shank " of Barbados.

degree every element of prosperity that may be
consistent with its future destiny as a free British
settlement.

The truth of the assertion, that the Colony has
retrograded under the British, cannot be more
correctly tested than by comparing its present
agricultural resources with those which it had
attained in former days. The period of the
meridian of its prosperity under French rule was
incontestibly that which immediately preceded the
Revolution. Now, we see by the St. Lucia
Almanac for 1789, printed on the spot, that the
number of sugar estates in that year was forty-
three ; whereas, at the present time, the number
is eighty-one. These facts are further detailed in
the following table :—

Parishes.	Sugar Estates in 1789.	Sugar Estates in 1843.
Castries . . .	6	9
Anse Laraye . .	4	6
Soufriere . . .	9	20
Choiseul . . .	0	5
Laborie . . .	5	8
Vieux Fort . .	8	10
Micoud . . .	1	7
Praslin . . .	3	1
Dennery . . .	1	4
Dauphin . . .	2	2
Gros-ilet . . .	4	9
	43	81

Here is an increase of thirty-eight sugar estates, which looks like anything but retrogression, especially if we consider that in 1789 the sugar establishments were upon a much smaller scale than at the present time. I am aware that in the same almanac the coffee plantations are stated at one hundred and forty-three, and that their present number does not exceed twenty; but I am also aware that in those days every garden that displayed a coffee bush was dignified with the name of a coffee plantation; while at the present time the coffee estates are chiefly confined to the quarter of Soufriere, and are upon a footing of surpassing magnificence. In 1789 the *matériel* of the sugar estates consisted of thirty-two water-mills, eighteen cattle-mills, and three windmills: now it comprises fifty-one water-mills, twenty-six cattle-mills, and six windmills, besides fourteen steam-engines, an improvement totally unknown at the period referred to.

Had St. Lucia continued a French Colony, it could not be expected that she should have made such rapid advances as Martinique, her elder sister and the spoiled child of their common mother country. Now, what are the present state and prospects of Martinique? As an agricultural country, its resources are immense,

its natural fecundity unbounded. As a West
Indian community, it yields the palm to none
other in political advantages and social improvement. As the France of " Outre-mer," and the
cradle of her colonial aristocracy, it still rules
pre-eminent in this hemisphere; but as a trading,
slave-holding Colony, it is on the brink of bankruptcy and ruin. Rotten at the heart, " as con-
cave as a covered goblet or a worm-eaten nut,"
it presents all the appearance of the " sepulchrum
dealbatum," all the tranquillity of the dormant
volcano. At the surface it is nothing but gaiety
and gaudiness—theatres, concerts, assemblies,
balls; within nothing but darkness and de-
spondency — debts, difficulties, and discontent.
Martinique is now what St. Lucia was in 1830—
a prey to the over-grown, all-absorbing vulture
of commercial credit, and nothing can save it but
the application of the same remedy—the introduction of the *saisie réelle.* This, however, is
not likely to be accomplished for some years.
The planters exercise an all-powerful influence in
the councils of the mother country; and they
who have all but succeeded in effecting the suppression of the beet-root manufactories, will have
little difficulty in staving off the day of reckoning
with their miserable creditors on the spot. In

this state of things Martinique should be prepared
to encounter one of two equally formidable evils :
either emancipation may be indefinitely postponed ; and then the slaves, sick of delay and
disappointment, will again have recourse to the
cutlass and the torch ; or it may be conceded
without compensation, and then the proprietary
body will be reduced to irretrievable ruin. There
are not ten planters in the island, fair and
flourishing though it seem in its present artificial
vitality, that could find the means of providing
for the cultivation of their estates under a system
of free labour.

Far be it from me, however, to wish to maintain the position, that St. Lucia has progressed
in proportion to its extent or capabilities. In fact,
not more than one sixteenth part of the island is
under cultivation, although it is susceptible of
being so to the summits of the highest mountains.
Little improvement has been effected in the old system of agriculture : few, if any, attempts have been
made to substitute mechanical for manual labour;
and even the plough and other implements of
agriculture, which might be employed with so
much advantage, are as yet scarcely known.

The chief exports at the present day are sugar,
coffee, cocoa, rum, molasses, and logwood.*

* See Appendix No. 2 to this Chapter.

Cotton, once a staple production, has been totally discontinued, although it still grows wild in many parts of the island. It is surprising that the cultivation of this product has not been resumed since the abolition of slavery. It requires but little labour and less outlay; is of quick growth; thrives in every season; offers a sure harvest and a ready market; and would yield a more remunerative return than the raising of ground provisions or any of those light branches of industry, in which most of the small farmers are now engaged. Nor would its cultivation necessitate the diversion of one shilling of capital, or one acre of land, or one hour's labour from their more lucrative investment in the great staples of the Colony. These remarks equally apply to the cultivation of tobacco, which was formerly carried on to a considerable extent, and should therefore recommend itself to the small settler with the test and security of experience. In 1841 Mr. Marchant, the owner of an estate in the vicinity of Castries, addressed a memorial to the Legislative Council, stating his intention to lay out the whole of his property in the culture of tobacco, and praying to be invested with an exclusive privilege for a period of ten years, for raising that article of production: but the Council refused to entertain his proposal, as tending to the establishment of a monopoly, and the project has in consequence been relinquished. To me it does not appear that the profitable cultivation of tobacco should require any such protection, as that solicited in this instance; and it is therefore the more to be regretted that the stimulus of Mr. Marchant's example, and the encouragement it would have held out to the less adventurous farmer, should have been lost to the community.

Sulphur is another of St. Lucia's treasures, which had long remained unheeded and unexplored : and, after all, it is to the skill and enterprise of strangers, Messrs. Bennett and Wood of Antigua, that the Colony is indebted for the development of this important branch of its natural resources. The attention of these gentlemen was first directed to the subject in 1836, and from the prospect held out, they were induced to purchase a small property in the neighbourhood of the *Soufrière*, whereon they formed the requisite establishment for working the mines. A reference to the tabular statement in the Appendix will show how successfully this undertaking had been prosecuted, and what vast sources of wealth its continued encouragement might have opened up to the colonist ; but in 1840 the sugar-grower took the alarm, and at his instigation the Legislative Council, with that stunted policy and exclusive regard to individual interests, which occasionally mark its proceedings, imposed a tax of sixteen shillings sterling upon every ton of purified sulphur to be exported from the Colony. This measure, however plausible on theoretical grounds, amounted in practice to an absolute prohibition, coupled as it was with the adjustment of the Neapolitan sulphur question ; and the consequence was that Messrs. Bennett and Wood, after incurring a heavy loss of time and treasure, had to break up their establishment and retire from the Colony.

The production of wine from grapes of native growth has been a subject of speculation for some time ; although it is very unlikely that it will ever be submitted to the test of a practical experiment. Not that the climate and soil are unfavourable to the culture of the vine ;—to be convinced of the contrary we have only to survey the variety and abundance of excellent grapes, produced, almost without culture, in the quarter of Soufriere ;—but because an experiment of that importance would require more capital and enterprise than any speculator in St. Lucia will be disposed to bestow upon it, so long as the

present staples continue to produce a remunerative return. This subject was first seriously
entertained in October 1841, on the occasion of
a visit from M. Correa da Costa, then on a tour
amongst the islands with the ostensible design of
establishing a " Wine Company." Pursuing his
favourite scheme with a tenacity of purpose
worthy of a better cause, this person had successively visited the whole of the islands ; and after
various attempts, more or less successful, to raise
subscriptions for his wine company, he at length
resolved to try his fortune amongst the St.
Lucians ; to whose notice he introduced himself by
the following communication through the press :

" The excellent clime and fertile soil of this
beautiful island have attracted my attention for
the purpose of cultivating its lands with sugar,
cotton, tobacco, Victoria wheat, indigo, cocoa,
vine grapes, and all kinds of vegetables and fruits:
and being informed by some respectable patriots that nine-tenths of the lands remain still
uncultivated, I wish I could ascertain whether,
in the event of forming a wine company in
British Guiana, or elsewhere in the West Indies,
I could reckon on a sufficient number of shareholders in this island for the establishment of a
branch of the said company here. Though I

could have already formed the ' West India Wine Company' with English capital from England; nevertheless, I would like to have at least two-thirds of the shareholders resident in the West Indies. At all events, either in British Guiana, St. Kitts, Grenada, St. Lucia, Jamaica, or Montserrat, a wine company will be formed positively in the next year.

" I will be very much obliged to you for the publication of this letter, and for some information on the subject."

After several years' travel in three quarters of the globe M. da Costa

> " Hath strange places cramm'd
> With observation, the which he vents
> In mangled forms"

upon all those who oppose his scheme. Jews, judges, and journalists, appear to have incurred his especial hate; and no sooner does he fail in any quarter to receive the looked-for support, than with true Quixotic chivalry he turns round upon his opponents and assails them in a heroi-comic diatribe in some local print. It happened that the shadow of his notoriety had preceded him to St. Lucia—the place of all others whose people were least likely to be led away by any

visionary projects of this kind ; so that "the
poor wine-maker" (as he modestly styled himself), encountered nothing but apathy or abuse.
Nor is this to be wondered at: a "chevalier
d'industrie" in every sense of the word—literally,
figuratively, and professionally—without capital,
without credit, without fortune, without friends,
pursuing the *ignis fatuus* of his wine company
from island to island, alternately laughed at and
lampooned by the press, what encouragement
could he have reasonably looked for in St. Lucia?
What support could he have expected to find in
the *ultima thule* of his peregrinations, after
having failed every where else ?

The cultivation of canes in halves, commonly
termed the *Métairie* system, is another agricultural speculation to which I shall advert in passing. It was first adopted in 1840, since which
period it has attracted considerable notice
amongst the islands, more perhaps from the encouragement given to it by the Minister of the
Crown, than from any correct appreciation by
the colonists of its peculiar merits, or of its applicability to their respective situations. On
this, as on almost every other question, there are
two opinions entertained in St. Lucia. The
planter who owns an estate, but is destitute of

the requisite capital to enable him successfully to
compete with his wealthier neighbour, is glad to
avail himself of the services of a few industrious
cultivators, on condition of dividing the profits of
the crop. In this way he derives a return, however scanty, from his land and the estate's machinery, which must otherwise have remained
idle and unproductive ; while the cultivator receives a price for his labour, which he might
have sought for in vain in the market. The
advocates of this system are all those who participate in its benefits, from the sinking planter
to the aspiring peasant : in their estimate it is
the only measure of salvation for the Colonies.
Its opponents are to be found amongst the capi-
talists and independent proprietors, supported by
the mercantile and shipping interests both in the
Colonies and the mother-country : by these it is
regarded as a ruinous speculation. Perhaps,
however, the true interests of all may be found
between these conflicting opinions. The system
has its advantages and its evils : the former are
sufficiently obvious. The worst feature of the
latter is the direct tendency to give an undue and
overstrained impetus to the growth and accumulation of wealth amongst the labouring population ; to induce consequent habits of indolence ;

by lowering the condition of the landowner, and elevating that of the labourer, to place both on a footing of equality ; thereby to increase the number of small farmers ; and ultimately to divert a large amount of capital and industry from the more legitimate, because more lucrative, cultivation of the staple commodities. It is a system in fact, which neither requires encouragement nor justifies restriction. Wherever there are proprietaries in a state of pecuniary destitution, and labourers disposed to take advantage of that circumstance, this plan of cultivating an estate will naturally suggest itself as the most advantageous for both parties. To attempt to restrict it in this case would be as foolish as unjust. But where no such circumstances exist— where the landholder is able to provide money-wages, or otherwise to meet the cost of production, the *Métairie* system, however commendable on general grounds of expediency or right, would be attended with ruinous consequences. Let the labourer have fair play : let him have broad and impartial justice ; let there be no undue restriction on the one side—no monopoly on the other : but, in the present condition of the Colonies and in a thinly-peopled country like St. Lucia, let there be no propping up of one class to the pre-

judice of the other—no creating of a distaste for
regular labour, and a steady but gradual advancement towards the profits and pleasures of an
industrious life.*

Immigration, the universal topic of the day—
the great panacea for commercial embarrassment
and agricultural distress—has received as yet but
little encouragement in St. Lucia. Too prudent
or too poor to embark in those bold schemes
which have proved all but ruinous to some of the
more independent Colonies, she has devoted her
energies and her resources, such as they are, to
the training and improvement of her own offspring and the encouragement of her native industry. In this she has so far succeeded that,
although money wages continue at a higher rate
than in some of the other islands, there is no lack
of labourers for the field; while many of the
freemen and artizans, who in the days of slavery
would have regarded manual labour as degrading,
are now seen in the foremost ranks, setting an
example of patient toil and assiduity to their more

---

* The only instance that occurs in Colonial history of the adoption of
the Métairie or Métayer system, is that of Prince Edward's Island, where
it appears to have been extensively acted upon at one period.—See
M'Gregor's British North America and Merivale on Colonization. The
latter describes it as " the primæval plan of division between landlord and
tenant, which dates from the very origin of civilization."

indolent neighbours amongst the newly-emanci-
pated classes.

The little that has been accomplished in the
way of immigration is entirely owing to the
exertions of private speculators. The first experiment was made by Mr. Muter, an extensive
merchant, shipowner, and landed proprietor, who
in 1836 imported five Irish families, consisting of
five men, four women, and eight children : but
he committed the fatal error—fatal alike to the
interests of humanity and of immigration—of
establishing them in the notoriously insalubrious
district of Roseau ; and this was the more un-
accountable in Mr. Muter, the owner of estates
in every part of the island, as the ostensible design
appears to have been the introduction of the
plough upon his estates. The consequence was
that the immigrants fell off one by one, victims
to the insidious fevers of that humid locality. In
1837 the same gentleman made another essay of
a similar nature. This time, however, the stream
of immigration was made to flow from Scotland ;
but, as in the former case, the immigrants, num-
bering eighteen persons, were located in the valley
of Roseau ; and notwithstanding the most lavish
expenditure in food, clothing, nursing, and
medical attendance, the experiment met with no

better success. In 1840 Mr. Muter made another importation, consisting of seventeen persons, from the same quarter, and with the like unfortunate results.

Mr. Henry King, the owner of a large coffee estate in the quarter of Soufriere, was the next adventurer in this novel field of speculation : and through his exertions and perseverance the colonists of St. Lucia have witnessed the practical adaptation to its climate of the constitution of the European labourer. True, Mr. King had many important advantages over Mr. Muter. First, he had the benefit, such as it was, of the experience derived from that gentleman's failure : secondly, his immigrants were all natives of Germany, who, though picked up in the streets of London, turned out to be persons of temperate habits : thirdly, they were located in one of the most salubrious spots in the island : fourthly, they were never engaged in any but the light occupations of a coffee estate, or their provision grounds : and lastly, they constantly received the domestic care and personal attentions of Mrs. King, a lady of distinguished benevolence and liberality. The result has been highly favourable : of twenty-nine German labourers, imported in 1840 and 1841, only two have fallen victims to disease. The others continue in excellent health, and by their industry and sobriety contribute to exalt the character of the free cultivator amongst the commonalty of St. Lucia. Their gardens, the only ones in the island that deserve the name, abound in every description of European vegetable and tropical fruit, with which they supply the Soufriere market, and sometimes even that of Castries, a distance of twenty miles from the estate.

The next immigrants were twenty-three Frenchmen and Savoyards, imported by M. A. J. Beaucé in January 1842. M. Beaucé is a foreigner who has purchased an estate in the quarter of Dennery, a locality that may vie with Roseau in point of unhealthiness: and being on a visit amongst his friends at Lyons during the summer of 1841, he appears to have prevailed upon some of the redundant population of that great manufacturing city to accompany him to St. Lucia as indented labourers. M. Beaucé had already acquired abundant experience of the insalubrity of Dennery during a residence of seven years; and he has but himself to blame for the failure of his immigration projects. In the course of two or three months after their arrival, five of the settlers were carried off by malignant fevers, and the

others became so alarmed that they deserted the
quarter. For their subsequent history and ad-
ventures we are indebted to M. Beaucé himself,
who has volunteered an account of the transaction
in a letter addressed to a friend in France through
the local press. In this document he descants
on the removal of those unfortunates from their
homes, and their consequent difficulties, and even
their death, with a levity and recklessness truly
harrowing. But the most objectionable feature
of the business was the promise he exacted from
them in France, as one of the conditions of their
engagement, that they would inviolably adhere
to the Roman Catholic religion. A man of extreme opinions in religion as in politics, M. Beaucé
appears to have been hatching some crude scheme
of theocratic colonization, modelled on the famous
Republics of the Jesuits : but, alas ! the similitude
between the man and his model is about as great,
as between the district of Dennery and the province of Paraguay.

The only other immigrants are one hundred
and ten Barbadian Negroes introduced in 1841.
Seventy-five of these are indented to Mr. Good-
man of Union Vale, twenty-seven to Mr. Todd
of Union, and eight to M. Lacorbiniere of Co-
rinth. They appear to afford satisfaction to their

employers ; but the outlay attending their removal and location has far exceeded the original esti- mate, and neither of these gentlemen has been tempted to repeat the experiment.

To these isolated efforts has immigration been hitherto confined ; nor, as regards Europeans, does it seem desirable that it should be further extended. Mr. King's disinterested labours, and for which he is entitled to the thanks of the com- munity, have incontrovertibly established the fact, that the climate of St. Lucia is by no means uncongenial to the constitution of the white labourer. But, unfortunately, amongst private speculators we shall always meet with more Beaucés than Kings ; and the blunders of the one have done more to damage the cause of im- migration than all the prudence and precautions of the other will ever accomplish towards its pro- motion. If we are to have any immigration at all, let it be of the right sort and upon a scale of systematic encouragement. Let the monied interests of the Colony, backed by their mercantile friends in Britain, take the subject in hand ; and let the local authorities come forward with proper measures to give it practical operation. If this cannot be effected, then St. Lucia must rest satis- fied to advance in her own quiet, plodding way, with her own natural population, and their natural means of increase.

Under all circumstances, but especially if immigration is to be systematically promoted, there is one preliminary question which it would be politic to set at rest; namely, the disposal of Crown or waste lands. During the early period of Emancipation the practice of " squatting" prevailed to an injurious extent, and the great facility afforded for its indulgence in St. Lucia was still further enhanced by the difficulty, nay in most cases the absolute impracticability, of determining the boundaries of private estates in the immediate contiguity of ungranted lands. This practice, as discouraging to the industrious labourer, as it was unjust to the *bonâ fide* landowner, soon gave rise to complaints and recriminations; and if it has now almost entirely disappeared, we owe that circumstance to the harmonising influence of exorbitant wages, whereby the squatters were enticed from their precarious seclusion in the woods to the more profitable occupations of the field. Now, the natural result of immigration upon a large scale would be to encourage squatting to an illimitable extent, as well by increasing the number of idle and disorderly persons, as by lowering the prices of the labour-market. The same cause which would increase the number of hands would necessarily depreciate the value of labour, and produce a corresponding diminution in its amount. In a word, the labourer who now considers it worth his while to work in the field for one shilling and sixpence per day, will, when immigration has reduced wages to ten-pence, either retire to cultivate his little garden, or, if he have none, betake himself to the woods.

St. Lucia on an approximative calculation contains 158,600 acres of land. Of these about 45,000 belong to private persons, and the remaining 113,600 to the Crown, including the *cinquante pas du Roi*,* specially reserved in all colonies of French origin. There are 9,900 acres in cultivation, of which 5,245 are planted in canes, 460 in coffee, 275 in cocoa, and 3,920 in provisions. There are moreover 3,000 acres in pasture. A general survey of the Crown lands, on the plan proposed by Captain Dawson in reference to New Zealand, would be a most desirable object; but it is doubtful whether, in a rugged and mountainous region like St. Lucia, it could be accomplished without considerable

* The " cinquante pas du Roi" comprise that belt of land that encircles the island, a breadth of fifty paces inwards from the beach.

expense. Perhaps the most economical course would be to have the survey made by the Government surveyor, who possesses the advantage of local information and a practical acquaintance with the limits of the different estates.

The commercial relations of St. Lucia extend chiefly to the United Kingdom, British North America, Barbados, Martinique, and the United States.* The traders are divided into what are called "Négocians" of the first class, "Négocians" of the second class, and "Négocians" of the third class, or "Marchands." With the Frenchman, from the trading prince to the travelling pedlar, every one is a *négociant*. There is nothing that flatters his vanity so much as this distinction: to this all his aspirations tend;—nothing from which he recoils with such instinctive abhorrence as the appellation of *boutiquier:* sooner than descend *in name* to this depth of commercial degradation he will set up for a " fourth-class " merchant. Even the common huckster has his dignity to support, and if he cannot properly style himself a merchant, he claims to be ranked as a "Commerçant." The *Commerçant* is that genus of trader, not incongruously denominated a storekeeper. If a man can only hire a large

* See Appendix, Nos. 3 and 4, to this chapter.

store (of which there is no lack in Castries) and
furnish it with a cask of salt fish and a firkin of
butter, he fancies himself a personage of some
importance and passes for such in the eyes of
many.   But, in point of fact, how few there are
who have any founded pretensions to the respectable calling of a merchant, in the British sense
of the word!   In St. Lucia their number does
not exceed half a dozen: all the others may be
fairly classed as shopkeepers.   Shopkeeping, in
truth, is the universal rage: what Napoleon is
reported to have said of the British, as a nation,
is more strictly applicable to the St. Lucians, of
whom it may truly be said that they are a colony
of shopkeepers.   Every second house in Castries
displays a shop of some description, or rather of
a nondescript character, crammed with every
imaginable ware, from a pipe to a prayer-book.
Even the most respectable ladies and the wives
of the wealthiest merchants deem it not derogatory to have a shop and hawk goods about the
streets.   Nor is this system confined to the
towns: on the abolition of slavery almost every
planter was induced to establish a shop upon his
estate, with the twofold object of attaching the
labourers to the property, and of drawing back in
exorbitant profits a portion of the exorbitant

wages he was compelled to give them in that early stage of the experiment of free labour. In some cases the speculation has proved a losing affair; but wherever the person in charge of the shop has been found trustworthy, and careful in not extending the credit system beyond the resources of the labourers, it has answered well.

Amongst the tradesmen and mechanics, the blacksmiths, masons, carpenters, and joiners occupy a prominent position; and their employment, owing to the destructive influence of the climate, is both regular and remunerative. A large proportion of the youth of the island are apprenticed to these trades, from whose ranks some of the planters and proprietors of the present day have risen to wealth and independence. Shoemakers and tailors are less favourably circumstanced, and must continue so, as long as the merchants of "every class" find it advantageous to import boots and shoes and ready-made clothing from Britain. The tailors labour under the additional disadvantage of having to compete with the *artistes* of Martinique, whose traffic is considerably enhanced by superior skill and a direct contact with Parisian fashions. The other inferior branches of industry—alike the refuge of the idle and the resource of the industrious—are fishing, cutting logwood, preparing charcoal, and plying the island boats. This last occupation is chiefly confined to the town of Soufriere by reason of its central position on the leeward coast.

From the influence which banking transactions have exercised on the economical condition of the Colony, I am induced to advert to the subject in passing. Two institutions of this kind have been formed in the West Indies within the last seven years, namely, the Colonial Bank and the West India Bank. The latter has not yet been extended to St. Lucia; but a branch of the former was established there on the 1st August 1837, and has since continued in operation. Like all novelties this establishment was hailed as a boon by the colonists, and many were the benefits it was predicted to confer in the various walks of speculation and trade. I regret to say, however, that far from realizing the anticipated results it has proved a fertile source of disappointment to some, injury to others, and ruin to many. The besetting error of the institution was the great facility it afforded for discounting bills and notes of hand. Allured by this bait a swarm of needy speculators suddenly started into existence, and with the aid of a few signatures which they could command on a system of reciprocity and mutual accommodation, they were enabled to obtain that encouragement at the Bank which should have been reserved for the *bonâ fide* trader. And to such an extent was this encouragement held out at one time, each note, as it became due, being redeemed through the artificial resource of a fresh note, that many were enabled to engage in extensive transactions without one shilling of available capital. The factitious system of credit thus created was not long confined to the mere speculator, who had little to lose and everything to gain. The honest but less adventurous trader, the slow but steady agriculturist were soon induced to embark their little capitals on the swelling tide of competition. Too soon, however, they became sensible of their dangerous position, and endeavoured to retrace their steps; but it was too late. The bank agents having opened their eyes to the vicious practice which had been introduced, resolved to cut down the system of " cash credits " to its legitimate proportions. This could not be effected without injury to the parties already engaged; and while the insolvent speculator was compelled to resume that penniless position, from which he should never have been tempted to emerge, the honest

trader and industrious planter found themselves
seriously involved either on their own account or
that of their friends. Even the bank itself did
not escape uninjured. Its losses may be stated at
£2,000 sterling—rather a heavy drawback upon
the profits of a branch establishment.

APPENDIX TO CHAPTER VIII.

No. I.

ESTATES DISPOSED OF BY JUDICIAL SALE BETWEEN THE
1st JANUARY, 1833, AND THE 1st JANUARY, 1844.

Name of Estate.	Acres of Land.	Date of Sale.	Price obtained.
			STERLING.
Terre Blanche	90	17 October 1833 ..	£1,000
Riche Fonds......	330	3 July 1834......	2,000
Mont d'or	583	23 October 1834 ..	2 040
Bonneterre	353	15 January 1835 ..	400
Ressource........	187	26 February 1835..	1,860
Bath	100	5 March 1835....	680
Grand Rivière	346	8 October 1835 ..	820
Beauséjour	333	8 October 1835 ..	1,600
Saphir	690	15 January 1836 ..	1,680
St. Catherine	133	14 January 1836 ..	740
Bastille	100	18 February 1836..	3,380
Balambouche	587	18 February 1836..	6,640
Volet	333	24 February 1836..	1,340
Pointe	423	24 March 1836....	2,400
Malgrétout	37	24 March 1836	3,000
Chateau Belair ...	167	24 March 1836	3,100
St. Pierre........	100	28 April 1836	2,820
Réunion	333	7 July 1836......	1,940
Fond d'or........	607	7 July 1836......	6,240
Belle Plaine......	217	28 July 1836......	3,600
Anses Noires	273	28 July 1836......	1,680
Esperance	220	18 August 1836....	600
Incommode......	500	8 September 1836..	2,980
Morne Belair	307	15 September 1836..	1,320
Perle	500	15 September 1836..	2,020
Bastille..........	54	6 October 1836....	600
Anse Cochon	200	6 October 1836....	720
Mondésir........	400	20 October 1836....	1,280
Vide Bouteille....	133	20 October 1836....	2,000
Source	133	17 November 1836..	1,260
Ravine Claire	220	15 December 1836..	1,480
Anse Mahaut	333	15 December 1836..	1,200
Diamond	363	26 January 1837 ..	4,540
Desgatiere	430	26 January 1837 ..	2,560

Name of Estate.	Acres of Land.	Date of Sale.	Price obtained.
			STERLING.
Mount Pleasant ..	387	26 January 1837 ..	£2,420
River Dorée......	313	9 February 1837 ..	2,940
Savannes	500	20 April 1837......	840
Beauchamp	367	20 April 1837......	2,460
Perle	243	30 May 1837	1,640
Riche Bois	333	19 September 1837..	1,120
Bellevue	140	19 September 1837..	2,700
St. Urbain	500	19 September 1837..	2,020
Fonds	1670	17 October 1837 ..	5,840
Réunion	300	8 February 1838 ..	1,220
Parc............	137	8 February 1838 ..	720
Rabot	200	15 May 1838	1,000
Lacaye..........	417	9 October 1838....	980
*Beauséjour	333	20 December 1838..	1,800
Belair	300	24 January 1839 ...	160
Two Friends	293	5 February 1839 ..	1,000
Corinth	283	5 February 1839 ..	3,000
Ressource	284	2 April 1839	1,540
*Ravine Claire....	220	2 April 1839	·820
Bosquet d'or	380	7 November 1839..	310
*Bellevue........	140	4 December 1839..	1,200
Bois d'orange	410	17 December 1839..	1,900
*Bastille	54	17 December 1839..	520
Barbier	40	21 February 1840 ..	160
Grand'Anse......	1250	21 February 1840 ..	960
*Diamond	363	9 June 1840	2,300
Beauséjour	273	7 July 1840	1,420
Blackbay........	510	1 September 1840..	2,620
Mont d'or	580	17 November 1840..	3,060
Union Praslin	840	5 June 1841	2,020
Riche Fonds	330	15 June 1842	4,500
Bosquet d'or	270	15 June 1842	200
Ressource	282	15 June 1842	750
Savannes	500	15 June 1842	950
*Union Praslin ...	840	8 September 1842..	1,400
Union de Micoud..	1740	8 September 1842..	900
Mondésir........	400	22 September 1842..	3,250
Riche Bois	333	22 September 1842..	70
Peru............	401	27 October 1842....	2,000
*Beauséjour......	333	18 May 1843	870
Terre Blanche....	90	6 July 1843	500
Beauchamp	367	5 October 1843....	2,670

The Estates marked thus * were re-entered upon and re-sold in default of payment of the instalments accruing upon a previous sale.

No. II.

A RETURN OF THE PRODUCE EXPORTED FROM THE COLONY OF ST. LUCIA BETWEEN THE 1ST JANUARY 1826 AND THE 1ST JANUARY 1844.

Years.	Sugar (lbs.)	Coffee (lbs.)	Cocoa (lbs.)	Rum (galls.)	Molasses (galls.)	Logwood (tons)	Cassava (brls.)	Cotton (lbs.)
1826	9,070,273	227,311	98,343	35,200	225,050	1,514	..	1,735
1827	8,531,828	230,584	79,275	47,680	235,440	1,164	8	3,220
1828	9,815,144	217,146	75,275	33,910	263,017	1,211	814	1,000
1829	8,957,870	385,359	93,793	57,785	219,097	1,277	279	2,300
1830	11,239,814	377,262	153,340	40,523	230,123	708	99	..
1831	7,671,723	193,087	98,090	34,544	210,150	972	59	334
1832	5,154,982	297,165	51,925	5,450	139,960	967	..	800
1833	4,890,040	235,164	91,048	12,130	142,320	784	..	50
1834	7,008,678	242,370	60,620	8,520	194,542	595	713	450
1835	5,553,585	106,665	49,218	16,228	155,373	402	..	..
1836	3,732,600	121,598	47,950	2,000	83,840	171	..	..
1837	4,687,200	85,740	48,591	15,800	106,614	118	..	..
1838	5,533,320	135,008	38,590	6,930	110,002	109	..	..
1839	5,151,108	145,832	54,639	11,340	119,300	218	..	..
1840	3,683,820	303,820*	82,293	9,900	73,200	206	..	..
1841	4,677,350	67,251	78,225	10,900	103,800	132	..	..
1842	6,384,365	144,791	55,175	9,910	124,900	102	..	..
1843	5,065,195	35,320	48,279	180	112,340	40	..	..

540 tons of sulphur were exported in 1836; 60 tons in 1838; and 160 tons in 1840.

* It is supposed that some portion of the coffee of 1840 was smuggled into St. Lucia from Martinique and shipped as the produce of the former island.

No. III.

A RETURN OF THE VALUE OF IMPORTS AND EXPORTS OF THE COLONY OF ST. LUCIA, FROM THE 1ST JANUARY 1830 TO THE 1ST JANUARY 1844 :—

Years.	Imports.			Exports.		
	Sterling.			Sterling.		
	£	s.	d.	£	s.	d.
1830	133,551	12	4	97,277	18	11
1831	103,868	5	9	78,235	9	3
1832	102,182	1	7	72,796	13	11
1833	108,076	16	0	71,580	14	10
1834	123,144	11	0	86.982	14	0
1835	114,593	15	0	88.750	12	6
1836	121,103	14	4	79,962	1	8
1837	121,304	5	3	85,019	19	0
1838	114,893	6	10	85,140	17	8
1839	108,939	12	11	97,762	15	0
1840	114,537	12	7	86,296	5	0
1841	105,340	10	8	105,466	13	0
1842	106,859	15	0	107,914	19	0
1843	70,360	13	11	96,290	6	3

No. IV.

A RETURN OF THE SHIPPING EMPLOYED IN THE TRADE OF ST. LUCIA FROM THE 1ST DAY OF JANUARY 1830 TO THE 1ST DAY OF JANUARY 1844 :—

	Shipping Inwards.			Shipping Outwards.		
Years.	No.	Tons.	Men.	No.	Tons.	Men.
1830	424	19,910	2,458	393	20,889	2,412
1831	364	17,297	2,088	424	18,735	2,372
1832	335	13,933	1,802	339	14,191	1,889
1833	282	13,013	1,610	313	13,466	1,750
1834	308	13,705	1,734	353	15,585	2,067
1835	359	16,361	2,030	360	16,002	2,075
1836	349	13,168	1,928	379	13,166	2,194
1837	335	13,043	1,994	337	13,005	2,119
1838	321	13,508	1,960	337	12,995	2,119
1839	308	12,638	1,874	317	13,151	1,968
1840	265	11,329	1,656	282	11,548	1,769
1841	245	11,726	1,555	256	11,771	1,611
1842	243	10,879	1,578	251	12.216	1,577
1843	260	12,772	1,642	263	14,348	1,683

CHAPTER IX.

THE first Court of Judicature of which we have any account was established about the middle of the eighteenth century. It was called the Court of Sénéchaussée, and was presided over by a *Sénéchal*, exercising a jurisdiction in civil as in criminal matters, tantamount to that ordinarily vested in a Judge of First Instance. In all criminal cases there was a right of appeal to the head of the local Executive, and in civil affairs to the "Conseil Souverain" of Martinique. The other functionaries attached to this tribunal were a *Lieutenant-Sénéchal*, with power to act in all cases of incapacity of the President ; a *Procureur du Roi*, or King's Attorney, specially charged with the prosecution of police offences; a *Substitut du Procureur du Roi;* a *Greffier*, or Registrar, and two or three *Huissiers*, or Bailiffs, to carry its orders into execution. There were, moreover, some half dozen practitioners at the Bar, combining the functions of advocate and attorney; and about an equal number of Notaries Royal.

On the surrender of the Colony to the British on the 26th May 1796, this tribunal was replaced by certain provisional committees, appointed to administer justice in the peculiar circumstances of the Colony. These, however, appear to have given but little satisfaction ; and on the 1st July 1800, a proclamation was issued by Brigadier-General Prevost, for re-establishing the courts of justice, conformably to the laws and usages of the French monarchy. By this proclamation it was further provided, first, that there should be instituted a local appellate jurisdiction, similar to that prevailing in Martinique; secondly, that in all matters, wherein the subject of litigation should exceed the sum or value of £500 sterling, an appeal should lie to the King in Council; thirdly, that all questions relating to trade should be determined according to the law of England, in terms of a regulation to be framed for that purpose; and lastly, that there should be vested in the Governor for the time being an exclusive right to take cognizance of all offences against public order and the safety of the Colony.

The Sénéchaussée continued in full activity until the 31st December 1831, when it was superseded by the present judicial constitution: and it is but justice to the laws of France, by which its proceedings were regulated and its jurisdiction defined, as well as to the functionaries who presided in it, to state, that the business was generally conducted with efficiency and zeal. There were few men better qualified for his office than M. Romain Juge, the late Sénéchal; and the pains-taking honesty of purpose, which he applied to the hearing and investigation of even the most trivial case, will long live in the grateful remembrance of the suitors in St. Lucia. The Court met once and sometimes twice every week, and sat the whole day. Of the mass of business disposed of no one, unacquainted with the spirit of litigation that prevails in a French colony, can have any adequate idea. And yet, with a tribunal on the spot whose duty it was to take cognizance of every appeal, upon payment being made into court of the trifling sum of £4 sterling, to be forfeited as an "amende de fol appel," it is surprising how few of his decisions, comparatively speaking, were appealed from, and how few even of these were reversed. Nor was it in the civil department alone that the Sénéchal's exertions were taxed. To him was likewise assigned the difficult and responsible task of preparing the *instruction criminelle*, or preliminary investigation, in every case cognizable by the Supreme Court; and afterwards of sitting as a sort of grand jury (having two other gentlemen, generally members of the Bar, associated with him) for the purpose of deciding whether or not the case should be sent for trial before the higher court.

The Court of Appeal, or Conseil Supérieur, was composed of twelve councillors. On the senior member, or dean, devolved, *virtute officii*, the functions of president, and in his absence on the next in seniority. The councillors were selected from amongst the influential merchants and planters, and officiated as a jury in all cases, both civil and criminal. Six, besides the president, formed a quorum. To this tribunal were attached an Attorney-General and a Registrar in chief. The qualifications of councillor did not necessarily imply a legal education, and the candidates appear to have been selected rather for their respectable standing in the community, and their general acquaintance with the business of life, than for any professional experience or acquirements. Indeed there were never more than two lawyers to be found in their ranks at any time; and these might have been the presiding Judge and the Attorney-General, but were as likely to be any other two councillors. The office was, however, one of considerable importance; and the influence and honors it conferred were deservedly looked forward to as objects of ambition and rivalry by the leading men in the community. The proceedings of this Court, which were conducted with senatorial gravity and decorum, were carefully minuted on four sets of books. The first contained the deliberations, or quasi-administrative transactions; the second the ordinary business of the Appeal Court; the third the *arrêts au rapport,* being the judgments pronounced in certain causes, whose intricacy or importance required that they should be referred to one of the councillors for his special report; and the fourth contained the record of the criminal prosecutions. On the whole, those old-fashioned courts worked with admirable efficiency; and keeping in view the reforms which subsequent changes in our social condition would have naturally suggested both in their composition and machinery, it is a question whether they were not better adapted to the circumstances of a distant dependency, like St. Lucia, than its present judicial constitution or any other that could be devised.

Pre-eminently distinguished amongst the Presidents of the Court of Appeal was the late Sir John Jeremie, a name alike endeared to the cause of humanity and the interests of justice. After a course of legal study at Dijon in France Mr. Jeremie was practising at the bar of Guernsey, his native country, when in 1824 " his eloquence and abilities having attracted the notice of the Government, he was selected for the office of First President of the Court of Appeal."* For this important post no one possessed higher qualifications. Combining all the vivacity and shrewdness of the Frenchman with the unflinching honesty and independent bearing of a Briton, he brought with him to the discharge of his laborious duties an extensive knowledge of the English and French languages, an

* Duncan—History of Guernsey.

intimate acquaintance with the laws and usages of both countries, quick penetration, untiring activity, and unbounded zeal. His first care was to improve the civil, criminal, and commercial institutions of the Colony, while he restored confidence in the administration of justice, by a series of "judgments and decisions which cost him days and nights of patient investigation, and which for power of thought, felicity of illustration, and searching sagacity, as applications of law, may be studied as models. To say that he was the ablest judge that ever presided in St. Lucia is to say little indeed. Wherever you turn your eyes you meet the proofs of his activity in the discharge of the administrative duties which at one time devolved on the First President. The high roads opened up and levelled; the paving and drains for the salubrity of Castries, the erection of the Protestant church—all attest his unwearied and zealous labours."* Nor was the sphere of his usefulness confined to St. Lucia. Placed on the pinnacle of judicial power in the centre of the Archipelago, he shone forth a " light for all nations" over the still dreary and tempestuous horizon of West Indian slavery—

* Address of Chief Justice Reddie to the Bar of St. Lucia on the death of Sir John Jeremie.

infusing a spirit of moderation into the colonial laws, and spreading far and wide those feelings of sympathy for the Negro race, which were destined ere long to usher in the glorious day of their deliverance from bondage.

From the moment of Mr. Jeremie's installation in the Court of Appeal, which took place on the 28th February 1825, he appears to have devoted his whole energies to the attainment of one great object—the reconstruction of the social edifice, then fast tottering under the combined effects of unmitigated slavery and commercial dilapidation. In a preceding chapter I have already glanced at some of the reforms introduced by him for the purpose of giving stability to the trade of the Colony; and it now remains for me briefly to notice his more valuable services in the cause of his fellow-man.

Thirty years of modern civilization had smiled upon the fortunes of St. Lucia, and the *Code Noir* with all its monstrosities was still in active operation. In vain had the victims of colonial prejudice and persecution looked forward, under the benign influence of British philanthropy, for some mitigation of this oppressive code. In vain had the appeals of religion and the cries of humanity been heard. The colonists, intent upon

perpetuating the privileges of caste, had turned a
deaf ear to every entreaty ; and while the slaves
were daily subjected to every species of outrage
and cruelty, a system of restriction, the most
stringent and degrading, continued to weigh down
the energies of the coloured classes. In this state
of affairs Mr. Jeremie presented himself to the
people of St. Lucia, charged with the noble but
arduous mission of revising the slave laws. He
found the inhabitants divided as it were into two
hostile camps : on the one hand were prejudice
and power ; on the other disability and degradation : yet, notwithstanding the fearful magnitude
of the evil, and the numerous difficulties with
which it was beset, he succeeded in dealing a
heavy blow to the colonial régime, suppressing
some of its most glaring abuses; introducing practical ameliorations ; and obtaining for the people
of colour a substantial participation in the civil
and political rights of Englishmen. In a pamphlet
entitled " *Recent Events at Mauritius*," published
on his return from that Colony in 1835, his services to this much injured class in the West
Indies are thus forcibly stated :

" Ten years ago a legal distinction, broad and
galling, existed between the free classes throughout our Negro Colonies—the distinction of

colour. It was said to be interwoven with the whole framework of society and inexpugnable. It seemed to him a fertile source of weakness, and should it continue to endure until emancipation were granted, likely to shake to its foundation that part of our empire. As a grievance it was politically more pregnant with danger than slavery itself. Yet had it drawn comparatively little attention, and though occasionally a voice had been raised against it, nothing had been practically effected. It was after four years' experience, and having well weighed and witnessed the consequences, that Mr. Jeremie drew up and submitted to Sir George Murray an argument in which this grave colonial question was treated in all its bearings. This at once caught the clear and quick eye of that eminent statesman : it met with his approbation, and without a struggle or a murmur the curse of Ham disappeared from the western world. Sir George Murray commenced with St. Lucia, and within six months not one British West India Colony persisted in this mistaken and outrageous policy. Deep-rooted as it was said to be, it met its deserved fate ; and men only wondered and continue to wonder how for two centuries their prejudices could have rendered them so blind to their true interests."

Mr. Jeremie's labours in this noble cause did
not fail to raise a fierce opposition against him
in St. Lucia ; and after six years of active and
useful exertion as a legislator, a statesman, and a
judge, he retired from the Colony on the 1st of
May 1831. " On his return to Europe he published four *Essays on Colonial Slavery*, pointing
out with admirable clearness the general features
of slave communities, the ameliorations introduced
in St. Lucia, and the practical steps to be taken
in order to effect the final annihilation of slavery.
This tract, which contained the results of personal
experience, honestly and fearlessly declared, produced a great sensation on the public mind ; and
doubtless contributed, in no unimportant degree,
to promote that great measure of emancipation
which has shed an imperishable lustre on the
name of England."*

For some time previously to Mr. Jeremie's
retirement the administration of justice in the
West Indies had engaged the serious attention of
the Imperial Government. Some comprehensive
scheme, alike calculated to meet the wants of
each particular community, and the contemplated
changes in the social condition of all, had been
sought for ; and for some time it was thought

* Duncan—History of Guernsey.

that the project of itinerant judges might be carried out with comparative advantage. On a closer examination, however, of the various conflicting interests involved, the adoption of this plan was postponed to a more fitting opportunity. To meet the existing emergency it was proposed to resort to a less sweeping measure in the formation of a revised system of judicature for the Crown colonies, whose judicial institutions were considered more defective than those of the other islands, while their similarity of condition and identity of interests appeared to admit of the same remedy. The result was the promulgation of a Royal Order in Council, bearing date the 20th June, 1831, which continues in operation as the Charter of Justice for St. Lucia. By this Order the Sénéchaussée and Court of Appeal, as well as the several offices connected therewith, were abolished; and in their stead was instituted a tribunal, styled the Royal Court, composed of a Chief Justice and two Puisne Judges for civil causes; and of these three Judges and three Assessors for criminal causes. There was established at the same time an inferior civil court, called the Petty Debt Court, with original jurisdiction in all matters wherein the sum in dispute should not be less than £3 3s. nor exceed £20

sterling; and an inferior criminal court, called
the Court of Police, having jurisdiction in all
criminal affairs to the extent of awarding punishments, with or without hard labour, for any term
not exceeding three months; or fines not exceeding £20 sterling; or whipping not exceeding
thirty-nine lashes. At these limits commenced
the jurisdiction of the Royal Court, extending in
the last resort to the sum or value of £500 sterling. From all decisions involving interests of a
higher or graver nature there was a right of appeal
to the Sovereign in Council.

When this Order was promulgated in St. Lucia
Mr. John Paynter Musson occupied the office of
First President, to which he had been promoted
on the departure of Mr. Jeremie. Mr. Musson,
who was a native of Bermuda, had been brought
up at the English Bar, and had already filled the
important office of Attorney-General in Barbados.
He was distinguished for urbanity of manners, an
extensive knowledge of English law and practice,
and an easy and dignified elocution. His qualifications for the Bar or the Bench might have en-
sured success in any *English* colony; but he was
totally destitute of all knowledge of the French
laws or language; and it was therefore to be regretted that he should have consented to accept

the highest judicial office in a Colony under the influence of both. The perplexity of his position was not a little increased by the changes effected under the Order in Council of the 20th June, less on account of any difference between the functions of President and those of Chief Justice, than of the difficulty of organising the new machinery and putting it in regular motion. True, he was supported by two other Judges ; but while one of them, M. Mallet Paret, from his long experience, both as a lawyer and as Procureur du Roi, was the best selection that could have been made ; the other, Mr. William Henry Grant, was quite the reverse—being a person utterly ignorant of the French language, without the slightest professional knowledge of the laws of the country, or indeed of any country—one, in short, whose only recommendation for the exalted office of Puisne Judge in the Supreme Court was his being the intimate friend of Mr. Musson, and his having formerly been a Justice of the Peace in Barbados.

The first measure, if not the only one, that marked Mr. Musson's judicial career, was a scheme for the consolidation and amendment of the laws of the Colony—a scheme which, strange to say, received the sanction and encouragement of the Governor and Council. That there should

have appeared a necessity for revising the slave-
code and the criminal jurisprudence, no one, at
all acquainted with the anomalous and defective
systems which still prevailed in reference to these
cardinal questions, will venture to deny: but that
the codification of the entire body of the laws
should have been resolved upon, will appear no
less incredible, than that such an undertaking
should have been entrusted to one who was ignorant even of the " titles " of those laws, and, if
pointed out to him, incapable of comprehending
them in the only language in which they are
written. Little indeed did Mr. Musson suspect
that the system which he undertook to revise
comprised nearly the whole of the French laws
previously to 1789—the accumulated experience
of ages—the united wisdom of France's proudest
lawgivers and statesmen, her Colberts, her
L'Hopitals, her D'Aguesseaus ;—and that those
laws were scattered over a vast number of authorities—the Coutume de Paris ; the Code de la
Martinique; the Ordinances, Declarations, Edicts,
and Letters Patent of the French monarchy ; the
Decrees of the Council of State ; the Instructions
and Decisions of the Colonial Ministers ; the
Regulations of the Conseil Souverain of Martinique; Pothier, Merlin, Ferrièrc, Joussc, Domat,

Serpillon, Pigeau; the local Ordinances; English
commercial law; Acts of the Imperial Parliament; and Orders of the Sovereign in Council.
Had it been otherwise, it is but charitable to
suppose that he would have recoiled from a task
of such magnitude and responsibility. Happily
the prompt interposition of Viscount Goderich
spared the Colony the exhibition of a piece
of Utopian legislation unparalleled in colonial
history.

Meanwhile the cessation of business consequent
on Mr. Jeremie's departure, the installation of a
new President, the time thrown away upon fruitless projects of codification, the creation of a new
judicial establishment, and the inability of a
majority of the Judges to discharge efficiently the
functions of their office—these and other causes
had been productive of much delay and disappointment in conducting the public business.
By an arrangement calculated to bring the
administration of justice into derision, the whole
weight of the department had been thrown upon
Mr. Justice Mallet Paret, whose business-habits
and indefatigable zeal enabled him to sustain it
for a time in comparative efficiency. Even mere
matters of routine and questions of the most
trivial import were referred for his decision, while

his colleagues were content to share the responsibility and divide the emoluments. This state of things, however, could not last: a feeling of discontent began to prevail. Some of the leading men in the community took advantage of the effervescence of the public mind to prefer charges against Mr. Musson. An investigation was ordered; but before it was brought to a close he was recalled by the Minister of the Crown. On the 5th November 1832 he took his departure for England; and three months after, Mr. Grant, now totally unable to maintain his ground in the absence of his patron, was superseded by the appointment of a gentleman of the English Bar.

Mr. Musson was succeeded in the Chief-Justiceship by Mr. Jeffery Hart Bent, First Puisne Judge of Trinidad, and for many years Chief Justice of Grenada. In the circumstances of the Colony a better selection could not have been made; nor indeed could there have been found, throughout the wide range of our West Indian possessions, a gentleman better qualified for the judicial office under any circumstances. Upright, impartial, and single-minded, in Mr. Bent were happily blended, in a high degree, the ability and tact of the sound, constitutional lawyer, and that spirit of independence so emi-

nently characteristic of the true English judge.
Having spent many years in the exercise of various
judicial functions in New South Wales, his experience in both hemispheres was only surpassed
by his integrity, and *that* was as much above
suspicion, as it was beyond the reach of slander.
Punctilious to the extent to which punctiliousness
is a virtue in the judicial character; and yet
active to a degree almost incompatible with his
delicate state of health, he infused into the different offices, connected with the courts, a taste
for regularity and order, which continues to be
productive of the most beneficial results even to
this day.

On Mr. Bent's arrival in February 1833, he
found that a large arrear of business had been
allowed to accumulate, while the local spirit of
litigation, ever active and prolific, had just received
a fresh impulse both from the promulgation of the
Ordinance for authorising the seizure of real property, and from the announcement of the project
for the abolition of slavery, to be accompanied by
a distribution of compensation moneys. It required all the activity and efficiency of Mr. Bent,
ably seconded though he was by Messrs. Hanley
and Burke, Puisne Judges, to cope with the vast
difficulties of the emergency. Every week there

was a sitting of the Royal Court, at which from
thirty to fifty causes were set down for hearing;
and there were weekly sittings of the Police
Court, the Petty Debt Court, and the Manumission Court, besides a multiplicity of petitions
at chambers. To form an adequate idea of the
amount of business actually disposed of, it would
be necessary to inspect the records of those
different courts; but some impression may
be derived from the return appended to this
chapter.*

Mr. Bent's services, extensive and valuable as
a Judge, were considerably enhanced by his
labours as a legislator. Amongst the many useful
objects that engaged his attention the system of
criminal practice is deserving of particular notice.
This important branch of legal science was no
doubt greatly indebted to Mr. Jeremie for the
improvements which he introduced in 1827; but
it was still defective in many of its most essential features. In Mr. Jeremie's day, too, there
existed an obvious necessity for cautious and
gradual progression; whereas the gigantic strides
that were now being daily made towards the
political regeneration of colonial society, seemed
to call for a corresponding measure of legal

* See Appendix, No. I., to this chapter.

reform. The great defects of the system, as it still prevailed, consisted in the multiplicity of empty and vexatious forms with which it was encumbered; the tedious preliminary procedure called the *instruction criminelle;* the objectionable practice of cross-questioning prisoners; the examination of witnesses by leading questions, and the trial of accused parties by *contumace.* Many of the forms were worse than useless, and had actually gone into disuse in France, in whose penal institutions they had had their origin. The "instruction criminelle" was admirably calculated to defeat the ends of justice, as well by creating unnecessary delay in bringing the really guilty parties to trial, as by subjecting to the cruelty of a criminal prosecution many a person whose innocence might have been easily ascertained by the adoption of a more expeditious procedure. Again, the interrogation of prisoners, although in some particular instances successfully employed as an instrument for discovering the truth, had amounted in general practice to a species of torture, as revolting in its application as it was pernicious in its results. Its effects in France are amply illustrated in the history of criminal prosecutions in that country.* As to the practice of putting leading questions to witnesses, while it could not fail to give offence to those of a truth-telling disposition, it served as a handle to the malignity of others. And finally, prosecution by " contumace," or default, was at best an useless procedure. If the outlaw never surrendered himself to justice, it remained without effect, and if otherwise, he had to be tried over again. In October 1834 Judge Bent drew up and submitted to the Legislative Council the draught of an Ordinance, enacting the total abrogation of this antiquated code, and substituting English practice and rules of evidence, as far as local circumstances permitted. This ordinance continues in operation ; and for fulness of detail, perspicuity, and precision, may be truly regarded as the best piece of legislation that has ever emanated from the legislature of St. Lucia. As a system of criminal practice it is superior to those which have obtained in the other colonies ; and, in the absence of trial by jury, is the best safeguard of the lives and liberties of the inhabitants.

In May 1836 Mr. Bent was appointed Chief Justice of British Guiana, and was succeeded in

* See " Causes célébres," *passim.*

St. Lucia by Dr. John Reddie, the present Chief
Justice.

About a year before Mr. Reddie's appointment
Lord Aberdeen had effected an important alteration in the composition of the Royal Court.
Since the days of Mr. Grant the office of Puisne
Judge had been filled by persons, regularly
brought up to the law, whose professional acquirements and experience were the surest gua-
rantees for the faithful discharge of their important functions. Now, however, it was arranged
that whenever the office should become vacant,
it should be filled up by the appointment of
unprofessional and unsalaried Judges, to be
selected from amongst the merchants and
planters in the Colony. It would be idle to
deny the vast inferiority of this machinery to
that supplied by men of legal education. No
one could be more thoroughly convinced of this
than the enlightened statesman then presiding
over our Colonial destinies; and there can be no
doubt that, *cæteris paribus*, his Lordship would
never have given the preference to such an
arrangement; but there were many cogent
reasons for its adoption at that particular juncture—first, the dearth of professional men at
the disposal of Government, occasioned by the

retirement of Mr. Justice Mallet Paret, the decease of Mr. Justice Burke, and the appointment of Mr. Justice Hanley to the consolidated offices of Secretary and Treasurer ; secondly, the difficulty of finding two gentlemen in England, sufficiently acquainted with the French laws and language, to undertake the duties for the moderate salary of £600 sterling ; thirdly, the success which had attended the experiment in other colonies, where the services of gentlemen, unlearned in the law, aided by a professional chief, had been found adequate to the efficient administration of justice; and lastly, the saving of £1,200 sterling per annum at a period when the colonial revenue was called upon to meet the heavy expense of the newly-created police establishment.

On his arrival in St. Lucia Dr. Reddie found this system in full operation. In the commencement it appears to have worked with sufficient efficiency ; but as litigation continued in connexion with the sale of the estates and the distribution of the Compensation funds, it was attended with much inconvenience. There were two principal assistants associated with the Chief Judge ; and yet a necessity arose almost every Court-day for the appointment of fresh assistants, who in their turn were soon to be supplanted by others. One Judge was a merchant, another a planter; and each had his own important concerns before the Courts; a third was connected by ties of consanguinity or business with the litigant parties; a fourth resigned, in consequence of some attack made upon him by one of the local journals; a fifth died; and a sixth left the Colony. In this way there was a continual movement going forward on or about the bench; and it often happened that the business of a single sitting could not be disposed of without the shifting and shuffling of five or six Judges from one side to the other. Had such a system produced no more mischievous consequence than the weekly conversion of the sanctuary of justice into a species of serio-comic exhibition—a sort of judicial phantasmagoria—it should have been long since reformed by the common sense of the community. But its pernicious effects may not stop here: it may ultimately impair, if not annihilate, one essential element of justice—that in which Justice has its breath, its very being—the confidence of the public in the administration of the laws. At first commissions only issued *pro re natâ*, or as each case of vacancy, from death, absence, or other incapacity,

occurred—a mode of proceeding which appeared
to be in accordance with the spirit of the Charter
of Justice ; but as the occasions for new Judges
increased, this plan was found inconvenient, and
recourse was had to the more expeditious one of
appointing Judges, without reference to the business before the Courts.   These were styled *Juges
suppléans*, that is, persons empowered to supply
the place of the other Judges, in all cases of incapacity, whether actual or contingent.   Nevertheless, the number of appointments was very
great.   Incredible as it may appear, no less than
sixty-two Judges were appointed in the space of
eight years ;   until at length every man in the
Colony, of any standing or respectability, could
exhibit a Commission of Puisne Judge in the Supreme Court.

Another great element in which the present
system appears defective is the prosecution of
appeals to the Sovereign in Council.   Under the
Royal Order of 20th June 1831 there is a right
of appeal from all decisions of the local tribunal,
involving any title or interest above the value of
£500 sterling ; while the right of seeking redress,
by petition to the Sovereign, is maintained in all
its sacred inviolability.   But it is no less an undisputed fact that recourse is seldom had to either

remedy, and that few appeals are followed up to a final issue. The cause of this is twofold : first, the delay in preparing the case in England, and presenting it before the Judicial Committee ; and secondly, the heavy expense heretofore attending its prosecution. Since the promulgation of the present Charter of Justice, a period of twelve years, sixty-four petitions of Appeal have been filed in the Royal Court. Of these forty-nine have been abandoned or withdrawn in the Colony, and fifteen transmitted to the Privy Council; but of the latter only nine have been followed up to a final decision.

Various measures for improving the administration of justice have recently attracted public attention both in the Colony and the Mother Country. Amongst the most prominent are the introduction of the English language ; the institution of Circuit or itinerant Judges ; trial by jury, both in the civil and criminal branches of the department ; the establishment of Courts of Reconciliation ; the formation of an Assistant Court of Appeal; and the substitution of English law for the present anomalous and antiquated codes. Of these measures, however, the only one that has yet been adopted is the change of language, which after a sturdy opposition from the gentlemen of the bar and a few influential French residents, was finally effected on the 1st January 1842. This is by far the most important reform that could have been introduced. Its advantages, social as well as political, are beginning to be appreciated by all classes ; and it will serve as a stepping-stone to other improvements, which would have lost much of their practical utility had they been ingrafted on the French language. In truth, it was bad policy not to have made the change at once, at the cession of the island in 1814. No advantage could be gained by delay, and the result has shown that the members of the legal profession were as little prepared for it in 1842, as in 1814. How does the case stand even at this moment ? Of the seven gentlemen practising at the bar, two only are able to address the Court in tolerable English, while the others are driven to every possible expedient to supply their lack of appropriate phraseology—continually interlarding their discourses with Latin, French, and even Scotch terms. The following speeches of Counsel may be taken as specimens of the most approved style :—

May it please the Court.

This is an action on behalf of your humble *servitor*, the Honourable William Singleton, trading

under the *copartnery-firm* of Singleton and Co.,
to recover damages against the *defender*, Mr.
Philip Pajol, under the following circumstances.
My client is the owner of a lumber-yard in this
town, comprising about two *carrés* of land, and
surrounded with a stone-wall. The *defender* occupies a house and yard conterminous with this
lumber-yard, and is at present building and erecting an oven right against the said wall, to the
great risk of the *pursuer*, and the *nuisance* of his
property; and is using the said wall for letting
in stones, whereon to rest and support the timbers
of the said oven, in the very teeth of the law,
and contrary to the rights both of property and
servitude extant in the person of the *pursuer*.
[Burge vol. iii., p. 407 (A), and p. 408 (F)].

The *pursuer* has repeatedly desired the *defender*
to desist, and represented the danger to the said
lumber-yard, in the event of a spark falling from
the chimney upon his shingles (the top of the
said chimney being just on a level with the piled
wood of the *pursuer*, and to windward of the
same) which danger may extend to the town and
even to the shipping in the bay; but the said
defender persists, *vi et armis*, in the execution of
his undertaking, to the wrongous usurpation of,
and encroachment upon, the *pursuer's* wall.

The *pursuer* further begs to state that he had a *signification* served upon the *defender* by the Marshal's *huissier*, calling upon him, in the name of the Queen and of justice, to desist:— and what was his reply? This honourable Court will be horrified when I state that he said he would make no reply at all!—which amounts *ex facie* to nothing more nor less than a high contempt of the Court's dignity. Of course, it is not for me to say what the Court, in its sapience, ought to do with this contumacious contemner of of the law; but this I will say that a more aggravated case of *rebellion à justice* has never come under my notice!

The *pursuer's conclusions* are, therefore, that the Court may be pleased to *interdict*, prohibit, and *discharge* the said Pajol from proceeding with his said erection—failing which, within the delay of three days from the *deliverance* of the Court, that he be *decerned* and *ordained* to pay to the *pursuer*, in real and *effective* money of this Colony, and even *par corps*, the sum of one hundred pounds sterling, in name of damages, for the torts inflicted on the *pursuer*, together with all legal *accessories*, under *protestation* to add and eke—As *accords* of Law!

Before I resume my seat, and to avoid all *chicane* as to the meaning of the word " wall," I beg to refer the *defender* to Dr. Johnson's Dictionary.

DEFENCE OF PAJOL.

May it please the Court.

I appear in this case for Mr. Philip Pajol, the *defender*. Your Honors have heard the *plaidoirie* of my learned *confrère;* and certes a more extraordinary piece of forensic *fanfaronnade* has seldom been exhibited in a Court of Justice ! Well might the uninitiated exclaim : " Oh ! the glorious unintelligibility of the law !" The *pursuer* first proceeds to raise a foundation of lumber, and thereupon he erects a Babel of words—crowning the whole with a chimney, to show that his arguments must end in smoke. It will be no difficult task, I apprehend, to demolish his *echafaudage*, and without expatiating *de omnibus rebus et quibusdam aliis*, after the fashion of the *adverse* party, I shall grapple at once with the facts of the case.

Somewhere about the year one thousand seven hundred and sixty-five, the *defender's auteur* purchased the lot of land adjoining that of the *pursuer* (and here I may observe, *en passant*, that the Honourable Mr. Singleton has proceeded

on a false narrative of the extent of his lot, which
only comprises a *carré* and a half). The *defender's auteur* engaged himself with the *auteur* of the
pursuer to have a *mitoyen* wall constructed between their respective lots. Now, my client's
auteur, qua bonus pater-familias, has punctually
implemented his part of the contract, while the
pursuer's has failed to do his. It is, therefore,
abundantly obvious that Pajol has *de facto*, as
well as *de jure,* the *dominium* of the wall in question. If the *pursuer* has gone to sleep, instead
of *implementing* his part of the engagement, he
must take the consequences ; *vigilantibus, non
dormientibus, inserviunt leges.* I humbly apprehend that the position of the parties must be
reversed ; and that, *mutatis mutandis*, my client
is entitled to damages for breach of agreement
and *warrandice.* In further elucidation of this
position, I request the Court to cast an eye over
the *hypothecary inscription* in the *dossier* of my
client, which I now submit on the Court's *bureau.*

Here I might pause for the Honourable *pursuer's*
retort to these *dilatory* pleas ; but from a note
which has just this moment been placed in my
hands, I am prepared to bring forward a *peremp-
tory* exception. It now turns out that the wall
in question is the *pro-indiviso* property, not of

the *defender*, as I had been led to believe, but of the Demoiselle Adelaide Coco ; and that the *defender* merely conducts the erection at her request. Therefore the *requéte* introducing the *instance* is egregiously *inept*—it is *in gremio* a perfect nullity, and must fall to the ground. Therefore the *defender* has been most unwarrantably, I might have said illegally, dragged into Court, and is entitled to damages (Domat. vol. iv. titre v.—*de damnis et impensis*). Wherefore I move the Court to grant me *acte* of my *reserves* to prosecute, *en tems et lieu*, for the gross, wanton, and unprovoked libel that has been levelled against my client's character.

My learned brother has referred us to Johnson's Dictionary—the *convenient* pocket edition, I apprehend, which he carries about him ; but if he will take the trouble to *feuilleter* the folio edition with notes and annotations, it may throw some light upon the meaning which *ought* to be attached to the word " wall." That he will find in my *study*, to which I beg to refer him *brevitatis causâ*.

My *conclusions* are : *primo*, that it may please the Court to interdict the *pursuer* from molesting and disturbing my client in the quiet and peaceable erection of his oven—or rather Miss Coco's oven—and the necessary walls and chimneys of the same; *secundo*, that the *ordinance* of the Court *ad factum prestandum* be *cassed*, rescinded, and annulled, inasmuch as the fact has become *imprestable*; *tertio*, that the *pursuer* be *decerned* and adjudged to empty his hands into those of the defender, of the sum of £200 sterling, in lieu of damages, for the injury inflicted on his fair fame, by the acts and proceedings of the *pursuer*, and the said *defender* be *reponed* and restored thereagainst *in integrum*; and *quarto*, by way of *subsidiary conclusions*, that the *pursuer* be dismissed *simpliciter*, under the law of common sense, save his recourse against *qui de droit*.—And this is justice!

The applicability of the circuit system to the West India islands, generally, continues to be a subject of inquiry; although there is as little likelihood of its practical adoption, at the present day, as there was in 1822, when the subject was first propounded. The plan would appear to be to form the Colonies into two great judicial divisions, to be styled the Windward and Leeward Circuits—the one to comprise Barbados, St. Lucia, St. Vincent, Grenada, Tobago, and Trinidad; and the other Dominica, Antigua, Montserrat, Nevis, St. Christopher, and the Virgin Islands. The

establishment in each circuit would be composed
of a Chief Justice and two Puisne Judges; the
chief and one puisne to reside at Barbados, for
the Windward Circuit; and at Antigua for the
Leeward Circuit: and there would be a resident
Puisne Judge in each island, to be invested with
the jurisdiction of a Judge of First Instance, in
the absence of the other two; and during their
periodical visits to be associated with them in the
Supreme Court. Experience and the particular
circumstances of each colony might suggest some
slight modifications in the details of the measure;
but taking this as the outline, there can be no
doubt that it would be a vast improvement on
the present system. The radical vice of our
West Indian communities is the inducement held
out to the resident Judge to engage in the exciting
conflicts of local partizanship. One day he
descends into the arena of politics, wrangling for
popularity with the crowd: the day after he
ascends the judgment-seat, environed with all the
imposing gravity of a " sage of the law," to decide
upon the lives and liberties of his fellow-citizens,
perhaps his personal opponents. For the mischief
thus perpetrated there is now but one remedy—
an appeal to the Sovereign in Council, at incalculable delay and expense: whereas, under the

proposed circuit scheme the resident Judge would see the propriety of keeping aloof from local feuds. His political predilections would be restricted within the circle of his private intercourse; or, if vented on the bench, would find a prompt and efficacious check in the revision of his proceedings by two other judges, wholly inaccessible to local influences.

In this respect the measure would prove an invaluable boon to the islands generally : but in order that a colony, like St. Lucia, governed by the laws of a foreign country and of a by-gone age, should obtain a full and substantial participation in its advantages, one of two important objects must be first secured. Either the laws of the Colony, local as well as foreign, must be entirely replaced by English law ; or care must be taken that one of the judges going the circuit shall be adequately conversant with those laws. If these circumstances are overlooked, the circuit Judges will be a worse-than-useless institution. They will mistrust their own judgment upon questions of local law or practice : they will refer all intricate points to the superior experience of their colleague on the spot, and will ultimately adopt all his decisions. By this means the resident judge will be the sole arbiter of the fortunes of the inhabitants, and there is no conceivable mischief that he may not accomplish with absolute impunity. Complaints might be made, but where would the blame attach! The visiting Judges would naturally plead their inability to unravel the mass of local incongruities : "they must take the law from their colleague on the spot;" and the latter would as naturally reply that " he is but one of three, and can only accept his share of the responsibility."

An important question remains to be solved— How is the Colony to contribute its proportion towards the expenses of the circuit establishment? Indeed, I am aware that this has been an insuperable difficulty in some of the islands, to whose refusal to vote the necessary funds the postponement of the scheme is mainly ascribable. So far, however, as St. Lucia is concerned, the question is of easy solution. The cost of the present judicial establishment* amounted originally to £2,400 sterling, which the Colony did not hesitate to provide during the four years of its greatest financial embarrassment. Since 1835 this amount has been reduced to £1,200— being the salary paid to the Chief Justice. Ap-

---

* By judicial establishment I mean the Judges. All the other officers of the department would have to be continued on their present footing.

portioning therefore the provision for the Circuit
Courts, according to the scale laid down by Lord
Glenelg for the other colonies, the quota to be
contributed by St. Lucia would amount to about
£1,300 sterling, exclusive of £600 for a resident
Judge. This would give £700 more than the
present reduced establishment, and £500 less
than the original provision. To cover this additional outlay recourse might be had to the
surplus revenue of the Colony, which would be
more profitably employed in securing the blessings of prompt and impartial justice, than in the
prosecution of those numerous projects, of a
chimerical or questionable utility, on which it is
now annually thrown away.

The possibility of extending to St. Lucia the
benefit of trial by Jury has become a question of
intense interest. It was initiated in March 1843
by the Right Honorable Sir Charles Grey, Governor in Chief, whose statesmanlike views have
received all encouragement and support from Colonel Clarke, the present Lieutenant-Governor.
The question for consideration was the practicability of assimilating the institution of Assessors
to that of Jurors ; and with a view to facilitate
this inquiry it was recommended that the Law-
officers of the Crown and other public servants

should be requested to report their opinions. To
me, amongst others, this honor was vouchsafed,
and the view which I ventured to express is contained in the following extract of a letter, addressed to the Colonial Secretary on the 10th
April 1843 :—

"On the advantages of trial by Jury, moral as well as
political, it would be idle to expatiate in this place. I apprehend there can be no difference of opinion in any quarter as to
the paramount importance of the institution itself, sanctioned
as it is by the wisdom and experience of the most enlightened
legislators and statesmen of modern times. The only question
is its practicability in the present condition of St. Lucia.

"Any plan for assimilating the institution of Assessors to
that of Jurors must be considered in connexion with the character of the inhabitants, their language and that of the Courts
of Justice, the state of the laws, the diffusion of knowledge,
the standard of moral feeling, and the value attached to the
obligation of an oath. There is a population of 26,000 souls*
in St. Lucia, which is amply sufficient to furnish the numerical
competency required for the establishment of trial by Jury:
but, owing to the influence of counteracting causes, it is doubtful

---

* When this Letter was written, the general opinion was that the population fell little short of the round numbers here given. A census has
since been taken, according to which it would appear that the population
does not exceed 20,694 souls. My conviction is, however, that no reliance
can be placed on this census. To the ordinary difficulties, with which
such operations are beset in every country, and especially amongst the
migratory population of a West Indian community, there was superadded
in this instance an insuperable obstacle, arising from the impression, that
the census was intended as the basis of a system of taxation for 1844.

whether more than six persons, capable of serving as jurors, could be found to sit upon every trial. There is neither public spirit nor public opinion in this island. Unlike the purely British communities of Barbados and Antigua, or the purely French communities of Martinique and Guadaloupe, the inhabitants of St. Lucia are divided not only by colour (a characteristic feature of all West Indian communities) but also by country, by language and by religion. French is the language of the people; English that of the Courts of Law. I am aware that some improvement has taken place in this respect under the system of instruction pursued in the Mico schools; but it is entirely confined to the rising generation.

" From the list of Jurors it would be necessary to exclude, 1st, all public functionaries, as being generally, and often una-voidably, mixed up in local politics and party feuds; 2ndly, all aliens; for, however competent foreigners may be to be asso-ciated as Assessors with three British Judges, they would be but ill qualified to exercise the essentially English privilege of sitting in judgment upon the lives and fortunes of British subjects, without any control from the Bench: 3rdly, all persons convicted of infamatory offences; 4thly, all persons, whose character for honesty or veracity may have been im-peached: 5thly, the whole labouring population of the Colony, who, whether considered with reference to the little progress of education, the prevalence of sorcery, or their ignorance, generally speaking, of the obligations of an oath, must as yet be held to be incapable of discharging the important functions of Jurors.

" By carefully revising the list of Assessors a considerable number of fit persons might be added; and arrangements might be made for having six instead of three to sit on every trial; but in the peculiar circumstances of the Colony, it would be impossible to obtain a greater number, without either swelling the list with the names of parties, totally incapable of serving; or subjecting the respectable inhabitants to serious inconvenience and expense, by establishing a standing jury of the same persons for the trial of every case. The accomplishment of even this partial change would involve, as a necessary sequence, the abrogation of the present Charter of Justice, not only in reference to the institution of Assessors, but to the constitution of the Court itself. The Juror should be made judge of the fact; and the Judge, merely judge of the law; instead of being, as now, both judges as well of the fact as of the law. And finally, the machinery of three Judges should be set aside as cumbrous and inconvenient—one professional Judge being sufficient to interpret all questions of law.

"Under all the circumstances, however, I am humbly of opinion that trial by Jury can only be beneficially substituted for the institution of Assessors, when it can be established to the full extent to which it prevails under the sanction of the laws of the mother country; and that any partial introduction of it, unaccompanied by the moral and intellectual improvement of the population, would but ingraft an additional anomaly upon our present confused and complicated system of jurisprudence."

Of the opinions expressed by the other officers of Government—the Members of Council, the Law-officers of the Crown, the Stipendiary Magistrates—I can only speak from public report. Some, it would appear, enamoured of the present order of things, for the sake of present advantage, pretend they foresee in this, as in every other measure of reform, the possibility of a disarrangeɹent of their blissful *statu quo*. Even a partial change would be regarded by them as an invasion of vested rights—to be opposed by every argument that sophistry can sanction or selfishness suggest. Others, led away by a love of change for the sake of change, look at nothing but the popularity of the measure. "It is the boast of Britons—the terror of tyrants—the palladium of the rights of Englishmen. It has conferred immense benefits on other countries : therefore it must be good for St. Lucia. By all means let us have trial by Jury—the measure, the whole measure and nothing but the measure." But as to the practicability of the thing itself, or its possible adaptation to the circumstances of the Colony, that is an idea that never troubles the imagination of this set of politicians.

The establishment of "Courts of Reconciliation" owes its origin to the late Governor in Chief, Sir Evan Murray Mac Gregor, whose paternal solicitude for the improvement of the labouring classes was amongst the chief characteristics of his administration. The idea of this institution, as adopted in Barbados, appears to have been suggested by the following paragraph in Sir Arthur Brooke's " Travels in Norway:"—

" In Norway a Forligelses Commission, or Court of Reconciliation, over which the Sheriff or his Deputy presides, is established for the púrpose of settling disputes and differences of every kind. Into this Court all civil actions must be brought in the first instance; and they cannot be tried at law before they have appeared there. It consists of a Jury, formed of the principal and most respectable peasants in the neighbourhood. These examine the merits of the case, hear what the plaintiff and defendant have to say, and give their advice accordingly. In nine cases out of ten the differences are made up, and the necessity of going to law, with its heavy expenses, prevented. If the parties acquiesce in the advice and opinion of this Jury, there can be no appeal afterwards : but if not satisfied, they are not in any way bound by their decision, but may proceed at law. In this Court no expense whatever is incurred. It is of recent date, having been formed in the reign of Christian VII., and the good that it does is incalculable. In fact, in consequence of its beneficial effects very few cases are referred to a higher tribunal. As an instance of this the *Amtmand* of Nordland mentioned that in one morning 130 were thus disposed of, without the necessity of their being brought before him in his judicial capacity."

Upon this model Sir Evan planned his Courts of Reconciliation; and without intending to detract in the slightest degree from their value in Norway or even in Barbados, it must be confessed that the attempt to introduce them into St. Lucia is somewhat premature. The gist of the question lies in the words: " principal and most respectable peasants," and their relative import in Norway, Barbados, and St. Lucia. In Norway the great majority of the peasants can read and

write : with them education and respectability go
hand in hand : their juries are no less competent
to decide than the litigant parties are to appre-
ciate their decision.   Hence the Forligelses Commission is in high esteem, and works with
admirable efficiency.   It is, in fact, to the Nor-
wegians, under an otherwise defective system of
laws, what trial by Jury is to Englishmen.   In
Barbados the experiment has partially succeeded,
because there education and respectability have
partially taken root : it were surprising, indeed,
if the peasantry of the most densely peopled
country on the globe did not furnish some materials for an institution of this kind.   But the
case is quite altered when we come to St. Lucia,
whose peasantry, equal only to one fifth of that
of Barbados, is scattered over nearly double its
superficial extent—a peasantry to whom education and respectability are only known by name,
or by an ardent desire to participate in their
advantages.   Here the experiment has totally
failed.

And after all what would be the practical results of such an institution in any West Indian
community ? If, as the name implies, its functions
are to be confined to the *amicable* adjustment,
by arbitration or otherwise, of all disputes and

questions amongst the commonalty, it appears to me that that duty would be much more efficiently performed by the Stipendiary Magistrate or any of the inferior tribunals of the country, than by a dozen of illiterate labourers, under the guidance and dictation of a Sheriff's officer. If, on the other hand, its jurisdiction is allowed to extend to the assessment of damages and the investigation of questions of a civil nature, then, assuredly, a Court of Reconciliation would be but another name for trial by Jury; and with all deference for some of the more sanguine friends of the Negroes, it is not to be denied that to introduce trial by Jury amongst them at the present day would be to flatter their vanity at the expense of their better judgment.

Another obstacle in the way of those Courts of Reconciliation is their unavoidable expense. The avowed object of establishing them at all is to protect indigent labourers against the heavy cost of litigation. If there is to be no saving of expense, it is admitted that it would be more advantageous to refer all questions at once to the constituted tribunals. Now, where shall we find a peasantry disposed to devote their time and attention in this way, without fee or remuneration? And since such a sacrifice has been

deemed unreasonable as regards the more enlightened portion of the public, with what show
of justice are we to demand it at the hands of
untutored peasants, mostly depending for their
daily means of support upon the time they
should thus give away for the public good ?
Upon this plan one-half of the labourers would
be constantly engaged in adjusting the quarrels
of the other half : and although it may be very
well for the principal and most respectable Nor-
wegian peasants, or other patient children of
the north, to dispose of " one hundred and thirty
cases in one morning," I apprehend that that
would be a feat of rather difficult execution for
the indolent sons of a tropical region.

The formation of an " Assistant Court of Appeal" from the decisions of the local magistracy
is an experiment which is about to receive practical application in St. Lucia. This jurisdiction
was first established in Barbados in July 1838,
under the auspices of Sir Evan Mac Gregor, and
its extension to St. Lucia was recommended in
August 1841 by Messrs. Drysdale and Laffitte,
Special Justices, on the ground that the legal
institutions of the Colony did not afford sufficient
protection to the labouring classes against the
injustice and wrongs to which they were daily

exposed by the decisions of the local Justices. I regret that I cannot concur in opinion with those gentlemen as to the existence of the alleged evil, or the expediency of the proposed remedy. No doubt, there may occasionally be found amongst the local Magistrates some wayward and ignorant persons ; but as a body they are deserving of every confidence, and their proceedings are marked by sound sense and humanity. The evil for which a remedy should have been sought was not the want of a Court of Appeal—the Supreme Court of Civil Jurisdiction being invested by law with that character : neither was it the want of legal advisers—the Special Justices being appointed and paid for the express purpose of assisting the peasantry with their advice : but it was the heavy expense attending the prosecution of appeals before the Supreme Court—an evil for which an efficacious remedy could have been found in the reduction, or even abolition in favor of the labourers, of the different fees (all ultimately accruing to the public Treasury), without resorting to the creation of two new appellate jurisdictions.

There remains the vexed question of a change of the laws. It is a general practice amongst civilized nations to guarantee to a conquered or ceded country the continuance of its institutions, as they are found to prevail at the time of the conquest or cession. Under British rule are excepted all laws and usages that may be opposed to public morals or the constitutional law of the realm—such being held to cease from the moment the imperial authority is proclaimed. On the cession of St. Lucia this principle was strictly adhered to, Great Britain reserving her natural right to make such subsequent alterations as time might suggest, and sound policy approve.* In the exercise of this right the laws of St. Lucia have undergone some important modifications. Independently of the great and glorious change effected by the final abrogation of the Slave Code, and the laws respecting the coloured classes, we have witnessed the introduction successively of English commercial law ; the mortgage law ; the " saisie-réelle ;" English rules of practice and of evidence in criminal matters ; the substitution of the English Justice of the Peace for the French Commissary Commandant ; of the Provost Marshal for the Huissiers; the creation of the office of Coroner; the adoption of the British currency of pounds,

---

* The laws of a conquered or ceded country are liable to be altered by Orders of the Sovereign in Council, Acts of the Imperial Parliament, Proclamations of the Sovereign, and Letters Patent under the Great Seal. —See decisions of the Judicial Committee of the Privy Council, *passim.*

shillings, and pence, and the introduction of the English language in the Courts of Justice. Even trial by Jury, as far as the mere laws are concerned, might be established without conflict or collision.

There are two other vital points which are said to call for revision and reform, viz. : the Bankrupt Law and the Press. It is alleged that the whole amount of relief afforded by the former consists in a sort of *cessio bonorum,* but of such questionable expediency, that owing to the degradation attached to it, the insolvent has but a choice of evils—physical death within the walls of a prison, if he disdain the *cessio,* or civil death without, if he accept it. As to any law regulating the Press, I believe it would puzzle all the sages of the law in St. Lucia or elsewhere to point out in what it consists or where it is to be found. Surely, the Censorship, as it prevailed in France before the Revolution, is about as applicable to a British Colony in the middle of the nineteenth century, as are the laws of Louis Quatorze on the subject of duelling. With these exceptions (to which the improvements recently introduced in English jurisprudence might be easily adapted) the only important features of the old legal system that continue unreformed are, the civil law, as regulating the tenure and transfer of real property, and the penal law, as defining the nature and amount of punishment applicable to each crime or offence. Even with regard to the latter, no punishment can be inflicted of a more stringent character than would be awarded, under similar circumstances, by the law of England. No doubt, the civil law is an essential branch of the old system, and it is not to be denied that it is little better than a mass of complexity and confusion. Still the question remains to be answered : is the substitution of English civil law practicable ; and, if practicable, would it be politic ? In a word, are we to unhinge the entire social edifice, based as it is on the present law, for the doubtful advantage of erecting one mass of confusion upon the ruins of another mass, a little " worse confounded ?" A change of the law is not so easily brought about as a change of the language, although some appear to think the one involved in the other. The sooner the language of the Parent State is adopted, the better for all parties, conquerors and conquered. But the case is different as regards the laws : there is no reason why those of a distant dependency—the ivy which has grown up with and entwined its political structure—should not be better adapted to its wants and even its weakness, than the laws of the conquering state, however superior these may be as the growth of a richer and better-cultivated soil.

The principal authorities that regulate the civil law are the " Coutume de Paris," being a portion of the ancient *lex non scripta* of France—Jousse's " Procédure Civile "—Pothier's "Traité des Contrats "—Ferrière's " Dictionnaire de Droit," and his " Commentaires sur la Coutume de Paris ;" and Merlin's " Questions de Droit " and " Repertoire de Jurisprudence." The local laws down to 1803 are comprised in the five volumes of a work, entitled the " Code de la Martinique :" but many of them, as well as of the Ordinances of the French monarchy, have gone into desuetude or become wholly inoperative. Those still in force are chiefly police and municipal regulations. The same remark applies to the local enactments since 1803. Of about three hundred and fifty Ordinances, Orders in Council, Rules of Court, and Acts of Parliament, that have been promulgated since that period, no more than one-fourth are still in operation.*

Amongst the offices connected with the present judicial establishment are those of Attorney-General, Solicitor - General, Queen's Counsel,

* See Appendix, No. II., to this chapter.

Registrar, Provost-Marshal, Advocate, Attorney, Notary-Royal, and Administrator of Vacant Successions.

The Attorney and Solicitor-General constitute what, under the old French system, was denominated the *Ministère Public*. As *Procureur-Général* the former functionary was invested with considerable authority and importance. These, however, have now been cut down to the more slender, but more clearly defined, attributions of an English Attorney-General. The Solicitor-General is seldom called upon to act, unless in case of the absence or incapacity of the Attorney-General. Although a separate and independent officer, he appears to stand much in the same light towards the latter, as did the *Procureur du Roi* towards his prototype of the old school.

The office of Queen's Counsel was first called into existence in October 1837, in the person of Mr. P. F. Gahan, now one of the judges in the Supreme Court of the Bahamas; and again in April 1838, in the person of Mr. H. J. Glanville, the present Chief Justice of Dominica. This office has been for some years in abeyance.

The *Greffier en chef* of the Court of Appeal and the *Commis Greffier* of the Sénéchaussée are now merged in one Registrar for the whole island, with whom are deposited the several records of the abolished Courts,* the Slave and Manumission Registers, the Parish Registers, and the Compensation Papers. In addition to his varied duties in the Royal Court, the Court of Assize, the Police Court, and Petty Debt Court, this officer is further charged with the registry of deeds and hypotheques—by far the most delicate trust under the Government.

The office of Provost-Marshal-General was created in 1830, as a substitute for the *Huissiers* or bailiffs of the old *régime*. The Marshal is also the Accountant of the Royal Court, in which capacity the late occupant of the office, Mr. Henry M'Leod, was entrusted with the most arduous and responsible duties, which he constantly discharged with fidelity and care. This officer is assisted by deputies, appointed by himself, subject to the approval of the local Executive.

The functions of Advocate and Attorney are combined in St. Lucia. The number admissible to practise has varied from time to time. It was fixed at eight until July 1837, when an Ordinance was enacted for putting a term to the consolidation of the two professions, without prejudice to

---

* The public records are only complete since July 1800—all those of a previous date having been destroyed by fire in 1796.

existing rights. By this enactment the number of attorneys was to continue fixed at eight; while that of the advocates was left unlimited. The disjunction, however, of the two professions has not been adhered to in practice; for, in all recent admissions to the Bar, I find them combined as formerly. At present there are ten gentlemen in the Colony holding a commission of advocate and attorney; but of this number only seven are actually practising before the courts. The qualifications of an advocate, as defined by the Ordinance in question, are, to be a British subject, and to have been received as advocate in a supreme British court, or taken a degree at law in a British university: and those of an attorney, to be a British subject—to have attained the age of twenty-one; and to have been admitted attorney, solicitor, or writer to the signet; or to have practised before a British court; or served a clerkship of three years to an advocate in St. Lucia.

The office of Notary under the French law is one of peculiar trust and importance. In St. Lucia he is invested with the different functions confided to the Notary Public, the Conveyancer, and the Master in Chancery in England; and to the Writer to the Signet in Scotland. Though not of the order technically styled " gens de

robe," he is in point of fact "un homme de loi."
In some instances he even assumes the office of
Chamber-counsel, and acquits himself of it with
tact and ability. The duties of the Notary are
so intimately wound up in the legal system of
the Colony that the candidate for the office is
required to go through a course of study scarcely
less complicated than that of the barrister. Indeed the two professions are almost on a footing
of equality—the acquirements of the one being
reckoned a sufficient qualification for admission
to the other. In former days the appointment
of advocates, attorneys, and notaries, was vested
in the Head of the Executive, as President of
the Supreme Court in right of his office—a
privilege which he continued to exercise long
after it ceased to have any legal existence. By
a rule of Court of the 3rd February 1835 the
right to appoint, as well as the power to suspend,
is vested in the Judges of the Supreme Court.

Formerly all vacant successions were administered by one officer, styled a *Curateur aux Successions Vacantes.** This office was abolished
by the Order in Council of the 20th June 1831.
In February 1837, with a view to obviate the
inconvenience arising from the want of Adminis-

* See Appendix, No. III., to this chapter.

trators to the vacant successions, two officers were appointed by the Court to take charge of all those for which no letters of administration had theretofore been issued. Since that period, as each vacant succession has accrued, the administration thereof has been entrusted to some creditor or other party interested, on his giving security to the satisfaction of the Court.*

* See Appendix, No. IV., to this chapter.

APPENDIX TO CHAPTER IX.

No. I.

A RETURN OF THE CIVIL SUITS HEARD AND DETERMINED IN THE COLONY OF ST. LUCIA, BETWEEN THE 1ST JANUARY 1832 AND 1ST JANUARY 1844.*

IN THE ROYAL COURT.		IN THE PETTY DEBT COURT.	
Years.	No. of Suits.	Years.	No. of Suits.
1832 . . . 82		1832 . . . 53	
1833 . . . 266		1833 . . . 93	
1834 . . . 342		1834 . . . 67	
1835 . . . 251		1835 . . . 54	
1836 . . . 257		1836 . . . 62	
1837 . . . 196		1837 . . . 48	
1838 . . . 205		1838 . . . 55	
1839 . . . 203		1839 . . . 99	
1840 . . . 148		1840 . . . 73	
1841 . . . 147		1841 . . . 74	
1842 . . . 126		1842 . . . 65	
1843 . . . 100		1843 . . . 82	

* These Returns do not comprise the defaults and interlocutory or other judgments, of which there were three or four in every suit.

No. II.

LIST OF ORDINANCES, PROCLAMATIONS, ORDERS IN COUNCIL, RULES OF COURT, ACTS OF PARLIAMENT, AND GOVERNMENT REGULATIONS, IN FORCE IN THE COLONY OF ST. LUCIA ON THE 1ST JANUARY 1844.

1809.

July 1. Ordinance for regulating Parochial Meetings.

1811.

March 30. Ordinance concerning the paving of the town of Castries, and the cleansing of the streets.

November 17. Ordinance for regulating the pirogue service.

1813.

April 28. Ordinance prohibiting the construction of wooden houses in certain parts of the town of Castries.

1816.

July 2. Ordinance concerning aliens.

1817.

January 8. Ordinance for establishing a chain-gang.

1818.

November 17. Resolution of Council for regulating Attachments (saisie-arrêts) made in the hands of the Treasurer.

1819.

May 13. Ordinance for establishing a Protestant Minister.

1823.

October 23. Ordinance prohibiting the construction of wooden buildings in certain parts of Castries.

1825.

March 23. Royal Order in Council for establishing a Bishopric at Barbados.

August 3. Rules and Regulations for the Harbour Master.

1826.

March 20. Ordinance for amending the law of evidence in civil cases.

——— Ordinance requiring the inhabitants of Castries to provide themselves with portable hearths.

——— Ordinance for regulating the establishment of commercial houses by aliens.

August 14. Ordinance for establishing a summary mode of proceeding for the recovery of maritime debts.

1826

August 29.   Ordinance reserving all offices of trust and emolument for British subjects to the exclusion of aliens.

December 27.   Ordinance to establish English commercial law.

1827.

November 24.   Ordinance to establish regulations for the guidance of the notaries and others.

December 8.   Ordinance enacting that all live stock belonging to and employed upon an estate, shall be considered as immoveable property, and shall not be levied upon apart from the estate.

1829.

January 15.   Royal Order in Council for establishing a Registry of deeds and "hypotheques."

———   Royal Order in Council fixing the age of majority at 21 years.

July 3.   Ordinance for regulating the form and manner of registering deeds and hypotheques.

———   Ordinance containing rules and regulations for giving full effect to the Royal Order in Council of 15 January 1829 for establishing a Registry of deeds and hypotheques.

———   Ordinance to enforce the payment of costs of process when taxed.

1830.

February 6.   Order of Government appointing a Medical Board to examine the qualifications of persons applying for medical commissions.

April 3.   Ordinance to repeal all former regulations relative to the security required of parties leaving the Colony.

April 13.   Ordinance for establishing a Provost Marshal.

April 20.   Ordinance for the better regulation of Parochial Meetings.

1831.

June 20.   Royal Order in Council for abolishing the Sénéchaussée and Court of Appeal, and establishing a new judicial constitution.

1832.

March 2.   Ordinance for establishing a Court of Police and a Court of Small Debts.

April 21.   Rules and Regulations for the Court of Police.

April 28.   Rules and Regulations for the Small Debt Court.

August 15.   Royal Order in Council to amend the Order in Council of 20th June, 1831, with reference to Assessors.

August 27.   Ordinance to amend the local ordinance of the 13th April 1830 for establishing a Provost Marshal.

1833.

January 2.   Ordinance to establish regulations for the seizure of real property (saisie-réelle.)

(No date.)   Rules and regulations concerning Assessors.

April 17.   Ordinance for altering the security to be given by the Registrar of the Royal Court.

October 21.   Ordinance for facilitating the proceedings in criminal cases.

November 21.   Additional rules respecting Assessors.

1834.

February 4.   Rules of Court respecting " saisie-arrêts" and petitions of appeal.

September 8.   Ordinance to amend the laws concerning roads.

October 23.   Ordinance for abolishing the office of Commissary Commandant, and substituting the English Justice of the Peace.

November 17.   Ordinance to amend an Ordinance establishing the Court of Small Debt and the Police Court.

December 21.   Ordinance for enacting Regulations for the Police—Houses of Correction and Penal Gangs.

1835.

February 3.   Proclamation for altering the market day.

————   Rule of Court regulating the admission of persons to practise as " Procureurs," Advocates, and Notaries.

February 5.   Ordinance for removing the Court House, and providing for the better accommodation of the public officers.

1835.

August 24. Ordinance for providing more effectually for the general police of the town of Castries; for constructing and repairing the wharves; and consolidating and amending all laws and ordinances on this subject.

December 21. Ordinance for repressing the illegal intrusions of fugitive alien slaves.

1836.

May 4. Ordinance for altering and amending an ordinance, dated 8th September 1834, " for consolidating and amending the laws and ordinances respecting roads in St. Lucia."

July 18. Ordinance for altering and amending an ordinance intituled " An Order in Council establishing a Provost Marshal in Saint Lucia."

August 22. Ordinance for regulating the amount of salary to be paid to the " Greffier en Chef," or Registrar of the Royal Court; and providing for the salary of a sufficient number of clerks, and all other expenses attending the said office.

August 29. Ordinance to define and limit the powers and jurisdiction of the Justices of the Peace.

September 21. Proclamation for transferring the market place from the principal square to the north-west corner of the wharf.

November 28. Ordinance for establishing and regulating an assessment on all Protestants.

1837.

February 21. Rule of Court for appointing administrators to certain vacant successions.

June 26. Ordinance for regulating the professions of advocate and attorney.

July 11. Proclamation for altering the limits of the district.

November 24. Ordinance to amend an Ordinance for regulating the form and manner of registering deeds and other instruments.

1838.

January 2. Ordinance for depositing in the Colonial Bank certain funds belonging to suitors in the Royal Court.

1838

July 13. Ordinance for terminating the apprenticeship.

——— Proclamation for giving effect to the Ordinance for terminating the apprenticeship.

July 25. Ordinance for authorising the appointment of rural constables.

July 27. Ordinance to provide for the relief of poor persons, and to provide work for such as cannot get employment.

July 30. Ordinance to amend the Police Ordinances.

——— Royal Order in Council for regulating contracts of service by persons within the limits of the Colony.

——— Ordinance for laying a duty on licenses to be taken out by pedlars and travelling hucksters.

August 4. Act of the Imperial Parliament for the better government of prisons in the West Indies.

August 11. Proclamation for prohibiting the punishment of flogging on convictions before a Justice of the Peace.

September 7. Royal Order in Council for regulating the relative rights of masters and servants.

——— Royal Order in Council for the suppression of vagrancy, and for the punishment of idle and disorderly persons, rogues, and vagabonds.

——— Royal Order in Council to amend the marriage laws.

September 11. Rule of Court directing that all matters of form and routine shall be disposed of before one Judge.

October 6. Royal Order in Council respecting the unauthorised occupation of Crown lands.

December 12. Proclamation for fixing the value of the doubloon and the dollar.

1839.

February 16. Ordinance for regulating the duties of porters, jobbers, and watermen.

——— Ordinance to repeal the laws and ordinances respecting the militia.

——— Ordinance to amend an Ordinance entitled "An Ordinance for laying a Duty on Licenses, to be taken out by Pedlars and travelling Hucksters."

1839.

February 16. Ordinance amending an Ordinance dated 18 July 1836, entitled " An Ordinance for Altering and Amending an Ordinance, entitled ' An Order in Council establishing a Provost-Marshal.' "

February 20. Royal Order in Council for removing any doubts that may exist as to the construction of the Order in Council amending the marriage laws.

May 6. Ordinance enacting rules and regulations for the protection and better government of the police force.

——— Ordinance to amend an Ordinance providing for the deposit of certain public funds in the Colonial Bank.

August 31. Ordinance to authorise the enforcement of certain quarantine regulations.

November 19. Rules and Regulations for the guidance of the Colonial Treasurer and other public accountants.

1840.

January 25. Ordinance to amend the Ordinance of 6th May 1839, enacting rules and regulations for the police force.

July 3. Act of the Imperial Parliament for regulating the carriage of passengers in merchant vessels.

October 6. Quarantine regulations for St. Lucia framed by Sir William Pym.

November 19. Ordinance to promote and encourage steam navigation between St. Lucia and Great Britain for conveyance of mails and passengers.

December 3. Ordinance for authorising the appointment of Coroners.

1841.

April 1. Royal Order in Council for abolishing the currency of " Livres, sols, and deniers," and substituting the British currency of pounds, shillings, and pence.

June 18. Proclamation announcing the introduction of the English language, to take place on the 1st January 1842.

June 23. Royal Order in Council for giving validity and effect to all contracts of service made in the United Kingdom.

1842.

January 3. Amended regulations for the gaols.

1842.

January 5.   Ordinance for removing any doubts that may exist as to the obligation to publish Judicial Notices in the official Gazette.

January 26.   Rules of Court for regulating certain points of practice and pleading.

July 16.   Act of the Imperial Parliament to amend the laws for the regulation of the trade of the British possessions abroad.

1843.

January 4.   Royal Order in Council to amend the Order in Council of 20th June 1831, and to empower the local Legislature to pass laws for amending the constitution of the Royal Court.

January 4.   Royal Order in Council for extending to condemned or forfeited slaves the provisions of the Order in Council for regulating the relative rights of masters and servants.

No. III.

A RETURN OF THE VACANT OR INTESTATE SUCCESSIONS IN THE
COLONY OF ST. LUCIA, FROM THE RE-ESTABLISHMENT OF THE
OFFICE OF "CURATEUR AUX SUCCESSIONS VACANTES" IN
1808, TO ITS ABOLITION IN 1831 :—

1809.	Bouchet	Gréaux
Fraiche	Boucaud	Manuel
Canelle	Guérard	Loup
Laforce		Dame de Grenolach
Lamothe	1811.	Ducrest
Norroy	Baudez	
Thomas	Tetlow	1813.
Lamarque	Richelme	St. Jours
Garceau	T ole	Firebrace
John Robertson	Ardilier	Campaigne
Dame Francisque	Dame Ardilier	Bowen
Marain	Félin	Dame Rachelle
O'Neill	Courty	Nérée
	Floret	Dupleix
1810.	Hacquin	Lombard
Bonnard	Barker	Paret
Dugard	Dame Bachelier	George Howit
Silvecannes	Hubin	Pauline
Prunier	Dame Gerfroy	Dame Hebert
Abbé Bachelet	Spadon	
Dame Olivier	Vigès	1814.
Lafouasse		Barras
Dubonnaire	1812.	Dufond
Lougat	Azéma	Barrancy
Isnard	De Brossard	Tapisson
Dame Isnard	Dame Lanse	Louis Henry
Turpeau	Calliandre	P. Jupiter
Dame Lemaitre	Pimart	Normand
Dame Clement	Downing	Robert
Berrein	Beaupré	Ellis
Mc Duff	Borry	
Albert	Porter	

1815.

Ashburner
Aubert
Gras
Martin
Desruisseau
Sautelet
Dame Dubrocard
Guierre
Taillasson
Dame Taillasson
Leonard Pascal
Desinchères
Lamaze
Pellain
Dawson
Labusquière

1816.

Rivalz
Mackenzie
Heulan
Valentin
Desnoyer
Corneille
Emmisseker
Hall
Dalbarade
Gueyrard
Chapman
Deville

1817.

Roche
Laralde
Manon
Séguy

François
Boisjoli
Sanders
Fuzier
Leboiteux
Doyembourg
John Mc.Donald
Ranson
Labady
Battet

1818.

Ferret
Hardman
Saupin
Achon

1819.

Tierney
Poustis
Pélagie
Heloise
Spiller
Reforce
Lacrosse

1820.

Pierre Toraille
Raymond
Dame Toussaint
Desert
Le Bon
Biron
Legay
Mc.Cann
Kelly
Mills

Hardy
Favier
Postlethwaite
Vincent
Falvey
Beaufort
Forien

1821.

Pringle
Mouret
Leconte
Louis Confident
Dame L'Evêque
Chaigneau
Fontanier
Abbot
Dayot
Larcorbinière
Négrin
Houston
Sollier
John Mc Call
Laura
Nicol Rasco
Dame Malzair
Chevalier St. Omer
Dame Solard
Dame Desfontaines

1822.

Gaspard Levater
Guillent
Dame Schawbourg

1823.

Backhouse

John Lowe

Purrey

Germain Dussault

Boiret

Dubuisson

Samuel Brown

1824.

Joseph Chatterton

William Hill

Robert Croll

Thourayne

Dame Guillette

Vimeney

Jean Marie

1825.

Dame Gibelin

John Hossack

Vignal

Berté St. Ange

J. B. Pierret

Abbé Rossy

1826.

Rechou

Siméon

Chatinville

Le Breton

Genot

Celeste Cenac

Dame C. Cenac

Regis Bué

Marchant de Charmont

1827.

L. Bergopzoom

Ste. Croix Tinturier

Petit Dessourses

Dame Devaux

J. M. Berland

1828.

Dame Longuet

A. J. Tallarie

Marcelin Devaux

Pierre Guillette

Jh. Marragon

Dame Michot

Stanislas Bazile

Dugard Turgis

Rual Delomel

1829.

Laroche Duval

T. Ravenau

Joseph Evans

J. B. Allègre

William Keighley

R. Ireland

L. M. Duval

Jay de Presbois

Jh. Ardillier

1830.

Jh. Hamel

Morelles

F. Peterson

Anette Dyer

Mongouge

Dame Girard

Chatelain

E. de Rameau

J. B. Leveillé

No. IV.

A RETURN OF THE VACANT OR INTESTATE SUCCESSIONS IN THE
COLONY OF ST. LUCIA, FROM THE ABOLITION OF THE OFFICE
OF "CURATEUR AUX SUCCESSIONS VACANTES," IN 1831, TO
THE 1ST JANUARY 1844 :—

Vacant Successions.	Administrators.	Date of Appointment.
Francis Lafargue	Stephen Williams	5 December 1831
Christopher Johnston	Francis Taggart	28 November 1832
G. Mc Cullom	William Muter	13 December 1832
Jean Recour	J. B. Lartigue	3 December 1833
Edme de Rameau	D. G. Gordon	10 February 1834
Francis Kearney	James Macfarlane	25 February 1834
R. Scott and J. Wilson	F. Jongogne	3 June 1834
P. G. de Bonne	Charles Glandut	3 June 1834
E. P. Burke	W. J. Evans	18 November 1834
P. Guillette	J. B. Niochet	18 November 1834
L. Barthelemy	Louis Petit	13 January 1835
Thomas Rowe	R. C. Gordon	27 January 1835
E. O'Callaghan	R. C. Gordon	3 March 1835
Samuel Brown	Donald Shaw	7 April 1835
De la Busquière	R. C. Gordon	12 May 1835
D. Mc Pherson	D. Ferguson	19 May 1835
J. F. Rechou	J. A. Lestrade	28 July 1835
William John	Mrs. W. John	2 April 1836
M. de Charmont	J. H. P. Piet	21 April 1836
Dorigny Lacaze	Louis Lacaze	21 April 1836
Eugene Pierre	Widow E. Pierre	21 April 1836
A. Romanet	Charles Tallarie	26 April 1836
J. Babonneau	Edward Ruffin	26 April 1836
J. B. Germain	Widow Germain	3 May 1836
Dame Castagnié	A. de Brossard	14 June 1836
Brossard de Bois La Pierre	St. B. de Brossard	16 August 1836
H. C. Duvernay	D. Ferguson	19 August 1836
Dlle. Rose Pelet	Delle. M. Henry	20 October 1836
P. Fressenjat	D. Ferguson	20 October 1836
Dlle. Ferlicot	Nelson Vitalis	25 October 1836
C. M. Desrameaux	Edmond Jore	12 January 1837
George Baillie	F. Deroze	14 February 1837
Auguste Jay	Delle. Julie Jay	1 March 1837
E. P. Burke	Salvigny and Geneteau	4 April 1837
Eugene O'Callaghan	D. G. Gordon	4 April 1837
De la Busquière	D. G. Gordon	4 April 1837
J. F. Rechou	X. St. Martin	23 May 1837
Wm. Milligan	William Mc Kay	28 June 1837
V. V. de Bexon	Salvigny and Geneteau	2 August 1837

Vacant Successions.	Administrators.	Date of Appointment.
Dlle. Badère	Salvigny and Geneteau	17 August 1837
William Murch'e	Duncan Ferguson	20 September 1837
Peter Ferguson	Duncan Ferguson	20 September 1837
Henri Desfourneaux	Auguste Hosten	6 February 1838
M. J. P. Alexander	Salvigny and Geneteau	21 May 1838
Felix Dujon	J. B. Lartigue	9 June 1838
Delle. Duchon	Dlle. T. Chambon	10 July 1838
E. B. Ryan	Salvigny and Geneteau	17 July 1838
Delle. Félicité Lee	Salvigny and Geneteau	3 August 1838
William Barr	George Mackie	31 December 1838
James Gunsell	Salvigny and Geneteau	2 January 1839
Mrs. Butler	Henry King	22nd February 1839
James Kennedy	Salvigny and Geneteau	22 February 1839
David Watson	Salvigny and Geneteau	13 March 1839
Martelly Brothers	I. P. Leuger	2 April 1839
James Aughterson	I. P. Leuger	2 April 1839
Dame Gabalda	M. A. Meynier	7 May 1839
Dame Tiffeneau	Momfredo Mombelli	7 May 1839
James Watt	William Glen	7 May 1839
Baron d'Yvoley	Stephen Williams	29 July 1839
Alfred Bailey	Ch. Henry Cox	6 August 1839
Donald Mc Laurin	Thomas Clarke	6 August 1839
Osmond Varrein	Francis Dreuil	3 September 1839
Delle. Marainville	J. B. Joseph	4 December 1839
J. B. Loustau	Francois Loustau	23 December 1839
De la Busquière	M. Garner Todd	28 December 1839
E. de Rameau	M. Garner Todd	28 December 1839
P. Mc Cracken	I. Richardson	16 January 1840
Faget (mother and son)	Henry Mc Leod	7 April 1840
Pierre Marucheau	R. Marucheau	15 April 1840
James Jessopp	John Grant	17 June 1840
St. Elve Bellevue	Joseph Daubaignan	9 July 1840
Edward Lewis	Francis Dreuil	23 July 1840
Dame de Sablon	Réné Varrein	21 July 1840
C. M. Desrameau	Charles de Brettes	22 September 1840
Philip Fuzier	Frejus Fuzier	20 October 1840
Auguste Hosten	G. R. Plummer	3 November 1840
Abbé Chevalier	Godard and de Laubenque	19 July 1841
F. Siraudin	James Meynier	30 September 1841
James Aughterson	Francis Peter	26 January 1843
L. F. Doussard	Dame Doussard	6 June 1843

CHAPTER X.

Administration—Proprietary Governments—First French Governor—St. Lucia a Dependency of Martinique—Becomes the Seat of a General Government—The " Reign of Terror "—Military Commandants—The First Civil Governor under the British—Administrative Authority of the Conseil Supérieur—The Captain General, Colonial Prefect, and Grand Judge—Conflict of Jurisdiction—Establishment of the Privy Council—Creation of the Executive and Legislative Councils—Governors, Lieutenant-Governors and Administrators of the Government—Annexation of St. Lucia to the General Government of the Windward Islands— Practical Results—Taxation—Statistics of the Revenue and Expenditure—Financial Embarrassment under General Farquharson—Administration of Sir Dudley Hill—Liquidation of the Public Debt—Colonial Agents and Houses of Assembly—List of Governors from the earliest Period—Civil Establishment on the 1st January 1844.

THE administrative authority * has varied with the various political reverses of the Colony. From 1642 to 1650 it lay in the hands of the French West India Company, and from the latter period to 1664 in those of the Duparquets. In that year it was assigned to a new company, which held the reins until its suppression in 1674· The island was then annexed to the General Government as a dependency of Martinique. In 1718 it was placed under the proprietary rule of

* See Appendix, No. I., to this chapter.

Marshal d'Estrées; but in consequence of the rival pretensions of England and France, it was declared neutral in 1723, and its neutrality was confirmed by the Treaty of Aix-la-Chapelle in 1748.

The first regular Governor under the French was the Chevalier de Jumillac, who administered from 1764 to 1768. At the latter period the Colony was again annexed to Martinique, and continued so until its conquest by the British in 1779. During that time the administration was conducted by a Lieutenant-Governor under the superintendence of the Governor and Intendant * of Martinique. On its restoration to the French by the Treaty of Versailles in 1783, it was again formed into a separate and independent administration; and this order of things prevailed until the first outbreak of the Revolution. The "Reign of Terror" commenced in 1791 and continued at intervals until 1798, during which time the supreme authority was successively wielded by the Patriot Clubs under Mondenoix and La Crosse, the Committees of Public Safety under Ricard and Goyrand, and the Brigands under Hugues and Lacroix.

During the different periods of the British

---

* The jurisdiction of Intendant was in every essential respect similar to that of Colonial Prefect—an officer of subsequent creation : see page 394.

occupation the Government was administered by military commandants, subject to the control of the Commander-in-Chief at Barbados. General Prevost, appointed at the request of the inhabitants in 1801, was the first civil Governor of whom we have any mention. The following is a copy of his commission :—

" George the Third, by the grace of God of the United Kingdom of Great Britain and Ireland King, Defender of the Faith, &c.

" To our trusty and well-beloved George Prevost, Esquire, Brigadier-General of our Forces, greeting.

" We, reposing especial trust and confidence in your loyalty, courage, and experience in military affairs, do by these presents constitute and appoint you to be Lieutenant-Governor of the Island of St. Lucia in America. You are therefore to take the same into your care and charge, and carefully and diligently to discharge the duties of Lieutenant-Governor thereof, by doing and performing all and all manner of things thereunto belonging. And we do hereby strictly charge and command all our officers and soldiers, who now are or hereafter shall be in garrison there; and all our ministers, officers and loving subjects whom it may concern, to obey you as Lieutenant-Governor thereof. And you are to observe and follow such orders and instructions, from time to time, as you shall receive from us, or any your superior officers, according to the rules and discipline of war, in pursuance of the trust we hereby repose in you.

" Given at our Court at St. James's the twenty-fifth day of April 1801, and in the forty-first year of our reign.

" By His Majesty's command.

" PORTLAND."

General Prevost was assisted in the civil administration by the Conseil Supérieur, composed of twelve of the most respectable inhabitants. This institution combined the administrative, legislative and judicial functions, exhibiting the popular privileges of self-government and self-taxation ingrafted upon the aristocratic prerogatives of a Court of Appeal. It held the purse-strings of the Colony ; levied imposts ; controlled the public expenditure ; took the initiative in all measures of legal reform ; and often assumed and sometimes exercised the right of dictating to the Head of the Executive. By intendment of law the Sovereign was held to be present, and all decrees or arrêts ran in his name. On the right of the presiding Councillor was placed the *Fauteuil du Roi*, which was occupied by the Governor in his capacity of *ex-officio* or titular President. This happened whenever a necessity arose for communicating any ordinance of the local Executive, or any information on behalf of the Imperial Government. On such occasions the representative of Majesty repaired to the Court-House with unusual ceremony, accompanied by his Secretary and Aides-de-Camp ; and, taking his place on the Bench, proceeded to open the business of the day with a speech " from the chair," which was responded to in French by the Attorney-General, who performed the functions of speaker. The Governor then retired, and the other business, financial and judicial, was successively disposed of.

In the short space that elapsed between the restitution of the Colony to the French at the peace of Amiens in March, 1802, and its re-capture by the British in June, 1803, the machinery of Government was remodelled upon a new and somewhat complicated plan. It consisted (in addition to the Conseil Supérieur) of a Captain General, a Colonial Prefect, and a Grand Judge. These offices were created by an arrêté of First Consul Bonaparte, dated the 26th May, 1802, " for determining the manner in which the islands of Martinique and St. Lucia shall be administered." The Captain General was to command the land and sea forces, the national guards, and the gendarmerie ; to provide for the internal and external defence of the Colony ; to regulate promotion in the army and navy, as far as the ranks of Colonel and Commodore ; to conduct all communications with foreign powers both in the Antilles and on the continent of America ; to plan roads and fortifications ; to determine the expenses of the public service ; to appoint to all vacant offices in the several branches of the administration ; in a word, to exercise the powers and prerogatives usually vested in a Governor General, subject to the approval of the First Consul. The Colonial Prefect had the superintendence of the finances, the auditing of the public accounts, the direction and distribution of the civil officers of the Government, and the framing of regulations for their guidance. And the Grand Judge was invested with the surveillance of the Courts of law, and all offices attached thereto ; of the prisoners, their cleanliness and discipline ; and of all rogues, vagabonds, and disturbers of the public peace. These functionaries usually resided in Martinique ; and, on occasions of absence from that island or St. Lucia, the duties of Captain General devolved on a Commandant—of Prefect, on a " chef d'administration," and of Grand Judge on a Commissary of Government.

The restoration of the British authority was followed by the re-establishment of that system of civil government, which had obtained in the time of General Prevost ; and this prevailed without interruption until the close of 1816. In April of that year, during the administration of General Stehelin, the Conseil Supérieur showed a disposition to encroach upon the prerogatives of the

Executive. It assumed the exclusive right of interpreting the Royal Order in Council for establishing a slave registry ; expressed its dissatisfaction at the measures adopted by the Governor, particularly the provision which he thought proper to make for certain civil appointments out of the general funds of the Colony ; and concluded by a resolution for the reduction of his salary, on the alleged plea of public economy. These proceedings did not fail to give offence to General Stehelin, as well as to his immediate successor, General Douglass ; and on their return to England shortly after, they took occasion to report the circumstances to His Majesty's Government. In truth, so many changes had taken place during the previous twenty-five years, and such discordant elements of polity had been engrafted on the ancient institutions of the Colony, that neither the Governor nor the Conseil Supérieur could well understand the nature and limits of their respective jurisdictions. A British officer, invested with the ordinary powers of a civil administrator, was little disposed to brook dictation and control from any authority within his government ; and a Council, habituated to wield a sovereign* preponderance in all matters of

* The institution was originally styled the " Conseil Souverain." See Code de la Martinique vol. i. p. 10.

legislation and finance, was ever ready to take umbrage at the slightest encroachment on its peculiar province. Combining, as it did, the prerogatives of " King, Lords, and Commons," however compatible its existence might have been with the authority of a mere military Commandant, it was clearly opposed to that of civil Governor ; and this the Council should have known when it solicited that appointment for General Prevost in 1801. The result was what might have been expected : in October 1816 instructions were issued by the Prince Regent in Council for establishing the civil government upon a new basis, and Major-General Seymour was commissioned to carry them into effect. This officer assumed the command early in December, and on the 15th of that month he published an Ordinance embodying the principal features of the new system. By this enactment the jurisdiction of the Conseil Supérieur was strictly confined to its functions as a Court of Appeal ; while the purely administrative and financial branches were transferred to the Governor for the time being, aided by an executive and legislative body, styled a Privy Council, and composed of five of the principal proprietors. On Mr. Jeremie's appointment to the office of

First President of the Court of Appeal in February 1825, his name was added to the list of Privy Councillors, as first in rank, with authority to preside in the absence of the Governor.

Towards the close of 1831 the experience of the previous fifteen years had suggested certain modifications in the constitution of the Council. Much inconvenience appeared to have resulted, as well from the paucity of its members and the restricted sphere of action conceded to them in their legislative capacity, as from the indiscriminate extension of the executive functions to each and every Councillor. To remedy this it was resolved to abolish the Privy Council altogether, and re-cast its materials in the formation of two distinct and separate boards—the one to be styled the Executive Council, and to consist of the Governor, Colonial Secretary, Attorney-General, Colonial Treasurer, and Protector of Slaves; the other to be called the Council of Government, or Legislative Council, and to be composed of the Chief Justice and the other officers just named, together with five of the principal proprietors. This arrangement was carried into effect in April 1832, under the auspices of Major-General Farquharson, and has been continued to the present time. Owing, however, to the suppression of the office of Protector of Slaves in 1834—the consolidation of the offices of Secretary and Treasurer in 1836, and the discontinuance of the Chief Justice as a member of Council in 1838, certain alterations have taken place in the composition of the two Boards. At present the Executive Council consists of the Governor, the officer next in command, the Colonial Secretary, and the Attorney-General; and the Legislative Council (besides the five unofficial members) of the Governor, the Colonial Secretary, the Attorney-General, the Collector of Customs, and any other two persons holding office within the Colony, at the Governor's selection.

It is the special office of the Executive Council to give its advice in all cases connected with the administration of the Executive authority; and of the Legislative Council to assist in enacting laws for the order, peace, and good government of the Colony. In the former two members besides the Governor form a quorum, and in the latter six. The officials, or members holding office, take precedence of the non-officials, or members not holding office; and these rank between each other according to seniority of appointment. They are nominated by warrant under the sign manual, and are addressed both collectively and individually by the title of " Honourable "—a title which appears to have been first conferred on the Privy Councillors in October 1818, during the administration of Sir John Keane.* They are included in the commission of the peace in right of their office, and claim exemption from personal arrest during their attendance on the Board of Council. The proceedings of the Executive Council are public since December 1838 ; but they may be conducted with closed doors, if the President shall deem it expedient.

The authority of the Governor is defined by the Royal Instructions, which accompany his commission. He is empowered to make grants of land to the extent of one hundred acres ; to grant licences of marriage and probates of wills ; to remit offences, fines, and forfeitures. He has the presentation to all vacant ecclesiastical benefices within the Colony, and the superintendence (with the advice of the bishop of the diocese) of all matters relating to the celebration of divine worship, the erection and repair of churches, the maintenance of ministers, the settlement of parishes, the establishment of schools, and the

* Now Lord Keane of Ghuznee and Cappoquin.

education of youth. He issues his warrant for
the disposal of the moneys for the public service;
appoints to all offices within the Colony, subject
to the approval of the Sovereign; and may suspend any officer, subject likewise to the approval
of the Sovereign, but has not the power to remove
or dismiss. He presides in the Executive and
Legislative Councils, which he may convoke or
adjourn at pleasure; and proposes the laws and
other subjects for their consideration. He is not,
however, bound to adopt the advice of the Executive Council, but may act in opposition thereto
on his own responsibility. He is also restrained
from making laws in certain cases, specially reserved to the Crown, such as the naturalization
of aliens and the divorce of married persons.

Previously to 1834 the head of the Executive
bore the title of "Governor and Commander-in-
Chief," and his *locum tenens* that of "Officer
Administering the Government." The title of
"Lieutenant-Governor" appears to have been
definitively adopted on the appointment of Sir
Dudley Hill in June of that year, although that
officer continued to correspond directly with the
Colonial Office. Towards the close of Sir Dudley's
administration, which terminated in April 1837,
one of those political squalls, so peculiar to the

St. Lucia atmosphere, had been gathering for
some time; but it did not completely burst until
the end of that year, during the temporary command of Colonel Bunbury. Actuated by the
same honesty of purpose which characterised the
administration of Sir Dudley Hill, Colonel Bunbury did not exhibit the same tact and experience in the conduct of affairs. The rough,
" pioneering" system which he introduced, was
but ill calculated to allay the mighty elements of
opposition that had been stirred up against him
on every side. At length, goaded to desperation
by the difficulties of his position the Colonel
resolved to make a general onslaught upon his
opponents. The Chief Justice was suspended;
the First Puisne Judge was sent to prison; the
members of the Bar, refusing to plead before the
new Judges, were suspended *en masse;* and to
crown all, the French language was abolished by
beat of drum.

The clamour raised against these proceedings
soon found an echo in the Mother Country. As
usual, the Colonial Office was besieged by complaints and recriminations from both parties; and
deputations and doleance - mongers were not
wanting to represent the sentiments of the community. According to one faction the Governor

was the sole evil-doer. As things stood, the colonists were at the mercy of the first military officer who chanced to have the command of the troops, and who, being but a novice himself, was compelled to make St. Lucia the theatre of his experiments in " the art of governing," thereby perpetually encroaching either on the powers of the Court or the prerogatives of the Crown.

> " Whether it be the fault and glimpse of newness;
> Or whether that the body public be
> A horse, whereon the Governor doth ride,
> Who, newly in the seat, that it may know
> He can command, lets it straight feel the spur."

In the opinion of the opposite party the Chief Justice was the cause of all the mischief. Invested with almost despotic authority under the anomalous laws of a Crown Colony, he was naturally led to aspire to the supreme command : and whenever the Governor refused to resign the reins into his hands, he endeavoured to wrest them from him by force, intimidation, or intrigue. How far these considerations may have influenced the decision of the Colonial Minister it is not easy to determine. The general impression appears to be that Lord Glenelg had been contemplating for some time the annexation of St. Lucia to the government of the Windward Islands, and that the recent feuds did but precipitate a measure which had not yet received his Lordship's mature consideration. However this may be, in February 1838 orders were issued to restore men and matters in St. Lucia to their former position; and with a view to prevent a recurrence of similar proceedings, the Colony was included in the General Government, then under the adminis- tration of the late Sir Evan MacGregor. From that period the head of the local Executive has been a *Lieutenant-Governor* in reality, as well as in name.

After six years' experience of this change it may not be uninteresting to enquire what have been its practical results. First, we have the establishment of a controlling power more imme- diately accessible, on great emergencies, than the Colonial Office could possibly have been: and secondly, the avoidance to that department of those references on mere points of form, which are continually recurring in the management of a distant Colony. As drawbacks upon these, how- ever, it must be borne in mind that the emergency which called forth the measure of annexation was one of infrequent occurrence, and that many references, admittedly of a formal character, must continue to be the subject of correspondence between the Governor-in-Chief and the Minister of the Crown. But the principal drawback is the delay and loss of time. Under the old system a day or two after the arrival of the packet in the West Indies, the Governor of St. Lucia was in possession of the Sovereign's commands upon every question connected with his administration. Whereas, by the present arrangement the Despatches proceed to Barbados in the first instance, and must there be taken in rotation with those of that island, St. Vincent, Grenada, and Tobago. On an average it may be computed that there elapses a period of one month for every despatch, between the date of its arrival in Barbados and that of its reception by the Lieutenant-Governor of St. Lucia. Now, if we consider that about one-third of the despatches require neither note nor comment, and are ultimately forwarded, as received, " for the information and guidance of the officer administering the Government," it will be obvious that in many important cases the advantages of time and opportunity are thrown away, and the primary object of the measure itself—political centralization—absolutely frustrated. In this respect, and for any benefit to be derived from steam navigation, St. Lucia might as well have its existence in the middle of the

Pacific Ocean. With regard to the despatches which are accompanied by instructions or observations from the Governor-in-Chief, it must not be forgotten that St. Lucia is a Crown Colony, whose laws and institutions are essentially different from those of the other islands, included in the General Government; and that His Excellency's acquaintance with its local interests is necessarily less extensive than that of his Deputy on the spot. During the six years that the island has been under the tutelage of a Governor-in-Chief, His Excellency has paid it but one brief visit, and that was at the passing of the Emancipation Bill in July 1838. Sir Evan MacGregor, understanding that the measure was likely to encounter some opposition in the Legislative Council, took his departure from Barbados on the night of the 11th July, and came to anchor in Port Castries on the evening of the 12th. At one o'clock on the 13th he had taken his seat at the Board of Council: before five the Bill had passed without opposition; and as His Excellency re-embarked for Barbados at seven o'clock, well might he have indulged in Cæsar's thrasonical brag: " I came, saw, and overcame."

The same observations apply to such portion of the correspondence as originates in St. Lucia.

By the recent extension of steam navigation the Lieutenant-Governor would be enabled to forward his despatches to Downing Street, so as to receive a reply in the space of from two to three months ; but under the present arrangement he must wait for the regular opportunities for Barbados, which are not more frequent than those for England. If the point submitted for consideration be one of importance, in nineteen cases out of twenty His Excellency the Governor-in-Chief will call for additional particulars of information. A correspondence will thus arise and extend over a period of several weeks ; and ultimately the question will be referred to the Colonial Office, whence, after a lapse of six or eight months from the first application to the Governor-in-Chief, a decision will be received, *viâ* Barbados, which might have been obtained in less than three months by a direct reference to the Minister of the Crown.— This is the ordinary result in matters of importance : take for example the passing of an Ordinance to provide the " ways and means." The estimates, being agreed upon by the Legislative Council, are forwarded to Barbados by the first opportunity. Upon a subject involving so many questions of general policy as the different modes of taxation resorted to by the Colonial legislatures, it is natural that the Governor-in-Chief should offer such comments as his wisdom and experience may suggest. Accordingly, either the ordinance is sent back to be amended, or explanations are called for from the Lieutenant-Governor and Board of Council. In either case, what between sending the original papers to Barbados—their being considered there in rotation with business of equal importance from the other islands—the preparing and sending to St. Lucia of despatches in reply—the re-summoning there of the Board of Council—the forwarding of the amended ordinance or of the requisite explanations—and finally the copying of the whole proceedings in Barbados for transmission to Downing Street, a period of three months will have expired before the Estimates are fairly on their way to England.

In offering these remarks I would not be understood as recommending a return to the former system. There are contingencies that cannot always be guarded against, such as a political Judge or an inexperienced Governor, upon whom the existence of a Governor-in-Chief, at the short distance of one hundred miles, cannot fail to operate as a salutary check. Moreover, what has been refused to St. Vincent is not likely to be conceded to St. Lucia. But I am of opinion that a modification of the system might be effected with much advantage to the public service. Let the local Administrator, whether as Lieutenant-Governor, officer Administering the Government, or President, have authority to correspond directly with the Chief Department in Downing Street; and let the interposition of the Governor-in-Chief, instead of being extended, as at present, to the minutest details of the service, be restricted to cases of importance, in which his interference shall be solicited either by the Lieutenant-Governor, the Legislative Council, or the Supreme Court of Justice. By this means we shall preserve all the advantages of a Governor-in-Chief, without impairing the efficiency of the local Administrator.

By far the most important privilege of the Executive is that of levying taxes and disposing of the revenue. The earliest attempt at taxation of which we read was made in 1766. In accordance with the policy of the times, whenever a slave was slain at the " chase of the Maroon Negroes," or underwent the extreme penalty of the law under a sentence of a Court of Justice, the owner became entitled to compensation for the loss of his services. To meet the daily increasing demands of this nature a tax of about ten pence sterling was levied on the colonists with their consent. This fund was called the " caisse des Nègres Justicés :" it continued for many years to be provided for by a specific impost, but it ultimately merged into the general revenue of the Colony.

In 1767, the King of France, on receiving a favourable report of the progress made in commerce and agriculture, directed that a Court House, a Registry, and a Prison should be erected in the chief town of the island ; and to provide the necessary funds, an order was issued on the 21st December, for imposing a capitation tax upon all owners of slaves, at the rate of three livres, or one shilling and two pence half-penny sterling, for each able-bodied Negro, between the ages of 14 and 60. This tax was renewed from year to year until 1774, when in consequence of another favourable report of the progressive improvement of the Colony, his Majesty's Council of State ordered that the tax should be increased to nine livres for each slave, employed in the cultivation of coffee, cotton, or cocoa; and fifteen livres for each slave otherwise employed. This tax appears to have had no specific object connected with public edifices, or any other local improvement, but was applicable to the general

purposes of the administration.   At this period
St. Lucia was a dependency of Martinique, and
both were under the direction of Count de
Nozières, Governor-General, and President de
Tascher,* who held the post of Intendant, or
Chief Civil Administrator.   During the President's sojourn in St. Lucia, a short time before,
he had ample opportunities of becoming acquainted with the situation of the inhabitants;
and acting upon the conviction that the proposed
scale of taxation was greatly disproportioned to
the resources of the Colony, he resolved, in con-
junction with the Governor-General, to suspend
the execution of the King's orders.   It happened
that with this increase of taxation there was
coupled an increase of salary both to the Governor and the Intendant.   Nevertheless, these
functionaries with a rare disinterestedness addressed a memorial to the King, representing the
inability of the colonists to bear such heavy burdens, and declaring their own determination to
forego the increase of salary, if granted in consideration of the additional taxes.   The King informed them that the tax had nothing to do with
the increase of salary; and moreover, that he had
good reason to know that the Colony was in a

* The Father of the Empress Josephine.

condition to bear it. He commended them for their extreme delicacy, but refused to remove the impost. In the following year, however, they were more successful. Considerable expense had been incurred since the war in providing for the defence of the colonies, and orders had been received to levy contributions upon them to cover this expense. The portion allotted to St. Lucia was 60,000 livres tournois, or £2,400 sterling; but at the earnest solicitation of Count de Nozières and President de Tascher, that island was ultimately exempted.

The next extraordinary impost was established on the 23rd October 1788, under instructions from the King of France. Its nature and amount are not stated, but the proceeds were appropriated to the re-construction of the churches and parsonage-houses, destroyed by the hurricane of 1780; and the providing of a salary for the clergy, at the rate of 3,000 livres to each of eleven priests for the eleven parishes of the island. The revolution and rapine which soon followed completely annihilated the resources of the colonists; nor was it until 1805 that they were again subjected to any heavy burdens.* On the 8th

---

* In October 1803 the 4½ per cent. duties, imposed on the exports of the other British colonies, were extended to St. Lucia; but the colonists memorialised the Government on the ruined condition of their affairs, and the tax was discontinued.

October in that year General Brereton introduced a system of taxation, which with very slight alterations has been continued to the present time.

The expenditure, though varying but little in the aggregate annual amount, has undergone considerable mutations in its application and details. Until 1801 it was confined to the single item of "Nègres justiciés"—the civil officers of government being all paid by the fees arising in their respective offices. In that year the policy of remunerating public servants, by fixed salaries from the general revenue, began to be acted upon; although as yet the whole expense under that head did not exceed £500 sterling. The principle was first applied to the civil Governor, on the creation of that office in 1801; and subsequently, as the exigencies of the service appeared to suggest, it was gradually extended to the other officers, until at the present day every person holding a commission from the Government (with the exception of the Vendue-Master) is paid by a fixed stipend from the colonial revenue.* Of the fees formerly received some have been augmented, some reduced, some replaced by others, and some abolished altogether. The whole amount is now

* See Appendix, No. II., to this chapter.

paid into the Treasury for the general uses of the Colonial Government.

Amongst the extraordinary expenses incurred by the Colony I may notice the construction of Government House in 1819, at a cost of £3,474 sterling; that of the Gaol in 1826 at £5,417; that of the Protestant Church in 1830 at £2,980; and the purchase of the Asylum for the Poor in 1840 for £1,700. On the other hand, certain items of the ordinary expenditure have been greatly diminished. Thus the Chief Justice's salary, which was £2,000 sterling in the time of Mr. Jeremie, is reduced to £1,200; and the Governor's, which stood as high as £2,500 in the days of Sir John Keane, is now cut down to £500.

The subject of taxation has been occasionally a source of much irritation between the inhabitants and the local Executive. This irritation was first seriously manifested in December 1831, in connexion with the promulgation of the Order in Council of 2nd November, for regulating the duties of master and slave. Strange to say, that partial interference with the "vested rights" of the colonists engendered a fiercer spirit of opposition, than did, at a subsequent period, the absolute extinction of those rights: and they who, two years after, submitted without a murmur to the abolition of slavery, now vied with each other in demonstrations of the most virulent hostility. They held public meetings ; denounced the conduct of the Executive in the most violent terms ; closed their stores against the public officers ; entered into a correspondence with the inhabitants of Martinique to prevent the arrival of succours from that quarter; and finally carried their opposition to such lengths, that in the space of six months no less than fifty-nine of the principal planters were fined for contraventions to the Order in Council, in the aggregate amount of £1,395 sterling.

The excitement occasioned by these proceedings gradually subsided under General Farquharson's administration in the course of the year 1832. There was, however, one element of opposition to which the colonists continued to adhere, namely, their refusal to pay the colonial duties ; and all the tact and sagacity, for which the General was distinguished, failed to bring about a favourable result. Before the end of 1832 the Treasury was in a state of bankruptcy: some of the poorer officers of government were reduced to the most embarrassing straits ; while such private parties as held claims against the Colony had their bills returned with the words "*payable in plantation taxes*," written upon them by the Governor himself. Under the French laws the Executive had it in their power to proceed against the delinquents by distress and even by personal attachment—taxes being held to be what are termed " deniers royaux ;" but either from forbearance, or the apprehension of open hostility, or ignorance of the law, the authorities looked on with the utmost indifference, while the Government was rapidly sinking into discredit and ruin. If forbearance was the General's motive (and no one who knew him would give him credit for such a sentiment under such circumstances) he was ill requited ; for, some time after, an effigy of his Excellency, decked out in the characteristics of his usual military deshabille, was found hanging at the door of the Court House, with the words : "*payable in plantation taxes*," inscribed upon it.

When Sir Dudley Hill entered on the administration in July 1834 the Colony was in debt to the amount of £11,000 sterling. Among the many qualities which so eminently fitted that officer for the post of Governor, not the least distinguished were the active but considerate zeal, which he displayed in the apportionment and

collection of the taxes, and the economical discrimination with which he husbanded the revenue.
No Governor ever expended more money on improvements and objects of public utility; none
supported the dignity of his office with more
becoming display; none maintained the establishment upon a footing of greater respectability;
and yet, with nothing but the ordinary resources of
taxation at his disposal, he found means to liquidate nearly the whole of the debts before he
retired in April 1837.

Since the days of Sir Dudley Hill the financial
affairs of the Colony have become a theme of
frequent and acrimonious discussion, not only
within the walls of Council, but with the public
and the press out of doors. Taxation—heavy,
onerous, intolerable taxation—is the monster-
grievance; and almost every year gives rise to
some fresh complaint of excessive duties or dilapi-
dated finances. By the annexed table* it will be
seen that the revenue for the last twenty-seven
years has averaged £10,376 sterling per annum,
and the expenditure £10,445. How far the establishment may admit of reduction or augmentation in the present altered state of society, it is
not for me to determine. There are colonies

* See Appendix, No. III., to this chapter.

fully equal to St. Lucia in importance and com_
mercial enterprise, whose burdens would appear
to 'fall short of her's ; and there are others whose
expenditure is in proportion considerably higher.
With a view to alleviate the sufferings on this
head, whether real or imaginary, different schemes
have been propounded from time to time. As
far back as 1803, when the sting of taxation was
felt for the first time, the Conseil Supérieur urged
the expediency of having a Deputy or Agent to
represent the interests of the Colonists in the
Mother Country. The person selected for that
purpose was Mr. Inglis, a merchant then extensively connected with the Colony ; and although
the proposal was renewed in 1816, it does not
appear that he was ever recognised in that capacity. Some attempts have recently been made
to obtain the sanction of the Government to a
similar arrangement, but without success. It is,
however, believed that Sir George Stephen,
though not formally accredited by the Secretary
of State, is authorised to act on behalf of certain
influential parties connected with the Colony.

The establishment of an elective body, either
in the character of a Legislative Council, or
House of Assembly, has been suggested as a
remedy not only against excessive taxation, but

against every kind of mal-administration. It has been gravely argued that the members of the Legislature, as at present constituted, "represent no one but themselves;" that they are totally irresponsible to the community at large; and that the majority are the paid servants of the Crown, ever ready to out-vote the colonial section, upon any question that may involve the views or wishes of the Executive Government. In a word, the advocates of this scheme would claim for the Colony the exclusive right to legislate for its internal regulation and government. It would be idle to deny the great advantages of the elective principle, when brought to bear upon the sinews and civilization of the Mother Country, or indeed of some of our more vigorous colonial settlements; but I imagine it would be productive of a totally different result, if applied to the circumstances of this mixed and multifarious community. In point of fact, what has been its practical working in some of the smaller colonies? What good has been accomplished by their Houses of Assembly that has been unattainable to St. Lucia and Trinidad? Have their mimic Parliaments been any thing but drags upon the wheels of good government?

The observations respecting trial by Jury are

equally applicable to the establishment of a House of Assembly. There is no want of numbers : the population, though scanty for the extent of the island, is three times greater than that of Bermuda or Montserrat ; twice greater than that of the Bahamas ; and is equal to that of Tobago, or Grenada, or Dominica, or St. Kitt's —all endowed with Representative Assemblies. The great want is the want of education and enlightenment, without which the best political institutions may be perverted into engines of mischief and disorganization. Again, in a House of Assembly the proceedings should be conducted in the language spoken by the great majority of the members : French would therefore be unavoidably adopted in the Parliament of St. Lucia. Now, are we to be told in 1844, that forty years of progressive improvement— of British connexion and colonization—are to be jeopardized for the pleasure of converting a peaceable and comparatively prosperous settlement into a hothouse of Papineaus ?

APPENDIX TO CHAPTER X.

No. I.

GOVERNORS OF ST. LUCIA FROM THE EARLIEST DAYS OF ITS
COLONIZATION TO THE 1ST JANUARY 1844.

Name.	Title.	Year.
M. Duparquet	Governor	1651
M. Rousselan	Lieutenant-Governor	1652
M. Larivière	Governor	1657
M. Haquet	Governor	1657
M. Le Breton	Governor	1657
M. de Coutis	Governor	1658
M. d'Aigremont	Governor	1658
M. Lalande	Governor	1659
M. Bonnard	Governor	1660
Mr. Robert Faulk	Governor	1664
The Count de Blénac	Governor-General	1677
The Marquis d'Eragny	Governor-General	1691
The Marquis d'Amblimont	Governor-General	1697
The Count d'Esnotz	Governor-General	1701
M. de Machault	Governor-General	1703
M. de Phelypeau	Governor-General	1711
The Marquis Duquêne	Governor-General	1715
The Marquis de la Varenne	Governor-General	1717
The Chevalier de Feuquières	Governor-General	1717
Captain Nathaniel Wring	Governor	1722
The Marquis de Caylus	Governor-General	1744
M. de Longueville	Lieutenant-Governor	1745
The Chevalier de Longueville	Lieutenant-Governor	1759
The Chevalier de Jumillac	Governor	1763
The Count d'Ennery	Governor-General	1768
M. de Micoud	Lieutenant-Governor	1769
The Chevalier de Micoud	Lieutenant-Governor	1771
M. de Karny	Lieutenant-Governor	1773
The Chevalier de Micoud	Lieutenant-Governor	1775
M. de Courcy	Lieutenant-Governor	1775
M. de Joubert	Lieutenant-Governor	1776
The Chevalier de Micoud	Lieutenant-Governor	1776
General St. Leger	Lieutenant-Governor	1781
Major Chester	Lieutenant-Governor	1782
The Baron de Laborie	Governor	1784
Colonel de Gimat	Governor	1789

Name.	Title.	Year.
General Ricard	Governor	1793
Colonel Sir Charles Gordon	Lieutenant-Governor	1794
M. Goyrand	Commissary	1795
General John Moore.	Lieutenant-Governor	1796
Colonel James Drummond	Lieutenant-Governor	1797
General George Prevost	Lieutenant-Governor	1798
General George H. Vansittart	Lieutenant-Governor	1802
General Jn. Fs. Xavier Noguès.	Lieutenant-Governor	1802
General Robert Brereton	Governor	1803
General Alexander Wood	Governor	1807
Major Jacob Jordan	Acting-Governor	1814
General Francis Delaval	Governor	1814
General Edward Stehelin	Governor	1815
General Robert Douglass	Governor	1816
General Richard A. Seymour	Governor	1816
Colonel Edward O'Hara	Governor	1817
General Sir John Keane	Governor	1818
Major John Joseph Winkler	Acting-Governor	1819
General J. M. Mainwaring	Governor	1821
Colonel Nathaniel Blackwell.	Governor	1824
General J. M. Mainwaring	Governor	1826
Colonel J. M. Sutherland.	Acting-Governor	1826
General J. M. Mainwaring	Governor	1826
Colonel Lorenzo Moore.	Governor	1827
General David Stewart	Governor	1829
Captain G. A. E. Delhoste	Acting-Governor	1829
Captain Robert Mullen.	Acting-Governor	1829
Major Francis Power.	Acting-Governor	1829
Colonel J. A. Farquharson	Acting-Governor	1830
General George Mackie.	Governor	1831
Colonel M. A. Bozon	Acting-Governor	1831
Colonel J. W. Mallet	Acting-Governor	1831
Colonel M. A. Bozon	Acting-Governor	1831
Colonel John Carter	Acting-Governor	1832
General J. A. Farquharson	Governor	1832
Captain Charles Lewis	Acting-Governor	1834
Colonel John Carter	Acting-Governor	1834
Colonel Sir C. F. Smith	Acting-Governor	1834
Colonel Sir Dudley Hill	Lieutenant-Governor	1834
Colonel Thomas Bunbury.	Lieutenant-Governor	1837
Colonel J. A. Mein	Lieutenant-Governor	1838
Colonel Mathias Everard	Lieutenant-Governor	1839
Captain George Murray	Acting-Governor	1841
Colonel George Graydon	Lieutenant-Governor	1841
Captain William Caldwell.	Acting-Governor	1841
Colonel George Graydon	Lieutenant-Governor	1841
Colonel Andrew Clarke.	Lieutenant-Governor	1843

No. II.

CIVIL ESTABLISHMENT OF THE COLONY OF ST. LUCIA ON THE
1ST JANUARY 1844 :—

Salary of Governor-in-Chief		£500
,,	Lieutenant-Governor	500
,,	Chief Justice	1,200
,,	Colonial Secretary and Treasurer	600
,,	Attorney-General	200
,,	Registrar of Courts	400
,,	Provost Marshal-General	300
Allowances to do.		400
Salary of Inspector of Police		280
,,	Two Protestant Clergymen (£200 each)	400
,,	Eight Roman Catholic do. (£100 each)	800
,,	Surveyor-General	150
,,	Deputy Postmaster	100
,,	Harbour Master	150
,,	Lieutenant-Governor's Private Secretary	100
,,	Chief Clerk in Secretary's Office	150
,,	Assistant Clerk in do.	70
,,	Chief Clerk in Treasurer's Office	150
,,	Assistant Clerk in do.	100
,,	Copying Clerk in do.	70
,,	Government Interpreter	100
,,	Inspector of Invoices	100
,,	Government Printer	100
,,	Government Messenger	25
,,	Gaoler of Castries	200
,,	Turnkey of do.	50
,,	Gaoler of Soufriere	50
,,	Gaoler of Vieux Fort	50
Maintenance of Prisoners in Gaol		700
,,	Asylum for the Poor	600
Out-door Relief to Paupers		600
Police Establishment		1,000
Incidental Expenses		1,200
Rent of Government Buildings		200

No. III.

REVENUE AND EXPENDITURE OF THE COLONY OF ST. LUCIA FROM
THE 1ST JANUARY 1817 TO THE 1ST JANUARY 1844.

YEARS.	REVENUE.			EXPENDITURE.		
	£	s.	d.	£	s.	d.
1817........	8,305	4	7	11,188	17	3
1818........	9,553	14	7	10,694	6	4
1819........	11,471	1	9	14,391	9	8
1820........	10,300	15	0	7,336	10	8
1821........	9,886	14	2	8,091	19	9
1822........	9,448	14	2	8,031	12	1
1823........	10,713	4	5	6,687	17	9
1824........	6,825	12	5	8,530	5	6
1825........	10,986	8	5	11,345	10	4
1826........	12,978	8	6	13,096	0	1
1827........	10,007	14	0	11,405	4	0
1828........	11,487	19	5	10,791	16	0
1829........	11,348	18	0	10,999	1	7
1830........	11,308	1	7	11,451	7	2
1831........	9,718	19	2	11,627	16	10
1832........	7,072	0	5	10,657	3	2
1833........	7,745	16	6	8,788	12	0
1834........	8,148	18	0	9,540	13	5
1835........	11,116	2	10	9,105	17	7
1836........	12,321	16	10	8,876	14	0
1837........	10,733	7	2	9,950	14	0
1838........	10,869	5	4	11,034	11	2
1839........	11,856	18	4	12,236	14	6
1840........	12,613	12	1	12,836	19	4
1841........	11,603	2	2	11,408	12	2
1842........	11,451	3	0	11,409	13	5
1843........	10,274	12	11	10,505	12	10

FINIS.